MW00453132

Every Day With Jesus

366 INSIGHTS FOR ENCOURAGEMENT, SPIRITUAL GROWTH, AND PERSONAL VICTORY

Andrew Wommack

Harrison House
Tulsa, OK

Unless otherwise indicated, all Scripture quotations are taken from the King James Version of the Bible.

Scripture quotations marked NIV are taken from *The Holy Bible: New International Version*®. NIV®. Copyright © 1973, 1978, 1984, by International Bible Society. Used by permission of Zondervan. All rights reserved.

Cover design by Koechel Peterson & Associates, Inc., Minneapolis, Minnesota

12 11 10 09   10 9 8 7 6 5 4 3 2 1

Every Day With Jesus:
366 Insights for Encouragement, Spiritual Growth, and Personal Victory
ISBN 13: 978-1-57794-972-5
ISBN 10: 1-57794-972-2
Copyright © 2009 by Andrew Wommack Ministries, Inc.
P.O. Box 3333
Colorado Springs, CO 80934-3333
www.awmi.net

Published by Harrison House Publishers
P.O. Box 35035
Tulsa, Oklahoma 74153
www.harrisonhouse.com

Printed in the United States of America. All rights reserved under International Copyright Law. Contents and/or cover may not be reproduced in whole or in part in any form without the express written consent of the Publisher.

Jesus Was God
John 1:1-5,14

In the beginning was the Word, and the Word was with God, and the Word was God.
John 1:1

Jesus was not just a man sent from God, He was God. This is the most important statement of the New Testament. All other truths hang on this truth. If Jesus was only a man, then regardless of how good He was, His life could only provide a substitute for one other man. However, since He was God, His life was worth more than every human life since creation. Indeed, His life was worth more than the sum total of the universe He created.

Any compromise on the truth of Jesus' divinity will negate His redemptive work in our lives. Jesus was God manifest in the flesh. (1 Tim. 3:16.) Yet, this Almighty God came to dwell in a human body. He humbled Himself and took the form of a servant (Phil. 2:7), and His humanity truly made Him one of us. He suffered the same temptations and pressures that we suffer. (Heb. 4:15.) It was His divinity, however, that gave Him the power to save us completely. (Heb. 7:25.)

We must never let His humanity blind us to the truth that Almighty God Himself became our friend. (John 15:13-15.)

We must never let His divinity blind us to the truth that He knows exactly how we feel, and He deeply cares for us.

Let the Holy Spirit give you a true revelation of the deity and humanity of our Lord Jesus Christ throughout this new year.

You Have His Fullness
John 1:16-17

And of his fulness have all we received, and grace for grace.
John 1:16

The Christian life is not like an insurance policy that only pays off when we die and go to heaven. Every believer has now received the grace of God and the fullness of God. Everything He is, we now possess in our born-again spirits. We are complete in Him. (Col. 2:9-10.)

When we receive Jesus as our Lord, we are instantly changed in our spirits (2 Cor. 5:17), but many of us aren't aware of the change that takes place inside us. Thus, we continue to live by our physical senses and natural mind, and we are oblivious to the new, born-again part of us that has received the fullness of God.

You can't see or touch your spirit because it is spirit. Your spirit is the eternal, invisible part of you. However, when you choose to believe what the Word of God says about you, you will begin to know that in Christ Jesus you have everything you ever need or want. His Word is spirit and life (John 6:63), and as you abide in His Word, you will begin to live more and more from your spirit.

In your spirit, you are right now as you will be throughout all eternity. (1 John 4:17.) Praise the Lord! To the degree you renew your mind to this truth and believe it, you will actually experience God's fullness in this life. Proverbs 23:7 says that whatever you think or believe in your heart is what you are.

Pray the prayer of Ephesians 1:15-23 and let the Holy Spirit reveal "Christ in you, the hope of glory" (Col. 1:27).

The Sign of a Christian
John 13:31-35

By this shall all men know that ye are my disciples, if ye have love one to another.
John 13:35

This is an amazing statement by Jesus! The distinguishing characteristic of a Christian, according to the Head of all Christendom, is our love for one another. This doesn't appear to be common knowledge in the church today. Possessing true love for other believers isn't a top priority for most Christians. Yet Jesus said that this is the number-one thing that will show unbelievers that He's real and alive in us today.

The body of Christ has invested vast amounts of money and effort to reach the lost. We've built fancy churches, padded the seats, and air-conditioned the auditoriums to attract more people. We've traveled around the world and held mass crusades. Yet our love for each other, which Jesus said would represent Him the best, is lacking or non-existent. We have bumper stickers on our cars but no love in our hearts.

The first-century church didn't have tapes, books, or videos. Neither did they put bumper stickers on every camel that crossed the desert. They met in homes without the benefit of radio or television, but they made a tremendous impact on their world with the Gospel. How could this be? They had God's kind of love for Him and for each other.

Jude spoke of the early church meetings as being "feasts of charity" (Jude 1:12). Love abounded and so did the Gospel—and there's a direct relationship between the two. Choose to be a living advertisement for the Gospel today. As you allow His love to shine through for your brothers and sisters as well as the lost, unbelievers will know that Jesus is alive in you.

Faith Works by Love
Galatians 5:1-6

For in Jesus Christ neither circumcision availeth any thing, nor uncircumcision;
but faith which worketh by love.
Galatians 5:6

When Jamie and I started out in the ministry, we were so poor we couldn't even pay attention. I was believing God for prosperity with all I knew, but we constantly struggled. At one time, all we had to eat was a bag of Fritos™ and some Cokes™ that a friend had given us. We rationed them out for days.

Then Jamie took the car and our last seventy-five cents and went to the laundromat. While she was gone, I did some serious praying. It seemed like the Lord wasn't meeting our needs. I said, "God, I'd give my right arm to feed Jamie!"

He immediately responded, "I gave My Son to feed you." Then He reminded me of Luke 12:32, which says, "Fear not, little flock; for it is your Father's good pleasure to give you the kingdom."

That broke my heart. I realized that I had let circumstances deceive me about God's love for us. I had been trying to operate in faith without love. I repented and received God's love. When Jamie returned, I told her we would eat meat that day.

After church that night, a friend invited us to his house. He gave us over ten pounds of fish, potatoes, and other food. Just before midnight, we sat down to a feast. The amazing thing was that he had tried to bring us the food earlier that day, but when he came by our apartment, our car was gone, so he supposed no one was home. The only time our car was gone was when Jamie was at the laundromat washing clothes and God was showing me His love for us. At the precise moment I received His love, my faith worked, and our need was met.

Let God's love for you abound, and your faith will too.

Nothing Is Impossible
Luke 1:26-38

For with God nothing shall be impossible.
Luke 1:37

What a statement. If we just believed this the way Mary believed it when Gabriel spoke it to her, how different our lives would be. From birth we are trained to know our limitations. "You can't have this. Don't touch that. Don't put things in your mouth. You can't touch the fire." The list goes on and on. As we grow up, it's actually a sign of maturity to recognize our limitations and learn to live within them. It is a fact of life that there are limits to everything.

God, on the other hand, has no limits. When we enter into the realm of His supernatural power, we have to take off the limits we have learned through the years. We have to renew our minds with the truth that He is not like us. He can do anything. We have an awesome God Whose power is so great that we can't even comprehend it. He created the universe, and it didn't even tax His ability. Yet many times we find ourselves wondering if our situation is too hard for Him. We can't see how He can pull us through.

The Lord said to Jeremiah, "Behold, I am the Lord, the God of all flesh: is there any thing too hard for me?" (Jer. 32:27.) The answer is a resounding no! The only thing that limits God is our unbelief. (Deut. 7:17.)

Today, honor God by believing that nothing is too difficult for Him. Whatever you are facing, He is more than able and more than willing to help you and bless you.

Standing for What Is Right
Matthew 2:16-23

Then Herod, when he saw that he was mocked of the wise men, was exceeding wroth, and sent forth, and slew all the children that were in Bethlehem, and in all the coasts thereof, from two years old and under, according to the time which he had diligently inquired of the wise men.
Matthew 2:16

Satan was the real motivator behind Herod's actions. Ever since God first prophesied that a "seed" of a woman would bruise his head, Satan had been seeking to find and destroy this "seed" (Gen. 3:15). That "seed," of course, was Jesus, our Lord and Savior.

It appears Satan is able to perceive when God is making a major move in the earth. In the days when Moses was born, Satan moved Pharaoh to kill all the male children of the Israelite slaves. After Jesus was born, Satan motivated Herod to kill all the male children in Bethlehem. No doubt he was seeking to eliminate this "seed," the One who was going to bruise his head and strip him of all power and authority.

Once again, today we see children being slaughtered. This time it is through abortion. The Seed has already come and is multiplying Himself in every born-again believer, so Satan is trying to kill people before they can be born and then born again. He is also attacking our youth in unprecedented ways through violence and suicide. Is it possible he thinks this is the generation that will bring Jesus back? Is he, in desperation, trying to put off his doom by destroying this generation?

Today we need to have enough spiritual perception to recognize that what is happening to our children and youth is an indication of a great struggle in the spirit realm. While we pray, "Even so, come quickly Lord Jesus!" we must also stand for what is right.

Even Jesus Prepared
Luke 2:41-51

And it came to pass, that after three days they found him in the temple, sitting in the midst of the doctors, both hearing them, and asking them questions.
Luke 2:46

This is the only scriptural record of Jesus' childhood; yet, there is much we can learn from this brief account. At twelve years of age, His wisdom astounded the men who had spent a lifetime studying the Scriptures (v. 47). Remember that Jesus did not have full-time access to a copy of the Bible like we do today. He received revelation knowledge from His heavenly Father, but He had to visit the synagogue to read the scrolls of God's Word.

Even at the young age of twelve, Jesus had a clear understanding of who His real Father was and exactly why He had come to the world (v. 49). However, He also asked the scholars questions (v. 46). This is amazing when you realize that in Him are all the treasures of wisdom and knowledge. (Col. 2:3.) Although He was God, He inhabited a physical human body with a natural mind that needed to be educated.

We see that Jesus knew His call and purpose even in His early childhood, but He still had to study and prepare Himself for the work God had called Him to accomplish. He is doing the same thing with you, preparing you for what He has called you to do.

If you don't know what you are called to do, ask Him today! Then ask Him to show you what you can do to prepare your mind and heart for all He wants to accomplish through you.

Be Who God Created You to Be
Matthew 3:1-12; Mark 1:1-8; Luke 3:1-18

In those days came John the Baptist, preaching in the wilderness of Judaea.
Matthew 3:1

These Scriptures record the ministry of John the Baptist. He spent thirty years in the deserts of Judaea preparing for this ministry. Then it only lasted about six months before He baptized Jesus and men started following Him. Nevertheless, in those brief six months John turned an entire nation to God.

John did not take the normal approach and go where the people were. He was out in the wilderness and the people came to him. He had no advertisements other than the testimonies of those who had heard him. He wasn't a flashy evangelist wearing the latest styles of the day. He didn't do anything the way the religious leaders taught it was supposed to be done in their seminaries; yet it worked. In a few months, he stirred an entire nation to anticipate the coming of Jesus.

God accomplished this amazing feat through a man who was not "normal." Too often our "herd instinct" keeps many of us from being used by God. We are so afraid of what someone else will think about us if we do what He tells us to do and live by His Spirit and Word. We try to be like everyone else, and then we wonder why we are getting the same results as everyone else. That's not smart!

John was completely yielded to the Holy Spirit, and he succeeded against all the odds. Dare to follow the Holy Spirit, even if it means going against the crowd, and you will get supernatural results too.

How Does Faith Increase?
Luke 17:5-10

And the apostles said unto the Lord, Increase our faith.
Luke 17:5

The apostles requested the same thing from Jesus that millions of Christians ask for today. They want more faith. Jesus stunned them with His answer, just as the truth about faith stuns people today. He said they didn't need more faith. The faith they had was sufficient to uproot a tree and cast it into the ocean. They just weren't using the faith they had. (v. 6.)

Jesus went on to correct a wrong idea most people have about faith. Faith doesn't just show up and go to work for you. Faith must be told what to do; it is your slave. Masters don't request slaves to work; they make them work. That's the way you should view your faith. You don't passively hope faith will perform or tentatively ask faith to work. You take the authority you have in Jesus and command it!

The reason the disciples didn't see their faith work harder for them was because they hadn't demanded more from their faith. They thought believing for miracles was so hard, it took more faith than what they had. That's not true for them or for us. We have underestimated our slave. We have thought we needed many slaves; when the truth is, this slave (faith) is so powerful it can accomplish whatever we demand of it.

You know the faith God has given you works because you were born again by it. Now that you have experienced the greatest miracle in this life by the faith God gave you, don't go back to thinking your needs are too big for your faith. If you got saved by faith, you can be healed, delivered, provided for, and promoted by faith. Put your faith to work today, and don't let it rest until it gets the job done.

The Weapon of the Word

Matthew 4:1-11; Mark 1:12-13; Luke 4:1-13

And Jesus answered him, saying, It is written,
That man shall not live by bread alone, but by every word of God.
Luke 4:4

When the Holy Spirit led Jesus into the wilderness, it was so He could be tempted by the devil. How did Jesus respond? He answered every temptation with, "It is written." The Word of God is the sword of the Spirit (Eph. 6:17), and it is the only offensive spiritual weapon we have. Jesus showed us how to use it.

Since Jesus is the Word of God (John 1:1), anything He would have spoken would have been the Word. When He was tempted, He could have said, "Scat!" and the devil would have had to go. Nevertheless, He quoted the written Word of God each time, the same Word you and I have today.

This gives us great assurance that the written Word of God is sufficient for us. Jesus, in the face of the greatest temptations Satan could offer, did not need to say anything that was not already recorded in Scripture. The Word sustained Him and enabled Him to overcome all temptation to sin. It is likely that when He returns to this earth, He will just speak the written Word to destroy His enemies. No wonder Satan tries to keep us from studying and knowing God's Word!

God has given you the mighty weapon of His Word. When you speak the Word in faith, hell shakes. Satan and his minions have already experienced what the Word can do. They know its power. Now you need to know it and be persuaded of it too.

The Just Live by Faith
Habakkuk 2:1-4

Behold, his soul which is lifted up is not upright in him: but the just
shall live by his faith.
Habakkuk 2:4

The just don't use their faith occasionally or only when they're in trouble. The just live by faith. This describes faith as a part of our life that is as essential as eating or breathing.

When my wife and I first started in ministry, we struggled financially. We often used the phrase "living by faith" to describe our condition. Indeed, it took a miracle each day to eat, pay bills, or buy gas for our car. Even though our faith has grown to a level where we walk in blessings and don't have to use our faith to receive food each day, we still live by faith. Our faith is what enables us to relate to God and thereby minister to others, which in turn produces finances to meet our needs. Our whole life is consumed with faith!

You don't have to be a minister to live by faith. Everyone needs to fellowship with the Lord daily, which takes faith. We need to recognize God as our Source, and not rely only on our jobs. We need to depend on Him to handle the pressures of family and work that confront us every day. We need to walk in faith not just for ourselves but also for others. The people we encounter each day need the Lord.

You have other people's miracles on the inside of you that can only be released as you live by faith. Make a conscious decision to live by faith today. If all your needs are met, believe God to help someone else. As you practice living by faith daily, your faith will grow. And then when you're in need, you'll be ready to receive by faith. The just live by faith.

Hearing His Voice
John 10:1-5

To him the porter openeth; and the sheep hear his voice:
and he calleth his own sheep by name, and leadeth them out.
John 10:3

Jesus said that His sheep know His voice, and they do not know the voice of strangers (vv. 4,5). Yet it seems most Christians experience the opposite. The vast majority of believers hear the devil, the world, and their flesh loud and clear, but they have a hard time hearing the Lord. That's not normal Christianity.

Jesus painted a picture showing that His sheep are sensitive to His voice and hard of hearing when it comes to anyone else. That should be the typical Christian experience. So what is happening to us? Why does our experience seem to be so different from what Jesus said it would be?

We can be assured that the problem is our hearing, not God's speaking. He speaks to us continually in many different ways, but we often miss it. Psalm 19:1-4 and Romans 1:20 declare God speaks to us through creation. Each day has something new to say to us, but we are too busy to notice.

God also speaks through His Word, but few of us find the time to read it, study it, and meditate on it. We are too busy making time for television, the Internet, movies, work, sports, and a multitude of other things that fill our heads and hearts with everything but Jesus. Is it any wonder we don't hear Him or recognize His voice when He speaks to us?

Jesus said He is speaking to you and has equipped you to hear His voice. You just need to tune in! Make time today and every day to hear no other voice but His, and it won't be long before you hear Him more than anyone or anything else.

Knowing Who You Are
Matthew 4:1-11; Mark 1:12-13; Luke 4:1-13

*And when the tempter came to him, he said, If thou be the
Son of God, command that these stones be made bread.*
Matthew 4:3

Two of Satan's three temptations began with the words, "If you be the Son of God." Jesus was God, but He did have a human body that had to grow in the knowledge and wisdom of God. (John 1:1; 1 Tim. 3:16; Luke 2:52.) It took faith for the physical mind of Jesus to believe the witness of the Spirit within Him that He was the Messiah.

In Matthew 4:3, Satan attacked the most basic of Jesus' beliefs: who He was. Satan also knew He was hungry. Turning stones into bread must have been a temptation for Jesus, or Satan would not have used it.

Satan is very subtle in his temptations. It looked like he was trying to get Jesus to perform a miracle, but he was actually trying to make Jesus waiver in His faith concerning who He was. He tried to get Jesus to draw on the supernatural power of God to confirm His own identity, but it didn't work! Jesus knew who He was and never wavered in believing it.

Unlike Jesus, we sometimes fall for this trick of the devil. We may say we are arguing what we believe, but we are hoping to convince ourselves. Someone who really knows who they are in Christ does not have to prove anything to anyone because they have full assurance from God's Word that He loves them and values them.

Isaiah 30:15 says, "For thus saith the Lord God, the Holy One of Israel; In returning and rest shall ye be saved; in quietness and in confidence shall be your strength." Today meditate on God's Word and let the Holy Spirit build your confidence in who you are in Christ Jesus.

Prosperity Pleases Jesus
3 John 2

*Beloved, I wish above all things that thou mayest prosper and be in health,
even as thy soul prospereth.*
3 John 2

Jesus gave His life to deliver us from this present evil world (Gal. 1:4) and to give us an abundant life. (John 10:10.) Having walked closely with Jesus and being inspired by the Holy Spirit, John wrote that more than anything he wanted all believers to be healthy and productive. That's what Jesus died for. He said this would happen as our souls prospered, and our souls prosper as we live in His truth.

Jesus said that if we saw Him, we saw the Father. He and the Father were in agreement about everything and were One. Therefore, it stands to reason that anyone who loved us enough to sacrifice His Son to purchase our freedom would do anything for our welfare. (Rom. 8:32.) Yet today many people think God either delights in or is apathetic toward our poverty and sickness.

The Word of God makes it clear that your soul and the rest of your life will prosper as you open your heart to the love and provision of the Lord in every area of your life—spiritual, emotional, mental, social, and physical. Not believing this truth has caused many others to see God as only relevant to their eternal needs. However, the Word plainly teaches that your great salvation includes so much more!

As you believe, experience, and preach a full Gospel, you will see God's reality and power manifest in the here and now. You shouldn't reject what Jesus died to give you for any reason. He is glorified when you let Him prosper you. (Ps. 35:27.)

Today give Jesus pleasure by walking in a whole new level of prosperity.

Make Jesus Marvel
Matthew 8:5-13; John 20:24-29

Jesus saith unto him, Thomas, because thou hast seen me, thou hast believed:
blessed are they that have not seen, and yet have believed.
John 20:29

When I first became aware that the Lord did miracles today, I realized I had missed out on the supernatural in my Christian life. That made me want to make up for lost time by immediately receiving everything I could. I heard about visions, dreams, and angels appearing to people—and I wanted all of that! So I started praying for those things to happen to me. However, the Lord used Scriptures like the verses above to stop me in my tracks.

Jesus said that the greatest faith He'd ever seen was a faith that didn't have to see to believe. This faith was in the Word of God alone. (Matt. 8:10.) He told Thomas that he had believed because he had seen, but there was a greater blessing on those who believed by faith and not by sight. This means that we will walk in a greater degree of faith the more we are directed solely by God's Word.

That settled it for me. I wanted God's best. I knew that without faith it was impossible to please Him, and I wanted to operate in the highest form of faith. That's not to say I refuse visions and dreams—I've had both—but they are no longer my focus. God's Word is supernatural enough. If the Lord chooses to use an angel or some other means to speak to me, I'll listen, but I no longer require these things. God's Word needs no additional confirmation; it is the absolute authority in my life.

Today why don't you decide to walk in faith and believe God's promises no matter what you see or hear or experience. Have faith like the centurion, the faith that made Jesus marvel.

Satan's Power Is Limited
Matthew 4:1-11; Mark 1:12-13; Luke 4:1-13

And when the devil had ended all the temptation, he departed from him for a season.
Luke 4:13

The wording of this verse implies that Satan exhausted his arsenal of temptations on Jesus and then had to leave. We have mistakenly given him too much credit. He does not have a limitless number of temptations to pull on us. As 1 John 2:16 says, there are three areas where the devil tempts us: the lust of the flesh, the lust of the eyes, and the pride of life. Jesus' three temptations correspond to these three categories.

By giving Satan limitless powers and abilities, we have made him bigger than he is. The truth is, "There hath no temptation taken you but such as is common to man: but God is faithful, who will not suffer you to be tempted above that ye are able; but will with the temptation also make a way to escape, that ye may be able to bear it" (1 Cor. 10:13).

Satan would like you to think he is tougher than he really is. One of his greatest weapons is intimidation, but Jesus defeated him on every score. His teeth have been pulled! Now he can only roar as a lion seeking to devour uninformed souls who don't know their authority in Jesus Christ. (1 Pet. 5:8.)

Today, walk in the truth that whatever Satan is fighting you with is only temporary. Don't quit–and the devil will have to quit. In due season you will reap, if you faint not. (Gal. 6:9.)

Sharing Your Faith
John 1:37-42

He first findeth his own brother Simon, and saith unto him,
We have found the Messias, which is, being interpreted, the Christ.
John 1:41

Andrew was the first disciple of Jesus to share his faith and bring another to Christ. Look who it was that he brought—Peter, who became one of the greatest apostles of Jesus. He preached on the day of Pentecost and saw three thousand people born again. He healed a lame man at the gate of the temple and five thousand were born again as a result. He raised Dorcas from the dead, introduced Christianity to the Gentiles, and wrote two books of the Bible that have ministered to millions of people through the centuries.

Just think how many millions of people Peter touched, and how Andrew was responsible for it all. The accomplishments of Peter recorded in Scripture far outnumber those of Andrew, yet without Andrew, Peter would not have known Jesus. In the eyes of God, what Andrew did was just as important as what Peter did.

As the one who introduced Peter to Jesus, Andrew had a part in all Peter's exploits. Therefore, on the Day we receive our rewards from the Lord, Andrew will share every reward Peter receives.

You may not ever shake your world as Peter did his, but God has called you to share your faith with others as Andrew did. Who knows, one person you lead to Jesus could be another Peter.

God Abides by His Laws
Romans 3:19-31

Where is boasting then? It is excluded. By what law? of works?
Nay: but by the law of faith.
Romans 3:27

Paul speaks here of "the law of faith." Faith is a law. Just as there are laws in the physical world, there are laws in the spiritual realm also. Failure to understand this is at the heart of many Christians' frustrations. They don't understand why God doesn't do something to end their pitiful situation or that there are laws they must learn to obey.

A person who walks off a ten-story building shouldn't be upset with God when they fall. The law of gravity, which God created, can hurt or kill them if they don't respect that law and operate accordingly. Gravity-caused is not personal on God's part. The law of gravity is a constant God will not cancel for our convenience. If He were to stop gravity so the person walking off the ten-story building wouldn't get hurt, there would be untold other deaths from car and train wrecks. That's what makes gravity a law. It's constant and universal.

Likewise, there are laws God has to honor. He loves us and wants to answer our prayers, but He will not violate His laws to do it. There is a law of sowing and reaping in the physical world. The farmer who doesn't sow shouldn't be upset with God when the crop he prayed for doesn't grow. He didn't cooperate with the laws God established. In the same way, many Christians don't cooperate with God's laws for prosperity, healing, success, and joy; yet they can't understand why they aren't reaping positive results.

Today make it a priority to begin to learn and then operate according to God's spiritual laws. Then you will enjoy the blessings God wants you to have.

True Prosperity Isn't Selfish
2 Corinthians 9:1-15

And God is able to make all grace abound toward you; that ye, always
having all sufficiency in all things, may abound to every good work.
2 Corinthians 9:8

D o you think Jesus was selfish in any way? And yet, if you really study the Gospels, it is obvious Jesus never wanted for anything. Furthermore, He had so much money that He had to have a treasurer. (John 13:29.) Yet most Christians oppose financial prosperity because they equate it with greed. No doubt many Christians err in this regard, but it is the love of money that is the root of all evil not money itself. (1 Tim. 6:10.)

True prosperity as the Bible teaches and Jesus practiced it is not selfish or greedy. Jesus had a lot because He gave away a lot. As this verse says, the Lord prospers us so we can have enough to give to every good work. Those who are unable to give to everything they would like haven't yet reached the level of prosperity God has provided for them.

Another verse that makes this point is Ephesians 4:28, which says, "Let him that stole steal no more: but rather let him labour, working with his hands the thing which is good, that he may have to give to him that needeth." God prospers you so you can bless others. When you understand the biblical concept of prosperity isn't selfish at all, you want to prosper so you can be a blessing to others.

Believers who say, "I have enough and would never ask God for any more," reveal that they think prosperity is just for them. With that attitude, it would be selfish to believe for more money. They think they are being holy by just getting their bare needs met. But once they see that prosperity isn't only for them, that they can be a channel of God's supply to others, this "I have enough" attitude will be exposed for what it is: silly and self-righteous!

What is your reason for wanting to prosper? Is it all for selfish gain, or do you want to be a blessing to others? Today, instead of thinking about all your financial needs and desires, look around you and consider the needs and desires of others. Stir up a desire to meet those needs. Then you will have the right motivation to prosper. If God can get it through you, He'll get it to you.

Settle Your Doubts
John 1:43-51

And Nathanael said unto him, Can there any good thing come out of Nazareth?
Philip saith unto him, Come and see.
John 1:46

Nathanael suffered from a skepticism that afflicts many people today. Jesus is nothing more than someone who has caused a lot of trouble between people. All this "Jesus is the only way," talk is divisive, and many people think nothing good comes from Christianity. Like Nathanael, they are doubters.

It is to Nathanael's credit that he came to Jesus and gave Him a chance to prove who other people like Philip said He was. We can only speculate what it was that Jesus saw Nathanael doing under that fig tree (v. 50), but it is clear that it was something that proved beyond a doubt to him that Jesus was the Messiah. Jesus didn't rebuke Nathanael for his doubts; instead, He removed them.

Jesus is the Living Word, and His Word has an answer for every doubt that we or anyone we encounter might have. We need to be honest and forthright before Him as Nathanael was (v. 47), and we need to go to Him when we are plagued with doubts instead of running from or avoiding Him. Jesus knows what we go through in life; He's been there. (Ps. 103:14.) It is not a sin to doubt, but it becomes sin if we harbor those doubts, never go to the Lord with them, and allow unbelief to take hold of our hearts and minds.

Be like Nathanael today and bring any doubts you have concerning your faith to Jesus. Let the Holy Spirit teach you the truth from His Word. I guarantee that you will be changed.

Just Do It!
John 2:1-11

His mother saith unto the servants, Whatsoever he saith unto you, do it.
John 2:5

Mary knew Jesus like no one else did at this point in His life. Although it is certain she knew Jesus was no ordinary man, her request to provide the guests with more wine reflected her belief that He could do things others could not. Her instructions to the servants were, "Whatsoever he saith unto you, do it." This shows that she not only knew Jesus could work miracles, but she knew His way of doing things did not always conform to conventional thought.

Sure enough, Jesus told the servants to fill the pots with water and then take it to the governor of the feast. This defied logic. Everyone knew the guests wanted more wine, not water. Yet at Mary's bidding these servants did exactly what Jesus told them to do, and the results were wonderful. The water turned to the very best wine.

This miracle would not have taken place if the servants had not done what seemed foolish to them. The Lord's ways are not our ways, and His thoughts are not our thoughts. (Isa. 55:8.) To see His miraculous power in our lives, we must do whatever He tells us to do, regardless of how foolish it may seem.

The foolishness of God is always wiser than the wisdom of men, and the weakness of God is stronger than men. (1 Cor. 1:25.) Today, whatsoever He says unto you, just do it!

Faith and Hope
Hebrews 11:1-6

Now faith is the substance of things hoped for, the evidence of things not seen.
Hebrews 11:1

There is a direct relationship between faith and hope. You can't have one without the other. Faith gives substance to things we hope for. Remove hope, and faith has no goal to achieve. A story that illustrates this is about a hillbilly who wandered into a church service. As the people started praising the Lord, the temperature in the sanctuary began to rise. He saw an usher walk over to the wall and turn a dial on a little white box. Within seconds cool air blew out of a vent onto this hillbilly's face. Utterly amazed, he thought this must be one of the greatest things he'd ever experienced!

Immediately he asked the usher what the device was and how he could get one. The usher told him it was a thermostat and all hardware stores sold them. The man could hardly wait to get out of the church service and buy one. After purchasing a thermostat, he took it home and mounted it on the wall of his house; but no matter how much he turned the dial, cool air never came out.

This man didn't realize that the thermostat didn't produce the cool air. It only turned the power unit on and off. That's a beautiful picture of the way faith and hope work together. Hope is your thermostat. It activates your faith. Although your faith is the power that overcomes the world, hope is the victory your faith moves to achieve. Remove hope, and faith will never be activated. Faith must have a goal.

Let God build a strong hope in you today, and then release all your faith behind it.

There Is a Righteous Anger
John 2:12-14

And when he had made a scourge of small cords, he drove them all out of the temple,
and the sheep, and the oxen; and poured out the changers' money,
and overthrew the tables.
John 2:15

Jesus brought the message of "love your enemies" to the world and demonstrated it in such a way that some people have forgotten instances like this, when Jesus clearly showed anger.

Anger can be a godly emotion. Ephesians 4:26 tells us to "be angry and sin not." There is a righteous type of anger that is not sin. However, Ephesians 4:26 goes on to say, "Let not the sun go down upon your wrath." That doesn't mean it is all right to be angry during daylight as long as we repent by bedtime. Rather, it speaks of how to handle this righteous type of anger. We are never to let it rest. We are not to put it to bed, but we are to keep ourselves stirred up against the things of the devil.

Throughout the Bible we are told to hate evil. (Ps. 45:7; 119:104,116; Prov. 8:17; Rom. 12:9.) When we see the enemy kill, steal, and destroy, it should make us angry! The key to distinguishing between a righteous anger and a carnal anger is recognizing who or what is the object of our anger. Godly anger is directed at the devil with no consideration of self, but carnal anger is self-centered and directed at people who hurt or offend us in some way. (Eph. 6:12.)

If you are angry with anyone today, forgive them and turn them over to God. But if you are furious with the devil for hurting or harming you or someone else, you are in full agreement with Jesus. Remember that He hates all evil. For that reason He defeated Satan and all the demons (Col. 2:15), and He has purchased total peace and victory for you.

The Joy of Being Born Again
John 3:1-21

Jesus answered and said unto him, Art thou a master
of Israel, and knowest not these things?
John 3:10

Nicodemus was a highly educated man in religious matters, yet he didn't have the slightest idea what Jesus was talking about when Jesus told him, "Except a man be born again, he cannot see the kingdom of God" (v. 3).

Nicodemus' relationship with God was purely academic. He knew a lot about God, but he didn't personally know God. Being the Son of God, Jesus had a uniquely intimate relationship with the Father that intrigued Nicodemus. He sought to understand it, and Jesus told him that this same kind of relationship was available to him through being "born again."

Of course, Nicodemus asked in verse four, "How can a man be born when he is old? can he enter the second time into his mother's womb, and be born?" Jesus explained that being one with God spiritually happens only when a person's spirit is reborn and regenerated by the indwelling power of the Holy Spirit. He said, "Except a man be born of water and of the Spirit, he cannot enter into the kingdom of God. That which is born of the flesh is flesh; and that which is born of the Spirit is spirit" (vv. 5,6).

The number-one thing that sets Christianity apart from religion is the born again experience. We don't just have a sure way to get to heaven; we have been born from above. We have God's Holy Spirit living in our spirits, and we are in constant communion with the Father, Jesus, and the Holy Spirit. Our eternal life is not just after our physical bodies die; it is the quality of life and spiritual blessing that we live in from the moment we are born again.

Christianity is a relationship, not a religion. As a believer, you have the exciting privilege of having continual fellowship with God your Father and Jesus your Lord and Savior through the Holy Spirit who lives inside you. Today, enjoy being born again.

The Greatest Prophet
John 3:22-37

He must increase, but I must decrease.
John 3:30

Jesus said in Luke 7:28, "Among those that are born of women there is not a greater prophet than John the Baptist." I believe the story of John shows us the main reason Jesus called him the greatest prophet that ever lived.

John the Baptist spent thirty years in preparation for his ministry. He didn't enjoy the normal benefits of childhood or adolescence. He lived out in the desert, away from people and separated unto God. (Luke 1:80.) Then finally, for approximately six months he enjoyed success in ministry like no other man ever had. The multitudes flocked to the wilderness to hear him preach. He became the most influential man in Israel and was known to the Roman rulers.

Then one day he baptized Jesus in the Jordan River and proclaimed Him the Messiah. (Matt. 3:13-17; John 1:29.) From that moment on, the multitudes and even his own disciples began to follow Jesus in ever-increasing numbers. This would have destroyed most men; but when he was questioned about it, John replied, "He must increase, but I must decrease." Shortly after that he was imprisoned (Matt. 4:12), and after one-and-a-half years in a dark cell, he was beheaded.

John's greatness didn't lie in his own success but in the success of another. Jesus owed much of His success to the preparatory work of John. In our celebrity-conscious society, few people want to be the backup singer or the stage manager. We have adopted a mentality that unless we are in the limelight we are nothing. That's not the way Jesus sees things! He taught in Matthew 23:11, "He that is greatest among you shall be your servant."

Surely John the Baptist was the greatest prophet because he was a great servant to Jesus. His life and Jesus' commendation for him is all you need to inspire you to be a great servant to Jesus and everyone you meet today.

Act on Your Faith
James 2:14-26

Even so faith, if it hath not works, is dead, being alone.
James 2:17

On December 30, 1973, I hurt my back very badly. I experienced excruciating pain and couldn't straighten up. I could barely talk, and my shoulder blades were nearly touching each other. It was the night before I was to be ordained into the ministry, and all I could think about was what a terrible testimony this would be at my ordination.

I prayed in faith that I was healed, and then I began to resist the pain and the devil by acting on my prayer of faith. I did push-ups, deep-knee bends, bent over and touched my toes, and anything else I didn't feel like doing. There was improvement, but I didn't have a total release. I took a shower and was washing my hair to get ready for the service. It hurt terribly to bend my head under the spout, but I knew I was healed and was determined to act like it. In between the first and second rinse, all the pain left, and I was completely normal.

Imagine a person in a burning building. They believe they will die if they don't get out of the building, but they just sit there. That is crazy, isn't it? Likewise, faith without the proper action isn't genuine faith at all. We must act according to what we are believing. In my case, I needed healing in my back, so I used my back as though I was already healed–because I was!

People who say they believe God for prosperity, but don't give, are deceiving themselves. A person who says, "I'm healed," but continues to act sick and dwell on their symptoms, is killing whatever faith they have. A person who intercedes for someone and then worries whether anything will ever happen is not acting in faith. True biblical faith must be acted upon. Therefore, act on what you believe today.

The Light to See Where You Are Going

Mark 4:21-23

And he said unto them, Is a candle brought to be put under a bushel,
or under a bed? and not to be set on a candlestick?
Mark 4:21

When Jesus said this, He had just taught and explained the parable of the sower to His disciples. This teaching stresses the importance of God's Word in our lives. We can't bear fruit without putting God's Word in our hearts any more than a farmer can have a harvest without planting seeds. Then Jesus said that a candle must be put on a candlestick to shine its light. The Lord was still speaking about the importance of His Word.

"Thy word is a lamp unto my feet, and a light unto my path" (Ps. 119:105). Jesus was saying that God's Word is how He sheds light on all of our situations. Without the illumination of God's Word, we will stumble around in the dark. Furthermore, what's the purpose of having a light if we aren't going to use it? Why would anyone place a lamp under his bed or a basket and block the light? That doesn't make sense. But that's exactly what we often do with the light God has given us.

How many times have we neglected meditating on God's Word because of our busy schedules, and as a result we just stumbled blindly through our day? The influence of God's Word in our lives is not a luxury we can do without. It's as essential as light in a dark room. Light in the darkness enables us to function as if it were day–as long as the light is in a prominent place.

Your heart is the candlestick on which you set the light of God's Word. As you meditate on it day and night, there is no circumstance or secret that will not be clearly revealed to you through the light of the Word. (Mark 4:22.) You will see where you are going and not stumble today if His Word is shining brightly in your heart.

Your First Love
Revelation 2:1-7

Nevertheless I have somewhat against thee, because thou hast left thy first love.
Revelation 2:4

D
o you cringe at this passage of Scripture? Most Christians do because they know they don't love Jesus as they should, and this just reminds them of that. But Jesus wasn't speaking of returning to how we first loved Him; He was talking about returning to our revelation of how He first loved us. As the apostle John put it, "We love him, because he first loved us" (1 John 4:19).

Often, preaching is centered on how we should love others. Although this is certainly appropriate, the greatest and most distinguishing characteristic of a true Christian is their love for the brethren. (John 13:35.) But we can't give away what we haven't received. Until we have a true revelation of how much God loves us, we can't genuinely love others. Trying to do so without a vibrant, experiential love within us is like trying to give someone a drink from a well that's run dry. It can't be done!

The Christian life is not just hard to live; it's impossible to live in our own strength. True Christianity is not you and I living for Jesus, but Jesus living through us. (Gal. 2:20.) Nowhere is this more apparent than in loving other people. The kind of love Jesus commands includes turning the other cheek (Matt. 5:39) and forgiving those who crucify us. (Luke 23:34.) This kind of love is humanly impossible. We can only live this way by walking in the supernatural love that only comes from God.

Therefore, loving others is the fruit—not the root—of God's love for you. As you return to the joy of understanding how much God loves you the way you did when you first received Jesus as your Lord and Savior, you'll love others more accidentally than you ever have on purpose.

Little Is Much When God Is in It
2 Kings 4:1-8

And Elisha said unto her, What shall I do for thee? tell me, what hast thou in the house? And she said, Thine handmaid hath not any thing in the house, save a pot of oil.
2 Kings 4:2

By anyone's evaluation except God's, this poor widow's resources were woefully inadequate to meet her needs. Her tiny bit of oil was worth only a pittance, certainly not enough to get her out of debt and the impending slavery of her children. Reason would say her situation was hopeless, but Jesus said, "With God all things are possible" (Matt. 19:26).

The widow knew she had this oil. She's the one who told Elisha about it. No doubt, she had taken a complete inventory of all her assets and had dismissed them as insufficient to meet the need. But little is much when God is in it! She had failed to factor into her equation what God could do with what she had. The man of God opened her eyes to the possibility of what God could do, and she acted in faith. In the end, she not only met her present need but had enough left over to live off of the rest of her life.

Like this widow, we often fail to see the potential of what God has given us. We look at ourselves and what we have only in human terms. We fail to factor in the power of God and His love for us. With His blessing, a few fish and a couple of pieces of bread can feed thousands. But first, we must take that step of faith and use what little we have as He instructs us.

This woman's oil didn't multiply until she had borrowed the vessels and began to pour out what she had. She prepared for increase and then began to give. As she gave of what she had, the power of God multiplied it back to her abundantly.

Everyone has something. What do you have today? It may seem too small to do any good, but give what you have to God in faith and watch it grow.

Your Whole Heart to Make You Whole
John 4:4-26

Jesus said unto her, Thou hast well said, I have no husband:
For thou hast had five husbands; and he whom thou
now hast is not thy husband: in that saidst thou truly.
The woman saith unto him, Sir, I perceive that thou art a prophet.
John 4:17-19

It didn't take great discernment for the Samaritan woman to make this last statement. Jesus had just "read her mail." He told her the most intimate details of her life. Anyone could have perceived Jesus was a prophet after something like that.

This woman came to get a bucket of water and encountered someone who was more than just a man. God was speaking to her. What was her reaction? She changed the subject. She brought up a doctrinal issue concerning the proper place to worship—anything to get Jesus' attention off of her personal life.

We all have a tendency to build walls of privacy around the intimate details of our lives. We are afraid to let anyone, especially God, look inside. The truth is, God already knows our hearts! He wants us to give all of our hearts to Him. He wants us to share everything with Him so that He can make us whole.

Jesus brought this woman right back to the subject of her personal relationship with God. He told her that the place of worship or the forms of worship weren't important. God was looking for people who would open their hearts—even the hidden parts—to Him.

Today you can stay occupied with everything except the one thing that counts which is to worship God with your whole heart in spirit and in truth. Choose to do the one thing He wants you to do. Open your heart fully to Him, and just watch the living water of Jesus pour through you and make you whole.

Spiritual Food
John 4:27-46

But he said unto them, I have meat to eat that ye know not of.
John 4:32

Food is essential for life. Without it we can't grow and remain healthy. We get strength and vitality from food; however, the wrong food can kill us. Improper diets have killed more people than any disease.

Our souls need nourishment too. The things we think on and the desires we have are food for our souls. Jesus said, "Man shall not live by bread alone, but by every word that proceedeth out of the mouth of God" (Matt. 4:4). He valued spiritual nourishment more than He valued physical nourishment. He was thrilled to see the Samaritan woman and the people of her town respond to His gift of salvation. His disciples had come with meat for Him to eat, but He said what nourished Him was people coming to Him for salvation.

Likewise, we should set our desires on the things of God so that spiritual matters are more important to us than physical ones. The wrong diet for our souls is the leading cause of failure and depression in the lives of Christians. The Bible says that being spiritually minded produces life and peace, but being carnally minded produces death. (Rom. 8:6.) In our health-conscious society, many of us wouldn't dream of abusing our bodies with a poor diet; yet, we kill our souls by feeding on ungodly, worldly things.

Today, treat yourself to a healthy, spiritual meal. Read your Bible and get filled up with God's Word. Then go to the mall and lead some people to Jesus. You will discover the "meat" Jesus loved more than any natural food.

All Debts Canceled
Luke 4:16-30

To preach the acceptable year of the Lord.
Luke 4:19

This Scripture was written prophetically by the prophet Isaiah about 650 years prior to when Jesus read it in the synagogue. It was read in Jewish synagogues thousands of times but never by the person it referred to. With this pronouncement, Jesus began the year of Jubilee.

The year of Jubilee is described in Leviticus 25. It was a year when no farmers worked in their fields and everyone kept the Sabbath. The Lord gave the people a miraculous provision the year before every Jubilee year started, and that sustained them for three years until their crops could once again be harvested.

The year of Jubilee was different than any other sabbatical year because it only occurred every fifty years and all debts were cancelled. All property was returned to its original owner, and anyone who had been sold into slavery was set free. It was a year of new beginnings.

Jesus proclaimed "the acceptable year of the Lord," which was a spiritual jubilee. We now live in a time when all our debts to God because of sin have been cancelled, and all the things the devil stole from us have been returned. Even our slavery to the devil has come to an end through the redemptive work of our Lord Jesus Christ.

Rejoice today because you are in the time of continuous Jubilee!

The Chosen Ones
Matthew 4:13-22; Mark 1:16-20; Luke 4:31-32; Luke 2:36-40

Now as he walked by the sea of Galilee, he saw Simon and Andrew his
brother casting a net into the sea: for they were fishers.
Mark 1:16

Jesus never chose an apostle from among the religious people. Every one of His twelve disciples was from the secular world. It wasn't because God didn't love those who were religious; it was just that most of those who were part of the religious system didn't have much faith in Him. They were so tied up in their own holiness and the outward appearance of being religious that they left out a personal relationship with Him.

One of the most common mistakes religious people make is to put faith in themselves. They think God accepts and uses them because of their holy lifestyle or special abilities. Paul said, "But God hath chosen the foolish things of the world to confound the wise; and God hath chosen the weak things of the world to confound the things which are mighty; And base things of the world, and things which are despised, hath God chosen, yea, and things which are not, to bring to nought things that are" (1 Cor. 1:27,28). That describes the twelve.

People who recognize their own inabilities and weaknesses are more dependent on God out of necessity. That is the way God wants it. He is constantly searching for someone who recognizes they are nothing apart from Him. Then He can do something through them. (2 Chron. 16:9.)

Instead of thinking of all your responsibility today, respond to His ability. Empty yourself and allow Him to be everything to you. You will be surprised at how much you will accomplish and how much better you will feel.

Demons in Church
Mark 1:21-28; Luke 4:33-37

And there was in their synagogue a man with an unclean spirit; and he cried out.
Mark 1:23

Many people don't associate demon-possessed people with places of worship. Yet, most of the demons Jesus cast out were encountered in the synagogue. Why would demon-possessed people be there? In some cases, the people were there because they were seeking help. A church, like a hospital, should offer people the cure for oppression and possession of demons; therefore, it attracts those who are sick.

In other cases, the devil sows these types of people in the church to spread spiritual disease. A church that is teaching the true Word of God should either try to evangelize these people or make them so convicted that they will move on. Sad to say, demon-possessed people can thrive in many religious settings today.

We always need to show love for the sinner as Jesus did, but we should cut the devil no slack. If a person wants to keep an evil spirit on the inside of them, they should not feel at home in church! Like in Jesus' day, they ought to be agitated and bothered by the presence and power of the Holy Spirit in their midst.

Today, let the Spirit of God live through you as He did through Jesus. If there is a demon present in anyone, you will either make people mad or glad. God will either use you to send them packing or set them free. If you are truly walking in the Spirit, you will never be indifferent to the enemy. You will expose him and defeat him, just like Jesus did.

Great Ministry
Matthew 8:14-17; Mark 1:29-34; Luke 4:38-41

And he came and took her by the hand, and lifted her up; and immediately the fever
left her, and she ministered unto them.
Mark 1:31

How did Peter's mother-in-law minister to Jesus and His disciples? Did she sit them down and preach to them? Certainly not. Yet sometimes people think the only way we can minister to others is to admonish them with the Scriptures.

Peter's mother-in-law apparently ministered to them by serving them. The word translated *minister* is the same word that was translated *deacon* twice in the New Testament, and *serve, served,* or *serveth* eight times. Her response to receiving a great miracle was to serve lunch!

This story should humble us. We should never despise "the day of small things" (Zech. 4:10). We can minister mightily for the Lord by doing some of the menial tasks that many consider to be unimportant. Jesus said that even a cup of cold water given in His name would not go unrewarded. (Matt. 10:42.)

Many Christians are waiting for the important jobs to come along, so they can make a big impact or receive a lot of recognition. In the meantime, they pass by the lesser opportunities to be a servant like Jesus in so many different ways. They forget He said that in the kingdom of God, we won't be given any great opportunities until we are proven faithful in the small things. (Luke 16:10.)

Today, ask the Lord to show you ways you can minister to others by serving them in any way, big or small.

Expand Your Vision for Miracles
Luke 5:1-11

Let down your nets… I will let down the net.
Luke 5:4,5

Jesus had just used Peter's boat to preach to the people, and He wanted to bless him for this. He also wanted to show Peter how He could meet all of his needs. Jesus told Peter to let down his nets for a catch. At that moment, all the fish in the lake started swimming for Peter's boat.

Unfortunately, Peter couldn't believe Jesus' promise over the fact that he had been fishing all night and had caught nothing. He certainly wasn't going to have better luck now. Jesus was a wonderful preacher, but what did He know about fishing? Peter was the expert there. It's to his credit that he obeyed, but he didn't do exactly what Jesus asked him to do. Jesus told him to cast his nets, and Peter only threw in one net. He obeyed, but he wasn't expecting much.

As a result, all the fish Jesus sent to fill many nets jumped into Peter's one net. The net wasn't able to handle all the fish, and it began to break. This was the biggest catch of Peter's life, yet it could have been even bigger! The fish were actually fighting to get into his net, but his vision was too small.

We often miss some of God's supply because we do not embrace God's vision for our lives. The widow in 2 Kings 4:6 could have had more oil, but she ran out of vessels to fill. Joash, the king of Israel, could have completely destroyed his enemies, but he wasn't aggressive enough. (2 Kings 13:18,19.) Likewise, we often limit what God wants to do for us because we don't fully embrace all He promises us in His Word. (Ps. 78:41.)

What has He told you to do? Do it with all your heart, and make plans for big results. Your faith determines the manifestation of God's supply.

God's Kind of Love
1 Corinthians 13:1-13

Charity [God's kind of love] never faileth.
1 Corinthians 13:8 [brackets mine]

There is a big difference between a fallen human being's love and God's love. Sinful mankind's corrupt nature doesn't have access to or understand God's kind of love. The Bible says God is love (1 John 4:8), and any man or woman who does not know Jesus as their Lord and Savior does not know God's love.

People have written millions of songs, plays, movies, and stories about love, but many of them are not God's kind of love. Human love and God's kind of love aren't in the same class. Essentially, human love is selfish, and God's love is unselfish. Human love says, "I'll love you as long as you do what I want you to do or as long as I feel like it." God's love is unconditional.

First Corinthians 13:4-8 lists the remarkable characteristics of God's love. Even few Christians fully appreciate how unique His love is. We often think God loves us in the way we have been loved in the past, but that's not so. Our bad experiences often prevent us from accepting God's love. We lower Him to our level and think His love is conditional and proportional to our performance. That's how everyone else loved us, but not God. His love is like no other love we have ever experienced.

God's love never fails, even when we do. His love is unconditional. Since we didn't do anything to earn it in the first place, He doesn't withdraw it when we don't deserve it. He loves us because He is love, not because we are lovable.

Make the decision today to renew your mind in the area of God's kind of love for you. Ask the Holy Spirit to teach you what His love is all about. This is a revelation that will change your entire life!

Spiritual Dyslexia
1 John 4:7-21

No man hath seen God at any time. If we love one another,
God dwelleth in us, and his love is perfected in us.
1 John 4:12

Dyslexia is a condition that causes a person to see things backward. For instance, the word G-O-D looks like D-O-G to a dyslexic person. This can be a serious problem because there's a big difference between God and a dog.

Spiritual dyslexia is found in religious people, causing them to see the truths of God backward. Religious people believe everything happens because of them, but the Bible says everything happens because of God. First John 4:12 is a perfect example of this. Religious people want God to dwell in them, so they try to love others, thinking that will cause His love to dwell in them. But that is just the opposite of what John said.

Loving others doesn't cause God to dwell in us or love us; having God dwell in us and experiencing His love causes us to love others. Our acts of holiness don't cause God to love us, but experiencing His love causes us to act holy. This is the difference between religion and true Christianity.

Religion tells us what we must do to be right with God. True Christianity tells us that we are right with God through our faith in Christ, and right actions just naturally follow. We can't walk in the Spirit by denying the flesh any more than we can bring light into a room by shoveling out the darkness. We must turn on the light to drive the darkness away. Likewise, we must walk in the Spirit to keep from fulfilling the lust of the flesh. (Gal. 5:16.)

You can't give away what you don't have! To set someone else free, you must be free. Let the Lord fill you with His love today, and you'll automatically love others. Walk in the Spirit, and you won't fulfill the lust of the flesh.

He Loved Us First

1 John 4:7-21

We love him, because he first loved us.
1 John 4:19

I t's amazing how we miss the truth of this simple and straightforward scripture. God doesn't love us for what we do—we love God for what He's done for us. All error in spiritual matters hinges on this point.

Everything we do must be in response to God's love, not to obtain it. Any good deed, regardless of its merit, can be rendered unacceptable to God if our motives are to obtain His favor through what we do. He doesn't relate to us based on our performance. Praise Jesus! God commended His love to us while we were still sinners. (Rom. 5:8.) He loves us because He is love, not because we are lovable.

Only when we appreciate this unearned, unmerited love of God can we truly love Him in return. God is love (1 John 4:8) and all love comes from Him. Love doesn't originate with us. We can only give love to the Lord and to others after we receive it from Him.

Relax! You don't have to force yourself to love God. All you need to do is focus your attention on how much He loves you. As you begin to explore the depths of His love for you today, you will automatically begin to love Him in return. It's inescapable. Instead of focusing on what you should be doing for the Lord, focus on what He's already done for you. Then love and appreciation will flow freely from your heart toward your loving Father.

Express Love by Your Actions
1 John 3:13-19

*But whoso hath this world's good, and seeth his brother have need, and shutteth up
his bowels of compassion from him, how dwelleth the love of God in him?*
1 John 3:17

We live in an area with one of the richest deposits of gold in the world. It is estimated there is still twice as much gold in the ground as was ever mined. We have huge gold mines operating today. This has caused many people to try their hand at prospecting with the hope of striking it rich.

I remember when one of my Bible school students came running up to me and asked me to hurry out to his pick-up. He had the bed of his truck piled high with what he was sure was millions of dollars worth of gold. But it was just pyrite, or what we call "fool's gold." I couldn't help but laugh since I had tons of it on my property. Yet he was convinced he had hit the mother lode. It was weeks before he washed all that dirt out of his truck.

The real and the counterfeit look alike, but there is always a way to discern the precious from the ordinary. Gold is distinguished by the way it reacts to certain chemicals such as acid. The acid test for true love is action. Jesus said, "If ye love me, keep my commandments" (John 14:15), and then He gave us a new commandment: "That ye love one another; as I have loved you, that ye also love one another" (John 13:34).

It's easy to say you love someone, but how do you treat them? That's the test that distinguishes God's kind of love from all counterfeits. Make sure you love the Lord and others in Spirit and in truth, and treat them as Jesus would.

God's Kind of Love Is Content
1 Corinthians 13:1-13

Charity envieth not.
1 Corinthians 13:4

God's kind of love is not envious. The dictionary defines *envy* as "discontented desire or resentment aroused by another's possessions, achievements, or advantages." A person who is discontent or resents others who have more things, talent, or a better job, is a person who doesn't appreciate God's love for him or her. If they would receive God's love for them, a supernatural contentment would settle into their lives.

Discontentment is envy and is at the root of all temptation. Take Adam and Eve as an example. Before the devil could get them to sin, he had to make them discontented. That was no small chore. How do you make people who are living in perfection dissatisfied? They had no needs. They had never been hurt or abused. They couldn't blame their actions on their dysfunctional family. However, the devil made them believe they were missing out on something. He made two people, living in paradise, dissatisfied with perfection. That's amazing!

This shows us that contentment isn't a state of being but a state of mind. If perfect people living in a perfect world could become discontented, then certainly imperfect people living in an imperfect world can be discontented. That's why the Bible admonishes us to learn to be content in all states. (Phil. 4:11.) Only God's love will give us the contentment we desire.

Ask the Lord for a deeper revelation of His love for you today. Realize that any discontentment is envy, and God's love is the antidote for this crippling attitude. Being content in His love is what will keep you from temptation.

Love Isn't Boastful or Proud
1 Corinthians 13:1-13

Charity vaunteth not itself, is not puffed up.
1 Corinthians 13:4

The old English word *vaunteth* simply means "to boast." The New International Version translates this phrase as "it does not boast, it is not proud." In other words, those who are full of God's love don't think they are better than others.

I've been on the platform with a number of Christian celebrities, and some have thought they were better than others. They demanded better rooms, better cars, better offerings, and said things like, "Don't you know who I am?" That's not characteristic of God's kind of love!

On the other hand, I was once with a television personality who is famous in both the secular and Christian realms. He showed the love of God that is in his heart. Because of poor weather, the crowds were a fraction of what was expected; yet this man gave it all he had, just as if there were thousands there. He ministered to the people individually, and not just the pretty ones but those who were hurting the most. He showed true humility, which spoke volumes to me of the work God had done in his heart.

Of course, the supreme example of God's love expressed in humility is our Lord Jesus Christ. He was King of kings and Lord of lords, yet He regularly associated with the lowest of the lowest. It was God's love that compelled Him to lay down His life for us, and if we have His kind of love, we can do the same for others.

Today, be mindful of your attitudes toward people. Do you think you are better than some and not as good as others, or do you love everyone with the love Jesus has for you?

God's Love Behaves
1 Corinthians 13:1-13

Doth not behave itself unseemly.
1 Corinthians 13:5

One of the biggest lies the devil ever sold us is that love is an overpowering feeling that cannot be controlled. However, God's kind of love never acts in an inappropriate way. Greek scholar Fritz Rienecker says, "Unseemly means to behave indecently or in a shameful manner." God's love is tactful and does nothing that would raise a blush.

People who are so overwhelmed with love that they just can't control themselves, aren't overwhelmed with God's love at all. That unseemly love is devilish. It's selfish and full of lust. The old line, "We just love each other so much that we can't control ourselves," is more accurately rendered, "We are so full of lust that we can't control ourselves."

Understanding this will shine the light of truth on many of the lies Satan brings our way. Any time we are smitten with feelings for someone other than our mate, it is not God's kind of love. His love will never act contrary to His Word. God's kind of love will never leave us either. Anytime we feel like love is gone, all that really happened is that lust has gone. God's kind of love never fails. (1 Cor. 13:8.)

Ask the Lord to help you redefine what true love is—on His terms, not yours. Start with the assurance that His kind of love is not a rush of hormones that'll get you in trouble! His love will bring peace and abundant life.

God's Love Isn't Selfish
1 Corinthians 13:1-13

Seeketh not her own.
1 Corinthians 13:5

S atan has tried to counterfeit every good thing God has given us. He has succeeded in selling the world a corrupted, inferior type of love. Hollywood has been a big asset to the devil in this battle. Movies portray an emotional, sensual lust as "love," but it has no basis in reality. It causes people to long for some utopia where every sense is fully satisfied at all times, but human love can never fully satisfy anyone's deep need to be unconditionally loved. This is God's kind of love.

The most distinguishing characteristic of the true God-kind of love is that it's not selfish or self-serving. True love isn't getting what you desire; it is selfless and giving. Just look at Jesus, the greatest example of God's kind of love that the world has ever seen. The world will tell you that living selflessly is joyless and miserable, but Jesus was full of joy and never miserable. He demonstrated the secret to life is selfless love.

Jesus didn't come to this earth to satisfy Himself. Ultimately, He did receive great satisfaction by redeeming mankind back to God, but He became a human being for His Father and for us, not for Himself. He left all the splendor of glory and came to dwell in the most humble surroundings. He left the adoration of all creation to live for thirty years in relative anonymity.

Although some praised Jesus during His ministry, He endured the scorn and ridicule of the religious establishment. Then He suffered the ultimate rejection of crucifixion and took all the shame that went with being a condemned criminal. He did all of this because "God so loved the world, that he gave his only begotten Son" (John 3:16).

Test your love toward others today by asking yourself this simple question, "Am I saying or doing this for me or for someone else?" Focus on expressing love to others, and see how differently your day goes.

God's Love Doesn't Have a Short Fuse
1 Corinthians 13:1-13

Is not easily provoked.
1 Corinthians 13:5

D uring a weeklong meeting in a church of about 600 people, I taught on God's grace and longsuffering toward us, and many were set free. However, the pastor would lead praise and worship each night and then would conspicuously walk down the aisle and right out of the church. It was obvious he didn't like what he was hearing at all.

I tried to balance everything so that no one would think I was encouraging sinful living, but the pastor didn't stay for the messages. The last night of the meeting, I was desperate to penetrate his rejection of the teaching. He led a song that talked about how we should be loving and longsuffering toward others, forgiving them even before they ask for forgiveness. This was a song he wrote.

Before he left the platform, I asked him if he really believed what he sang. I asked if that principle applied even to those who treated us badly over and over. He was adamant that we should always forgive in all circumstances. Then I said, "Isn't it strange that some people believe God expects them to behave with more love toward others than they believe He shows them?" He got the point.

Another test of whether or not we are walking in God's kind of love is how patient we are. God's love is always patient. As true as this is with our dealings with others, it's even more true of God's dealings with us. God will not instruct us to do something that He is unwilling to do. God is not easily provoked. He's not the one with a short fuse. Many people think God is short-tempered, but that isn't the truth.

Meditate on God's longsuffering love for you, and let Him show you how patiently He loves you today.

God's Love Doesn't Keep Score
1 Corinthians 13:1-13

Thinketh no evil.
1 Corinthians 13:5

Many years ago, Jamie and I sat down to have a "discussion." We felt we needed to talk some things out. What we did was give each other a list of what we thought the other was doing wrong. Amazingly, this list went back years and included even the smallest acts. It became obvious to both of us that we had been keeping a mental ledger of all the things we thought the other was doing wrong.

This isn't God's kind of love. It is not the forgiving love of Jesus we are supposed to enjoy and walk in every day. Therefore, we made a decision to quit keeping score. No more storing up all the things that hurt us so we could use them in our next "discussion." At first this was scary. It was like taking all the ammunition out of our weapons, but then we realized that we weren't each other's enemy! We shouldn't have any weapons pointed at each other.

We made a decision not to dwell on the things we disliked about each other. We chose to think only on the good and let God take care of the rest. It's amazing how much of a difference this has made. The love of Jesus worked a lot better than our accusations and indictments to make our marriage a great one.

Thinking on evil only gives fuel to the fires of self-pity, anger, and bitterness that Satan wants to ignite within us. Thinking on the wrongs we suffer from others magnifies the offense until it becomes bigger than it actually is. The devil loves to take a small, splinter-size offense, magnify it to the size of a baseball bat, and then beat our brains out with it. Don't let him do it to you.

Decide today to quit keeping score of all the offenses that come your way. Forgive and go on, thinking instead on things that are pure, lovely, and of good report. (Phil. 4:8.) Then you'll enjoy His peace. (Isa. 26:3.)

God's Love Rejoices in Truth
1 Corinthians 13:1-13

Rejoiceth not in iniquity, but rejoiceth in the truth.
1 Corinthians 13:6

*R*ejoice means "to experience joy or pleasure." A great indicator of whether or not we are walking in God's love is what gives us pleasure. God's kind of love only gets pleasure from things in line with His Word, which is truth. (John 17:17.)

Those who receive pleasure from sin aren't full of God's love. It doesn't matter whether they are personally doing it or just watching others commit acts of sin. God's love is pure and evokes purity in everyone it touches. Therefore, it shouldn't give us pleasure to explore all the weird and perverse things that go on in the world today.

Christians should get no pleasure from watching talk shows that investigate every type of immorality in the world. They should never look to magazines and books that glorify relationships contrary to God's blueprint for their entertainment. Movies that exalt values other than God's values shouldn't provide amusement for His children either.

I'm not saying we must quit everything we're doing and be miserable. This is simply a thermometer for us to take our spiritual temperature. If we are rejoicing in iniquity and all kinds of evil things, we need a healthy dose of God's love. Once we are full of His love, nothing less will please us. His love will spoil us!

Ask the Lord for a revelation of His pure love for you today. Then let His love redefine what causes you to rejoice.

God's Love Can Bear Anything
1 Corinthians 13:1-13

Beareth all things.
1 Corinthians 13:7

Most people have unquestioningly accepted that there are restrictions on how far to go in loving others. It's like we build a fence and say, "Anything within this boundary I can take, but there are limits to what I can bear. After all, I'm only human!"

It is true that we are humans, and humans have limitations, but it's not true that we are only human. The born-again part of us is supernatural and full of God's love, which can bear all things. Look at Jesus. He loved and asked God to forgive the very ones who crucified Him. Then Stephen proved any believer could walk in the same love when he forgave those who were stoning him to death. God has given all believers the ability to operate in this type of love. (Eph. 4:32.)

God's love doesn't have any limitations as to what it can bear, believe, hope, and endure. Its sustaining power is limitless. Those who say they can't bear any more are simply revealing that they haven't yet drawn on God's supernatural love. They have been loving out of their natural, human love.

I want to encourage you today. There is an infinite supply of God's love within you that will never fail. All you need to do is look beyond yourself to the Lord and receive His supernatural love. He wants you to walk in His love more than you do.

Don't listen to your flesh, the devil, or other people who justify having limitations to how far you can love others. Instead, draw on the God-kind of love within you that bears all things. If you let His love flow through you, you'll have an endless capacity to love others.

God's Love Believes All Things
1 Corinthians 13:1-13

Believeth all things.
1 Corinthians 13:7

Did you know that God's love produces faith? Galatians 5:6 says that faith works by love. When we experience the love God has for us, faith comes as a natural by-product. If we are struggling to walk in faith, we are actually failing to stay focused on the infinite love God has for us. If God Almighty is for us, who or what can be against us? (Rom. 8:31.)

A young child in their father's arms isn't worried about anything. They trust their father completely and don't have a care in the world. They don't struggle to believe for their meals, clothes, or future needs. Their loving father takes care of it all. That's the exact comparison Jesus made to encourage us to trust God for our needs. (Luke 11:11-13.) A loving relationship with our heavenly Father is the key to a life of faith. If we have a problem trusting God in any area of our lives, that is an indicator that something is wrong.

When the warning light on the dash of your car flashes, you don't disconnect the warning light. Instead, you fix the problem that caused the light to come on in the first place. Then the light will automatically shut off. Likewise, a lack of faith is a warning light that indicates you aren't properly focused on the love of God.

If you want more faith to believe God today, attend to the place of intimacy with Him, where you are fully aware of His great love for you. Then your faith will be so abundant that you will just naturally believe all things.

God's Love Hopes
1 Corinthians 13:1-13

Hopeth all things.
1 Corinthians 13:7

Hopelessness is a terrible thing. God's Word says, "Where there is no vision, the people perish" (Prov. 29:18). Lack of hope is behind most, if not all, of the self-destruction we see in the lives of people today. Those who don't have a strong faith in the future throw today away without any consideration of the consequences. The destructive habits of people are rooted in despair or hopelessness. Jesus used the fool who said, "Let's eat, drink, and be merry" (Luke 12:19) as an example of someone without vision for his future. Those who don't live with one eye on the future are headed for disaster.

Why is it that most of society is without hope? It's because God's love is the source of true hope, and there's a genuine famine in the world today of the truth of God's love for us. On the whole, religion tells us of God's holiness and our relative unworthiness, but the true love of God is not a reality in the hearts of most people—even most Christian people. Luck and fate don't generate hope. Only knowing a personal, loving God is working all things for our good (Rom. 8:28) gives us true and lasting hope. God's kind of love hopes all things.

God has a perfect plan for your life. Regardless of where you are now—no matter how far off the track you may have strayed—God has a perfect course plotted for you to where you're supposed to be. (Jer. 29:11.) He loves you in spite of what you have or haven't done. As you believe this today, hope will spring up in your heart.

God's Love Endures
1 Corinthians 13:1-13

Endureth all things.
1 Corinthians 13:7

People are in a constant struggle to feel good about themselves, yet it seems life is full of pressures that repeatedly drive them to and beyond their ability to cope. They go past what they know to be the boundary of a proper response. Their drive to maintain self-worth excuses their actions. They say, "There are limits. I'm only human. How much can one person take?" Those who haven't tapped into God's limitless power supply will readily agree and let them off the hook for their selfish attitudes and actions.

The truth is that where our limits end, God's power begins. He does not abandon His children to their own resources. He lives in them, and He's placed His supernatural love and joy in them so they can endure all things. That means believers have no excuse for blowing up and giving up. We have God's ability to endure all things because we have His love which never fails.

This truth isn't meant to condemn; it's a liberating truth that will set you free. (John 8:32.) The temporary solace that comes from giving up or giving in will soon be swallowed by the harsh realities that arise from inappropriate behavior. As the apostle James said, "The wrath of man worketh not the righteousness of God" (James 1:20). Regardless of how good it may feel to give in to your carnal emotions, that surrender will only bring you grief.

Today if you will draw upon His love, God will empower you with supernatural ability so that nothing will be impossible for you. You can change the things that can be changed and endure the things that can't be changed. Live in His enduring love.

God's Love Never Fails
1 Corinthians 13:1-13

Charity never faileth.
1 Corinthians 13:8

How could Paul say this? In his day hatred, selfishness, oppression, and many other evils prevailed as much or more than today. Paul experienced the sting of persecution and had administered it to others before his conversion. Certainly, he had heard of the Christians who were burned at the stake and thrown to the lions by the Romans. In A.D. 70 the Romans completely destroyed Jerusalem, plundering everyone and everything in the city. Would Paul have changed what he wrote if these things had taken place before this letter to the Corinthians? Certainly not!

God is love (1 John 4:8), and He never fails. In our single frame view, it may appear that God doesn't always prevail, but that's not so. For example, take the persecution of the Christians in Paul's day. The 20/20 view of history shows us that many Romans embraced Christ and jumped into the theatre to die with the Christians who were being martyred. Christianity spread at a phenomenal rate under Roman persecution. In less than thirty years the Roman world was evangelized. In just three hundred years, the seemingly undefeatable Roman Empire was conquered by God's love, and Christianity became the official religion.

God never fails, and His love never fails. Individuals may fail to respond to His love and thus bear the consequences, but love never fails. It will always prevail in the end. We just need to give it time. We need to walk in all its attributes of contentment, patience, endurance, rejoicing in truth, believing all things–The Lord doesn't force everyone and everything into compliance because it isn't time for that yet. Now is the time of mercy, when the Lord is longsuffering and gives everyone ample opportunity to repent (2 Peter 3:9,10.) As we act in love, we use the strongest force in the universe. History has proven the power of love. If we just believe and exercise patience, love will never fail us.

Drawn by His Power
Mark 1:35-39; Luke 4:42-44

And when they had found him, they said unto him, All men seek for thee.
Mark 1:37

Jesus' ministry was only a few months old and masses of people were seeking Him out. This is astonishing when you realize that Jesus did not use any of the conventional methods of publicity. He had already rejected publicity during His first ministry in Jerusalem. (John 2:24,25.) There was no natural explanation for Jesus' success.

God is the one who promoted Jesus, and He used supernatural means to do it. It was not the slick techniques of Madison Avenue that brought the crowds; it was the awesome manifestation of God's power. Just the day before, Jesus had cast a demon out of a man at the synagogue in Capernaum. (Mark 1:21-28.) This caused the whole city to gather at Peter's house where Jesus healed every one. (Luke 4:40.)

Jesus' display of the miraculous power of God was the spark that the Holy Spirit used to light a fire in the hearts of these people. Jesus had this power because of His intimate relationship with His Father. He was in continual communion with Him. When He wasn't ministering to the people, He was in prayer with His Father.

As you seek to touch others with the new life you've found in Christ, understand that God will bring them to you if you allow Him to work supernaturally through you. Decide today that you will open your mind and heart to the power of the Holy Spirit, and let God confirm His Word with signs and wonders and miracles through you. It is easy to lead people to Jesus after they are healed, delivered, and given the wisdom they need in His name!

Only the Hungry Are Fed
Matthew 5:1-9

Blessed are they which do hunger and thirst after righteousness: for they shall be filled.
Matthew 5:6

In the natural world, we often eat even when we aren't hungry. All we have to do is turn sideways and look at ourselves in the mirror to prove this! In the spiritual realm, however, we must be hungry to be fed. One of the worst things that can happen to us is to become spiritually complacent.

Being hungry for the things of God is one of the best things that can happen to you. Most believers don't feel that way. They would rather have the feeling of being full and content all the time, but Jesus promised us fullness if we would first hunger. He said, "No hunger, no fullness."

Therefore, what many of us dislike is actually a sign of spiritual health. Longing for more of God is a healthy sign. We never hunger for God on our own. That is not a function of our fallen nature. Only our born-again spirits can hunger for more of God under the unction of the Spirit of God in us. (John 6:44.) It is the Spirit in us who draws us by giving us an insatiable appetite for everything God is and has for us.

Hungering for God doesn't cause God to move in your life; it is a sign He is already at work in you. Today, praise Him for spiritual hunger, and be encouraged and excited when you experience it. He won't make you hungry and then let you starve. He will make you hungry so He can fill you with His wisdom and blessings and love.

He Will Share His Reward
Matthew 5:10-12

Rejoice, and be exceedingly glad: for great is your reward in heaven:
for so persecuted they the prophets which were before you.
Matthew 5:12

Jesus said persecution should actually cause us to rejoice. There are many positive things about persecution, but one of the best reasons to rejoice is because of the reward awaiting us in heaven after we endure it, refusing to lose our faith in Him.

Jesus takes the persecution of His saints seriously, as can be seen during the Damascus road experience of the apostle Paul. The Lord asked Paul (then Saul), "Why are you persecuting me?" (Acts 9:4). He didn't say, "Why are you persecuting my people?" but "Why are you persecuting Me?"

It is not actually us that people are rejecting; they are rejecting the One we represent. We are the body of Jesus Christ on this earth. Whatever people say or do to us, they are saying it and doing it to Jesus. Therefore, Jesus promised to share His reward with us. Jesus will share all His glory and honor with those who have suffered shame for His name's sake. (Rom. 8:17.) What a great reward.

Focusing on the reward instead of the persecution can actually make you rejoice when people speak against you or mock you because of your faith. (Acts 5:41.) Paul actually longed to experience the fellowship Jesus provided to those who suffered for His sake. Paul knew he would not only know Jesus more intimately but also walk in His resurrection power. (Phil. 3:10.)

For all these reasons, if you encounter persecution for your faith in Jesus Christ today, lift up your head and rejoice! His reward is infinitely greater than any suffering you endure.

Salt Shakers
Matthew 5:13-16

Ye are the salt of the earth: but if the salt have lost his savour, wherewith shall it be salted? it is thenceforth good for nothing, but to be cast out, and to be trodden under foot of men.
Matthew 5:13

What is it that will be cast out and trodden under foot of men? Is it the salt, or is it possible Jesus is speaking about the world? If we as believers lose our preserving influence, if we fail to walk in the power of our redemption in Jesus, then there is no way He can reach out to the lost. The lost will be dominated by people who don't know Him or His salvation.

God works through His people. Another way of saying that is that Jesus works through His body. Although it is not our power that saves and heals and delivers people, it is His power in us. He cannot do anything without us. We are in a partnership.

Many believers spend a lifetime praying for God to move, not understanding that He is going to flow through them. It is not God who is failing to intervene; it is His people who are failing to cooperate and let Him flow through them.

Today you have Jesus living in you, and He wants to do amazing things through you. That means you are carrying around other people's miracles. Do not hinder or stop the miracles–big and small–that Jesus wants to do in you and through you. You are His salt. You preserve and give flavor to this putrefying world. So get out of the shaker, and let His life and love flow to someone who needs Him.

Exceeding Righteousness
Matthew 5:17-22

For I say unto you, That except your righteousness shall exceed the righteousness of the scribes and Pharisees, ye shall in no case enter into the kingdom of heaven.
Matthew 5:20

What did Jesus mean? Since the Pharisees fasted twice a week, does He mean we have to fast three times a week? Since they paid tithes on everything, including spices, does He mean anyone who fails to tithe is doomed to hell? No, definitely not. The Pharisees' righteousness was based on their actions. Jesus is advocating a righteousness that is based on faith in what He did for us.

Trusting in our own actions will never grant us access to God. We may be better than others, but who wants to be the best sinner in hell? We have all sinned and come short of perfection, which is what God requires. (Rom. 3:23.)

The only One who was ever good enough to earn right standing with God is Jesus. His righteousness is offered as a gift to anyone who will put his faith in Him as his Savior.

Jesus offers us a righteousness by faith that is so far superior to the self-righteousness that the Pharisees had, that there is no comparison. This is the righteousness that we need, and it is available to us only through faith in Christ.

Spiritual Fitness
Matthew 5:23-30

And if thy right eye offend thee, pluck it out, and cast it from thee: for it is profitable for thee that one of thy members should perish, and not that thy whole body should be cast into hell.
Matthew 5:29

Is Jesus advocating dismembering your body? Quite the contrary. To make a point, He is drawing on the universal drive of self-preservation that is inside every person. If you value your body so much that you would never sacrifice one of its parts, then you need to esteem your spiritual fitness much more.

Ever since the fall of Adam and Eve, our priorities have been misplaced. Great effort is put into preserving our physical lives while our spiritual conditions are often overlooked. They constantly get put on the back burner while we tend to more urgent matters of this life.

The physical body is just temporary. If we live seventy years or more, that is just a fraction of a second in all of eternity. Our spirits live forever, and the state in which they will exist eternally is determined by the choices we make in this life. If we choose to reject Jesus Christ as our Lord and Savior, our spirits will spend eternity in hell, separated from God forever.

On the other hand, if we choose to receive Jesus as our Lord and Savior, it means we have obtained eternal life with God. Our spirits will be alive to Him in this life and throughout eternity. This decision means we have put everything second to our spiritual wellbeing.

Today, choose to make your spiritual condition your top priority. Spend more time in the Word and praying and communing with the Father than you do in the gym working out. You will find that exercising your spirit brings greater health to every part of your being, including your physical body.

The Best Defense
Matthew 5:38-48

*But I say unto you, That ye resist not evil: but whosoever shall
smite thee on thy right cheek, turn to him the other also.*
Matthew 5:39

Would you rather have God defend you or defend yourself? That's
the choice Jesus offers here. "Turning the other cheek" is not a
prescription for abuse but rather the way to get the Lord involved
in your defense.

Many people believe these instructions of Jesus guarantee that others will
take advantage of them. That would be true if there was no God! However, when
we follow His commands, we know He is on our side. He said in Romans 12:19,
"Dearly beloved, avenge not yourselves, but rather give place unto wrath: for it is
written, Vengeance is mine; I will repay, saith the Lord."

When we fight back, we are drawing on our own strength; but when we turn
the other cheek, we are invoking God as our defense. Once we understand this, it
becomes obvious that these instructions are for our own good.

James 1:20 says that the wrath of man does not accomplish the righteousness
of God. Regardless of how appropriate our anger may seem or how much we think
our wrath could make a person or situation change, we will never achieve God's
best that way.

When you defend yourself, you stop God from defending you. When you
turn the other cheek to your enemies, you are releasing the power of God on your
behalf. Let God defend you today.

What's Your Motivation?
Matthew 6:1-4

Take heed that ye do not your alms before men, to be seen of them:
otherwise ye have no reward of your Father which is in heaven.
Matthew 6:1

The motive behind your gift is more important than the gift itself. Paul said if he gave all of his goods to feed the poor, or if he made the ultimate sacrifice of giving his own life for someone else, but it wasn't motivated by love, then his gift would profit him nothing. (1 Cor. 13:3.)

Many Christians give faithfully, but never see the hundredfold return Jesus promised because their motives are wrong. (Mark 10:29,30.) Paul said God loves a cheerful giver—not one who gives grudgingly or out of obligation. (2 Cor. 9:7.)

Jesus gave us the key to purifying our motives in this same teaching. He said, "But when thou doest alms, let not thy left hand know what thy right hand doeth" (Matt. 6:3). Giving in a manner in which you will not receive recognition for your gifts guarantees your motives are right and grants you the true joy that comes through selfless giving. (Acts 20:24.)

Ask the Lord to show you an opportunity today to give a kind word or a helping hand to someone who will not be able to repay you and where others will never know about it. This could be a motorist in a traffic jam, a co-worker, a spouse, a child who won't even notice your kind deed, or any number of other people. You will find that when you look for them, these opportunities are all around you.

Quality Prayer
Matthew 6:5-8

But when ye pray, use not vain repetitions, as the heathen do: for they
think that they shall be heard for their much speaking.
Matthew 6:7

Some of the most effective prayers are the shortest prayers. Jesus said, "Peace, be still," and the wind and the waves ceased. (Mark 4:39.) He said, "Lazarus, come forth," and Lazarus came back from the dead. (John 11:43,44.) On the other hand, today in many churches and prayer meetings, there is a new emphasis on the quantity of prayer instead of the quality of prayer. Jesus never advocated long prayers, and there are only a few instances where He prayed long prayers. This is not to say that communion with God is not important. It certainly is, but formal prayer is only one part of our communion with Him.

Many times we ask the Lord to speak to us, but He can't get a word in edgewise! We are doing all the talking. It is interesting that in Psalm 5:1,2 the words *prayer* and *meditation* are interchangeable. That means keeping your mind stayed on the things of God throughout your day is prayer. There are also times when you need to be still and know that He is God. (Ps. 46:10.) This is prayer too.

It is not the length but your heartfelt faith makes your prayer a quality prayer. Today when you pray, understand that God is not hard of hearing. You don't have to repeat something over and over to get His attention, and prayer is not a means for you to impress Him or anyone else. Simply communicate with Him according to His Word, and you will not only get answers but you will also grow up in Him.

Your Loving Father
Matthew 6:9-13

After this manner therefore pray ye: Our Father which art in heaven,
Hallowed be thy name.
Matthew 6:9

Although God was referred to as "our Father" thirteen times in the Old Testament, Jesus' frequent use of this title brings a whole new understanding of our relationship with God. Jesus referred to God as His Father over 150 times, and He spoke of God as being "our Father" thirty times. This infuriated the religious Jews of Jesus' day. They considered it blasphemy to call God their Father because they understood that to mean they were equal with God. (John 5:17,18.)

This title has become so common in the church today that many times we don't perceive its real significance. The revelation that we are instructed to call God "our Father" reveals the kind, gentle, loving nature of our God. (1 John 4:8.) Paul amplifies this by using the term *Abba Father* (Rom. 8:15), which is an affectionate term that a young child would use for their father. *Abba* corresponds to our English word *daddy*.

Jesus tells us what our relationship with God is and that we are to praise Him for it. It's a relationship that goes beyond any human relationship we could ever have on earth. It's a relationship of belonging to a Father who loves us because we are His, no strings attached.

Today when things get tough or when you need someone to celebrate with you, run to your Father God. Drop all pretense and formality and call Him "Daddy."

Your Treasure
Matthew 6:19-21

For where your treasure is, there will your heart be also.
Matthew 6:21

If we separate certain Scriptures from the rest of God's Word, they could be interpreted as saying that having money or wealth is wrong. However, there are other Scriptures that speak of riches as a blessing. What we learn from these two apparently opposite positions is that money is neither good nor bad. It is the love of money that is the root of all evil. (1 Tim. 6:10.) You can love money if you are rich or poor. Many people have committed the sin of loving money and they didn't even have a dime!

The love of things (covetousness) is idolatry, and this is what Jesus is addressing. Because it is so easy to lust after money and the things it can provide, God established a system whereby prosperity is a by-product of putting God first. As Matthew 6:33 states, "But seek ye first the kingdom of God and his righteousness and all these things shall be added unto you." We should no more reject the blessing of prosperity than we should covet it. Our treasure is Jesus, and as we love Him and serve Him only, all the material wealth we need will come to us.

The strength of a laser is that all the light is concentrated on one single point. Likewise, your strength as a Christian depends on how concentrated you are upon Jesus. You may know Him and also possess riches, but you can only serve one of them. You do not have the ability to faithfully serve both, and you will rely on one more than the other. Only one can have all of your heart and devotion.

The reason for not laying up treasures on this earth is so your heart will not draw away from Jesus and all He has for you. Today He is your treasure.

Don't Say It!
Matthew 6:25-34; Luke 12:22-32

Therefore take no thought, saying, What shall we eat? or, What shall we drink? or,
Wherewithal shall we be clothed?
Matthew 6:31

In this passage Jesus commands us not to worry or be anxious about our material needs being met. It would be impossible to have no thought whatsoever about our physical needs. Even Jesus thought about His need for money to pay taxes. (Matt. 17:24-27.) We are simply not to be preoccupied with riches or to spend our time worrying about the necessities of life. These things will be added unto us as we seek first the kingdom of God.

According to this verse, the way we take an anxious thought is by speaking it. Doubtful thoughts will come, but we do not sin until we entertain them and declare them. Speaking these thoughts is one way of entertaining them; therefore, don't speak any anxious thought!

It is imperative that we watch what we say. Jesus exhorts us to speak words in faith that line up with His Word because positive results will follow. If we speak words of doubt, we will eventually believe them and have the negative things that these words declare. There are no such things as "idle" words that will not work for or against us. Death or life is in the power of every word we speak. (Prov. 18:21.) Our words can be our most powerful weapon to release the power of God and defeat the devil, or they can become a snare of the devil. (Prov. 6:2.)

Today, watch your words. Refuse to entertain any thoughts of fear, anxiety, or worry about any situation you are facing. Instead, make a conscious effort to speak words that express your faith, trust, and confidence in the Lord.

Righteous Judgment
Matthew 7:1-5

Judge not, that ye be not judged.
Matthew 7:1

Although we often hear that we should not judge people, there are many examples of people judging others in the Bible. Paul prayed that our love would abound more and more in all judgment (Phil. 1:9), and Jesus and the disciples spoke of judging. So it is evident there must be a right way and a wrong way of judging.

In Luke 12:56-57, Jesus used the words *discern* and *judge* interchangeably. There is certainly nothing wrong with discerning or spiritually appraising a situation or person, and we are told to try the spirits. (1 John 4:1.) Judging as discernment is good. It is the condemning type of judgment that is wrong. We can defer passing a sentence on people to God, knowing only He can make a perfect judgment. (Rom. 2:2; Rev. 20:13.)

Jesus does not forbid judgment, but He warns us to be careful with how we judge someone else because we will be judged the same way. There are certain cases where we have to pass a condemning sentence, as Paul did or as a judge would do today. Pastors and elders are charged with rebuking and even disciplining church members, but it is not something to be done lightly. Judging is not aimed at the person but at the actions of that person. This warning constrains us to be certain that we have heard from God. We must not simply vent our own frustrations or personal biases.

Every Christian needs God's wisdom in making judgments. You can be confident today that the Holy Spirit will help you to spiritually discern or judge situations and people and then give you the courage and compassion to act according to God's Word.

God Answers Every Prayer
Matthew 7:6-8

Ask, and it shall be given you; seek, and ye shall find; knock,
and it shall be opened unto you.
Matthew 7:7

Prayer that meets the requirements outlined in God's Word is always answered. Many times we don't perceive the answer because it always comes in the spiritual realm before it is manifested in the physical realm. If we waver from our confident faith, then we abort the manifestation of that answer (James 1:6,7; Heb. 10:35), but God did answer. Everyone who asks receives.

In Daniel 9, Daniel prayed and waited a relatively short period of time to see his answer. In less than three minutes the angel Gabriel appeared and answered all of his questions. In chapter 10, Daniel prayed another prayer, and this time it took three weeks before an angelic messenger answered. What was the difference?

Most people believe God answered one prayer in three minutes and the next prayer in three weeks, but Daniel 10:12 says, "From the first day that thou didst set thine heart to understand...thy words were heard, and I am come for thy words." We learn later that Satan had hindered the angel from reaching Daniel. God was not the variable. He answers every prayer.

This is confirmed in Matthew 7:8, which says that everyone who asks receives. God answers, but Satan can hinder our prayers. Unlike Daniel, in the New Covenant we have authority over the enemy in Jesus' name, so we can bind the devil from hindering or stopping God's answer from manifesting in the natural realm. The truths of these Scriptures encourage us that God always answers our prayers.

Today when you pray, bind the devil and loose the power of the Holy Spirit by speaking God's Word into your situation. You can have full confidence and faith that God will answer your prayers. If you are waiting to see something manifest, don't doubt God! Recognize you are fighting an enemy and must persevere. Stand on God's Word until you see the answer.

Check the Fruit
Matthew 7:12-20

Wherefore by their fruits ye shall know them.
Matthew 7:20

The way you can tell whether or not a person is genuine is by the fruit they produce. This fruit is their lifestyle. Jesus made the point that you don't get bad fruit from a good tree, and you don't get good fruit from a bad tree. Many people say one thing, but their actions speak the opposite so loudly that you really can't hear what they are saying. If you are in doubt about receiving or following someone, look at the fruit they are producing.

In evaluating ministers and ministries, more attention should be given to the fruit they are producing. Fruit is the true test of ministers and ministries. If people are being saved, if lives are being changed, there is good fruit. Even though the minister may say something bad and make mistakes, the fruit is good. Therefore, you can say that the tree is good.

Every minister has shortcomings, just as every other member of the body of Christ does, but that doesn't mean their ministry is bad. When they say all the right things and seem sincere, but the lives of the people around them are shattered, torn, and in confusion and distress, then the fruit is bad. You can judge the effectiveness of a person by the fruit they are producing in their life, and you can judge the effectiveness of a minister by the fruit they are producing in their ministry.

Today, always make sure the fruit produced from your life is good first. Do you make a positive impact on people's lives? Do you turn people to the Lord or leave them hurt and confused? Examine your own fruit first, and then you will be able to properly examine the fruit of those who lead you in the church.

Healing Is God's Will
Matthew 8:1-4

And, behold, there came a leper and worshipped him, saying,
Lord, if thou wilt, thou canst make me clean.
Matthew 8:2

This leper believed Jesus had the ability to heal him, but he was not certain He wanted to heal him. Jesus showed him His willingness to heal, and since He is no respecter of persons, He established a precedent for us. (Rom. 2:11.) This leper did not know God's will concerning healing, but this is not the case with us. The Word of God is the will of God, and the Bible reveals it is always God's will to heal.

When Isaiah wrote, "With his stripes we are healed," in Isaiah 53:5, he was speaking of the physical healing of our bodies. Jesus provided for physical healing as well as forgiveness of sins. Many Scriptures mention the healing of our bodies in conjunction with the forgiveness of our sins. Healing is as much a part of our salvation as the forgiveness of our sins.

Nowhere do we find Jesus refusing to heal anyone. In light of His statement that He could do nothing of Himself but only what He saw the Father do (John 5:19; 8:28,29), His actions are proof enough that it is always God's will to heal. There are certain things Jesus suffered for us that we should not suffer. He died for our sins so we would not have to pay for them. (Rom. 6:23.) He took our sicknesses and diseases so we could walk in health. (Matt. 8:17; 1 Peter 2:24.) He became poor so we might be rich. (2 Cor. 8:9.)

If Jesus did all this for you, then you have a great life ahead of you! He has made every provision for you to walk in all He has provided for you today. Don't put it off a minute longer.

The Strength of Grace
Matthew 9:9-10; Mark 2:14-15; Luke 5:27-29

*And as Jesus passed forth from thence, he saw a man, named Matthew, sitting at the
receipt of custom: and he saith unto him, Follow me. And he arose, and followed him.*
Matthew 9:9

When we first come to Jesus, it is impossible to know everything that following Him will entail. We have no reason to be afraid of making a total commitment to Him because His undeniable love and care for us is fully evident every time we look at the Cross. We can forsake everything to follow Him! Once we make that decision, then He begins to live through us and we find a strength that is not our own and is equal to whatever test we may encounter. (Gal. 2:20.) It is called God's grace.

It is Christ living through us that is the secret of victorious Christian living. It is not us living for Jesus, but Jesus living through us. Failure to understand this simple truth is the root of all legalism and the performance mentality. The law focuses on the outer man and tells us what we must do. Grace focuses on the inner man and tells us what is already finished in Christ. When we focus on what we must do, we put ourselves under law; but when we focus on what Christ has done, we walk in the supernatural strength of His grace.

The Christian life is not just hard to live; it's impossible to live in your human strength. The only way to be like Jesus and do the works of Jesus is to let Jesus live through you. Just as the life of a root is found in the soil, a branch in the vine, or a fish in the sea, your true life today will only be found in union with Jesus.

Something New
Matthew 9:11-17; Mark 2:16-22; Luke 5:30-39

*And he spake also a parable unto them; No man putteth a piece of a new
garment upon an old; if otherwise, then both the new maketh a rent,
and the piece that was taken out of the new agreeth not with the old.*

*And no man putteth new wine into old bottles; else the new wine
will burst the bottles, and be spilled, and the bottles shall perish.*
Luke 5:36-37

Why didn't Jesus act according to the Old Testament religious traditions
and expectations? (Matt. 9:14; Mk. 2:18.) Jesus answered that
question in these two parables. He said He had come to do a new
thing that would not mix with the familiar Old Covenant ways. (Isa. 43:18,19; Jer.
31:31-34; Heb. 8:7-13.)

A new cloth sown on an old garment would shrink the first time it was washed.
Then it would tear away from the old garment that was already shrunk, making the
hole worse. This illustrated that Jesus did not come to patch up the Old Covenant
but to replace it with an entirely new one. (Heb. 7:18,19.)

New, unfermented wine had to be put into new wineskins to allow for the
expansion of gases within the skin as the wine fermented. An old wineskin would
simply burst from the gases produced by the new wine. The Old Testament laws
could never stretch enough to accommodate the New Testament truths of mercy
and grace. (Heb. 10:1-10.) Jesus completely set us free from the judgment of the Old
Testament laws. (Rom. 6:14; 7:1-4; 8:2; 10:3,4; Gal. 3:12-14,23,24; 5:4; Phil. 3:9.)
He replaced living by the Law outwardly with living by the grace of God within us.

Today do not make the same mistake these religious scribes and Pharisees
(Luke 5:30) did by trusting in your own efforts to produce your right standing with
God. Jesus did not come to accept your sacrificial acts! He came to sacrifice Himself
so that you could be free of sin and have a new life of grace in Him.

Living Holy
John 5:1-15

Afterward Jesus findeth him in the temple, and said unto him,
Behold, thou art made whole: sin no more, lest a worse thing come unto thee.
John 5:14

Jesus said that sin causes the tragedies of our lives. He asks us to live holy lives because if we give in to sin, we yield ourselves to Satan, the author of sin. Yielding to sin is yielding to a person—Satan. God doesn't impute sin to believers (Rom. 4:8), but the devil does. Therefore, our actions either release the power of Satan or the power of God in us.

Although God is not imputing our sins unto us, we cannot afford the folly of sin because it allows Satan to have access to us. When we sin, we give the devil an opportunity to produce death in our lives. The way to stop this is to confess the sin. First John 1:9 says that God is faithful and just to release forgiveness and wipe out that sin in our flesh. The blood of Jesus continually removes Satan and his strongholds from our lives.

Our sins don't make us sinners any more than the righteous acts of unbelievers make them righteous before God. Sin is a deadly thing that even Christians should avoid at all costs, but whether or not we sin does not determine our standing with God. Born-again believers are in Christ. They are not "in" the flesh even though they may choose to walk "after" the flesh from time to time.

What is your motive for living a holy life? You live holy supernaturally because your nature has been supernaturally changed. You have been given God's nature. Today, do not live holy in order to obtain relationship with God; live holy because of the relationship you already have with Him.

Rest in Jesus
John 5:16-27

And therefore did the Jews persecute Jesus, and sought to slay him,
because he had done these things on the sabbath day.
John 5:16

The Sabbath was first mentioned in Exodus 16 when the Lord started miraculously providing the children of Israel with manna in the wilderness. The Israelites were commanded to gather twice as much manna on the sixth day because God would not provide any on the seventh day. Shortly after this, the Lord commanded the observance of the Sabbath day in the Ten Commandments. (Ex. 20:8-11.) In this command, God connected the Sabbath with His seventh-day rest after creation.

As revealed in Colossians 2:16-17, the Sabbath was symbolic. According to Exodus 23:12, one of the purposes of the Sabbath was to give man and his animals one day of physical rest each week. Today's medical science has proven that our bodies need at least one day of rest each week to function at their peak. Deuteronomy 5:15 also clearly states that the Sabbath was to serve as a reminder to the Jews that they had been slaves in Egypt and were delivered from bondage—not by their own efforts, but by the supernatural power of God.

In the New Testament, there is an even clearer purpose of the Sabbath. In Colossians 2:16-17, Paul reveals that the Sabbath was only a shadow of things to come and is now fulfilled in Christ. Hebrews 4:1-11 talks about a Sabbath rest that is available to, but not necessarily functional in all, New Testament believers. This New Testament Sabbath rest is simply a relationship with God in which we have ceased from doing things by our own efforts and are letting God work through us. (Gal. 2:20; Heb. 4:10.)

The Sabbath is not a day, but rather a relationship with God through Jesus. Rest in His love, and let Him use you today.

About Those Scribes
Matthew 12:1-14; Mark 2:23; 3:6; Luke 6:1-11

*And the scribes and Pharisees watched him, whether he would heal on
the sabbath day; that they might find an accusation against him.*
Luke 6:7

The scribes copied the Holy Scriptures. They preserved the oral law in
written form and faithfully handed down the Old Testament. Ezra was
a scribe during the Babylonian captivity of the Jews, and he was a godly
man. The office of a scribe was a worthy one, but Jesus often rebuked the scribes
of His day for having gone beyond the job of copying the Scriptures. They had a
large volume of interpretations based on traditions. They added to the Scriptures
and thus made "the word of God of none effect" (Mark 7:13).

The scribes became an independent company of interpreters of the law and
leaders of the people. Even they sought to evade some of their own precepts. (Matt.
23:2-4.) They clashed with Jesus because He taught with authority and condemned
the external formalism they fostered. (Matt. 7:28,29.) They persecuted Peter and
John (Acts 4:3-7) and had a part in stoning Stephen. (Acts 6:12.) Although the
majority of scribes opposed Jesus, some did believe. (Matt. 21:15.)

The scribes appeared to be holy outwardly, but their hearts were far from God.
They missed Jesus, their Messiah, altogether. This can happen to us when we get
caught up in studying and knowing all about the Bible and forget our personal
intimacy with God. Our heads become filled with knowledge, and the Bible says
"knowledge puffeth up" (1 Cor. 8:1). We become proud, judgmental, and demanding
like the scribes.

Today let your heart be tender and receptive to the Holy Spirit as you read
God's Word. Worship Him as you study. Let your relationship with Him guide you.

His Amazing Mercy
Matthew 12:15-21; Mark 3:7-19; Luke 6:12-16

A bruised reed shall he not break, and smoking flax shall he not quench,
till he send forth judgment unto victory.
Matthew 12:20

God's mercy relieves the misery of fallen people. Many times His mercy is called *compassion* or *lovingkindness.* It is expressed toward sinners because of the misery sin has brought upon them.

Jesus compared the unbeliever to a "bruised reed." The reeds that grew in the marshy areas in the land of Palestine were very fragile and could be easily bruised or broken. The term "smoking flax" refers to a linen wick that was made from flax and burned brightly when floating on oil in an open lamp. However, when the oil was depleted, the flax would just smoke until the oil was replenished.

The meaning of these illustrations is that Jesus ministered in mercy to those who were bruised or broken by sin (Luke 4:18) and had lost their oil (spirit). He came to fill them anew. (Matt. 5:3; Acts 1:5; 2:4.) The Jews were used to the judgment of the law, but Jesus came to minister grace and truth (John 1:17), even to the Gentiles. (Matt. 12:18-21.) He came to take their sins away and light their spirits with His Spirit.

As believers, we know our great salvation was given to us because of God's mercy and not something we merited or earned. As the apostle Paul states, "Not by works of righteousness which we have done, but according to his mercy he saved us" (Titus 3:5).

Today you may feel like a bruised reed or a smoking flax, but no matter what you have done wrong or how you may have sinned, God's amazing mercy is available to you. Receive it and be restored! This is the victory Jesus came to give you.

The Law of Sowing and Reaping
Luke 6:17-49

Give, and it shall be given unto you; good measure, pressed down, and shaken together, and running over, shall men give into your bosom. For with the same measure that ye mete withal it shall be measured to you again.
Luke 6:38

This verse reveals God's law of sowing and reaping. It works in the spiritual realm as well as in the physical world. Just as we "give" seed into the ground to receive multiple seeds in return, so it is with everything we give. Whether it's money, possessions, emotions like love or hate, prayers, or our time, we will reap a harvest of whatever we give. We reap the same thing we sow, and we reap in proportion to how much we give. (Gal. 6:7,8.)

"He which soweth sparingly shall reap also sparingly; and he which soweth bountifully shall reap also bountifully" (2 Cor. 9:6). This law works on positive or negative things. If we sow condemnation, we will reap condemnation. However, when we catch ourselves in this sin, the greater law of God's forgiveness can help to overcome the harvest of condemnation we have sown. The negative things we have given don't have to come back to us if we apply the greater law of forgiveness. (1 John 1:9.)

Likewise, the good things we have sown can be voided if we don't continue in well doing. (Gal. 6:9.) If we pray for finances, God is not going to make counterfeit currency and put it into our wallets. He will use people to get the money to us. We need to believe the Lord hears and answers our prayers, and then pray for the people He's going to use to deliver the answer. This could mean an employer or the people who buy your goods.

Today, purpose in your heart to give whatever the Holy Spirit prompts you to give, whether it's your time, your compassion, your prayers, or your money. Do this in faith, knowing that you are operating in one of God's laws.

Whose Faith Was It?

Luke 7:11-17

And when the Lord saw her, he had compassion on her, and said unto her,
Weep not. And he came and touched the bier: and they that bare him
stood still. And he said, Young man, I say unto thee, Arise.
Luke 7:13-14

The widow's son being raised from the dead is often used to demonstrate that Jesus did some miracles without any faith from those receiving the miracle, that He could move by His faith alone. However, the prayer in Mark 6:5-6 shows that Jesus could not (nor would not) do many mighty works in His hometown because of the people's unbelief. Many other Scriptures reveal that faith must be present to receive from God. (Mark 11:23,24; James 1:5-7.)

Whose faith was present in this instance? First, the mother of the boy responded to Jesus in faith. For this woman to allow Jesus to interrupt the funeral procession and tell her to stop weeping has to be viewed as faith! These people were no different from mourners at funerals today. If she had rebelled at Jesus' intrusion, the crowd would have sided with her because of pity, but none of these reactions are recorded. Jesus was in command the moment she obeyed Him.

Second, it cannot be proven that a dead person has no choice in what happens. People don't cease to exist at death; they simply leave their bodies. The woman's son was very much alive in his spirit. Many people who have been raised from the dead have mentioned that they had a choice in whether or not to enter their bodies again. Although this principle cannot be verified by Scripture, it cannot be ruled out by Scripture either. We do know that when Jesus raised Lazarus from the dead, He didn't ask His Father to do it; He simply told Lazarus to come forth (John 11:43), so Lazarus heard Him. Interestingly enough, it was Martha's faith that brought the miracle. (John 11:22.)

Whatever you are facing today, have faith. Choose to believe that whatever God has promised He will perform and reach out in faith to receive your miracle.

Being Yoked To Jesus
Matthew 11:20-30

Come unto me, all ye that labour and are heavy laden, and I will give you rest.
Take my yoke upon you, and learn of me; for I am meek and lowly in heart: and
ye shall find rest unto your souls. For my yoke is easy, and my burden is light.
Matthew 11:28-30

Yokes were made of wood, with two hollowed-out sections on the bottom portion. A yoke rested on the necks of two oxen, which were hitched to a plow or a cart. Figuratively, a yoke symbolized servitude or submission. Jesus was admonishing us to submit ourselves to Him, for true rest comes from serving Him—not ourselves.

A new ox was often trained for plowing or drawing a cart by yoking him with an experienced ox. The yoke kept the young ox from doing his own thing, and he soon learned obedience to his master. In like manner, we are to commit ourselves to being yoked to Jesus. "It is not in man that walketh to direct his steps" (Jer. 10:23). We have to "bear the yoke in our youth" (Lam. 3:27) if we want to become mature Christians, but the comparison ends there. Unlike the sometimes harsh treatment oxen are given to bring them into subjection, Jesus is "meek and lowly in heart" and wins us by love. Jesus pulls more than His share of the load; therefore, our burden is light.

The most loving father in the world cannot compare with the love our heavenly Father has for us. Yet, many times we find it easier to believe in the willingness of a father, mother, or mate to help us than to believe God wants to protect us, bless us, and provide for us. Relatively few people really doubt God's ability, but they doubt His willingness to use His ability on their behalf. Their doubt and unbelief causes them to do without.

In these verses, Jesus assures you that His love and His willingness to demonstrate that love are far greater than you could ever experience in any human relationship. Not only does He want your love, but He wants you to let Him love you today.

The Unpardonable Sin
Luke 7:36; 8:3; Matthew 12:24-31; Mark 3:22-30

Wherefore I say unto you, All manner of sin and blasphemy shall be forgiven unto men:
but the blasphemy against the Holy Ghost shall not be forgiven unto men.
Matthew 12:31

In these passages of Scripture, Jesus said that blasphemy against the Holy Ghost was attributing the work of the Holy Spirit to the devil. Many people in the Bible did this, including Saul of Tarsus, who became the apostle Paul. However, in 1 Timothy 1:13 Paul said he received mercy concerning his blasphemy because he had done it "ignorantly in unbelief." Therefore, the blasphemy against the Holy Ghost that Jesus warned against must be willfully and knowingly reviling the Holy Ghost.

This parallels Hebrews 6:4-6, where qualifications are placed on those who can fall away from grace. This passage indicates that only a mature Christian can commit such a thing. Likewise, rash statements spoken against the Holy Spirit in ignorance or unbelief by those who don't really know what they are saying can be forgiven. This is not blaspheming the Holy Ghost.

From our human perspective, no clear line can be drawn as to when someone becomes accountable for blasphemies and has committed this unpardonable sin. We can be assured that God knows the hearts of all people, and He will judge righteously concerning this. His Word does show us that when anyone becomes a "reprobate," they lose all conviction from the Holy Spirit. (Rom. 1:28.) Therefore, anyone who is convicted and repentant over having possibly blasphemed the Holy Ghost has not yet reached the place where it is unpardonable; if they had, they wouldn't care.

If you keep your heart tender and sensitive to the Holy Spirit, you will not have any concern about committing this sin. Listen closely to Him today!

Worth It All
Romans 8:1-20

*For I reckon that the sufferings of this present time are not worthy
to be compared with the glory which shall be revealed in us.*
Romans 8:18

People suffer terrible things in this world. Just a casual glance at human history will reveal sufferings so unspeakable that we wonder how God will ever wipe away the tears from some people's eyes. (Rev. 21:4.) But this verse assures us that God's rewards will be much greater than our sorrows.

Many things in life come only through much effort and hardship. In childbirth, for instance, nine months of pregnancy isn't all fun, and the actual birth process involves pain and suffering. Yet Jesus said it's all soon forgotten because of the joy that the baby brings to the parents. (John 16:21.) Athletes endure suffering, yet all the afflictions of training are quickly swallowed up in the ecstasy of winning gold. The end result makes all the effort more than worthwhile.

That's the way it will be with us when we see Jesus. The worst injustice that any person in history has suffered is not worthy to be compared with the glory that awaits those who love the Lord. Anyone who doesn't see it that way is exalting their suffering over the eternal rewards they have in Christ. This can easily happen because it is so easy to feel the pain of the present, but they have never had a glimpse of the glory that awaits them. Certainly none of us have fully comprehended how wonderful eternity with Jesus will be. (1 John 3:2.)

Take joy in the truth that whatever you may be suffering today will fade into oblivion when you experience God's limitless blessings throughout eternity.

Your Faith Must Be in God
Mark 11:20-26

And Jesus answering saith unto them, Have faith in God.
Mark 11:22

T his verse is often used to teach that we must have faith in our faith. It's true that we need to understand and believe that the faith we have is sufficient to accomplish anything we need from the Lord, but this verse specifically teaches that our faith should be in God, not in our faith.

Our faith has to be in someone other than ourselves, or we are simply "New Agers." If our faith is in ourselves or our circumstances, we are doomed to fail. When our faith is in God, our faith is potent!

Hebrews 12:2 says we are to look "unto Jesus the author and finisher of our faith." Faith begins and ends with God. Faith is totally dependent on Him. A person whose faith is truly in God will not find it more difficult to believe for big things and easier to believe for minor problems. Everything is small compared to God's ability. He's limitless. If our faith is in God, then our faith should know no limits.

Is your faith in God? It's easy to tell. Can you believe for anything, or are certain things too big? If your faith is limited, then your faith isn't totally in God. You are still basing too much on yourself and others. When your faith is in God alone, nothing's impossible. (Mark 9:23; 10:27.)

You can limit God. (Ps. 78:41.) One of the quickest ways to do that is to have more faith in your ability to fail than in God's ability in you to succeed. Today put your complete faith in Him alone. That is the key to having a good day!

What Is in Your Hand?
1 Peter 5:5-11

Casting all your care upon him; for he careth for you.
1 Peter 5:7

My youngest son was almost three before he talked. There was nothing wrong with him—why should he talk when he had three people who got him whatever he wanted with only a point and a grunt? He was smarter than the rest of us, and this had to change.

Coming out of a public restroom one day, he tried to open the door but the spring in the door handle was too tight for him to turn. He looked at me and grunted, but I told him he would have to talk before I opened the door. He refused and wouldn't let go of the door handle. Others were waiting to get out, so now I needed to open the door. His little hand still clutched the door handle, and in order to turn it and open the door, I would have to squeeze his hand. I realized I had to get him to let go of the door before I could open it.

I had no sooner done that than the Lord spoke to me, "That's the way it is with you. You have your problems so tightly in your little hands, and I can't do anything about them until you let go." Wow! I instantly knew what He was talking about.

I had cares about finances for the ministry. I was thinking day and night about what I could do to turn the situation around. I hadn't cast my care on Him. I was still holding it tight in my little hands. I figuratively opened my hands and said, "Lord, I give this problem to You. You open the door." He did, of course, and our needs were supplied.

Are you keeping the Lord from intervening in your situation because you have such a tight grip on the problem? Let it go by casting all your care upon Him because He cares for you. He can handle your problems better than you can.

Beggar or Believer?
Mark 10:46-52

And they came to Jericho: and as he went out of Jericho with his disciples
and a great number of people, blind Bartimaeus, the son of Timaeus,
sat by the highway side begging.
Mark 10:46

Prior to this time, Bartimaeus had no option but to be a beggar. There was no cure for his blindness. But some people had told him about how a man named Jesus had healed blindness. Now that man was passing right by him, and Bartimaeus cried out to Him, calling Him the son of David. That showed that he recognized Jesus as his Messiah. This was his day. God in the flesh was passing by. Nothing else mattered!

Bartimaeus could have made a different choice. With all the people going by, he could have made more money begging that day than he would have made in months. This was the break of a lifetime. Beggars think that way. But Bartimaeus turned from being a beggar to being a believer that day. He wasn't thinking about an opportunity to succeed in his beggarly existence; he was thinking of a brand-new life, a life free from begging, an independent life where he could see to make it on his own and help others.

What choices are you making? Are you so occupied with continuing the status quo that you're missing the opportunity Jesus is giving you to change your life? Are you so busy making a living that you don't take time to study or pray? Are you unable to go to church because of the demands of your business? That would be like Bartimaeus not calling out for his healing because of his great opportunity to beg.

Don't let the demands of everyday life cause you to miss Jesus as He passes by you today. Throw off all your beggarly clothes and act like a believer.

How Desperate Are You?

Mark 10:46-52

And many charged him that he should hold his peace: but he cried the more a great deal, Thou son of David, have mercy on me.
Mark 10:48

It's amazing how much influence other people have on us. There is an intense desire for each of us to conform to those around us. We want to be part of the group. We don't like to stand out from the crowd. We want to be accepted. But the crowd is never going to go all the way with God. Those who receive God's best always have to buck the crowd.

Bartimaeus was compelled to conform to what others expected of him. Other men could choose where they wanted to live or what they wanted to do for a living, but a blind man had no choice but to beg. However, when Bartimaeus heard about Jesus and the miracles He was performing, suddenly he had a choice! He could choose to believe and be healed.

Inside that blind beggar's body was the heart of a believer. Bartimaeus longed for the day when Jesus would pass his way, and one day that came. He wasn't going to let anyone stop him from receiving his miracle, and the moment he knew Jesus was close by, he began to yell, "Thou son of David, have mercy on me!" Other people were embarrassed by his outburst, but he had spent a life of embarrassment and shame and wasn't about to continue that way. If he didn't make a spectacle of himself, things would never change. It was now or never.

There's something powerful about desperation when it is mixed with faith in Jesus. Are you desperate enough to do whatever it takes to touch Jesus and receive all He has for you today? Don't let anyone or anything stop you from receiving His best.

Prepare for Your Miracle
Mark 10:46-52

And he, casting away his garment, rose, and came to Jesus.
Mark 10:50

In Bartimaeus' day, beggars wore clothing that distinguished them as beggars. Therefore, when Bartimaeus cast away his garment, he was making a significant statement. He was saying, "I'm finished begging." He believed Jesus would heal his blindness, and he acted accordingly.

While he was blind, he couldn't see the clothing he wore; but other people could, and he was obligated by the culture in which he lived to wear clothes appropriate to his place in life. Beggars weren't like everyone else. They weren't productive members of society. They might have been tolerated or pitied, but they weren't admired. They definitely weren't allowed the same privileges as those who were normal.

Bartimaeus must have hated the differences that his blindness imposed on him. No doubt, he dreamed about what it would be like to have his sight. Once he heard that Jesus was healing the blind, he probably became very specific about what he would do if Jesus ever passed his way. One thing he knew for sure: If Jesus came by his place, he would let nothing and no one stop him from receiving his healing. He'd never go back to begging, and he probably thought about what he would like to do after he could see.

Bartimaeus knew Jesus would heal him and he would never need his beggar's clothes again. How convinced are you that He will heal you, change you, deliver you? Are you holding on to your "old clothes" just in case nothing happens and you have to stay in your beggarly existence? That's not faith! Meditate on God's promises until you see yourself receiving whatever you need. Then make no plans to go back to where you were before.

God's Truths Belong to You
Matthew 13:1-13

*He answered and said unto them, Because it is given unto you to know
the mysteries of the kingdom of heaven, but to them it is not given.
Matthew 13:11*

God's truths are hidden for His children, not from them. He has given us His mysteries, which are those truths that can only be understood by His children. Only born-again believers can receive divine revelation to know how the kingdom of God operates.

God wants all people to enter and enjoy His kingdom. He has given an open invitation to everyone to receive the spiritual rebirth that entitles them to the revelation of these mysteries of the kingdom. As stated in 1 Corinthians 2:14, a natural man cannot receive the things of the Spirit of God because they are spiritually discerned. Therefore, whoever rejects Jesus, rejects the source of all wisdom and knowledge. (Col. 2:3.)

God has reserved the deep understanding of eternal life for those who receive Jesus. We can then draw on His wisdom through the Holy Spirit inside our spirits to receive revelation from His Word and wisdom to live this life. In this way also, He safeguards His laws, upon which the universe is founded, from being misused by Satan and his kingdom of demons.

In this passage of Scripture in Matthew 13, Jesus spoke about those who have revelation knowledge of the mysteries of God. They will receive even more revelation and will walk in the abundant life He provided. (John 10:10; 2 Peter 1:3.) Those who do not continue to grow in revelation will eventually lose whatever truth they have and go into deception. God reveals His truths to us in stages, not all at once (Isa. 28:9,10), and we must keep seeking Him!

As you walk in the revelation of what the Lord has already shown you, He will reveal more of His truths to you. The truths of God are mysterious only to those who do not soften their hearts by seeking God with their whole hearts. As Jeremiah 29:13 says, "And ye shall seek me, and find me, when ye shall search for me with all your heart."

Guard Your Conscience
Matthew 13:14-23

For this people's heart is waxed gross, and their ears are dull of hearing,
and their eyes they have closed; lest at any time they should see with their
eyes and hear with their ears, and should understand with their heart,
and should be converted, and I should heal them.
Matthew 13:15

The word *waxed* means "to become gradually more intense or to increase." It shows this condition of the heart is not something we are born with or that strikes us suddenly. It has to be nurtured over a prolonged period of time. This is why we should not violate our consciences, even in small things.

Guarding your conscience will keep you sensitive to God and will stop your heart from becoming hardened. If you will stay sensitive to the Holy Spirit, even in the small things, then you will understand, continue to mature in the Lord, and become more and more whole.

Walking in the Spirit and not in the flesh affects your awareness of how much God loves you. If you sin habitually and make no effort to resist your flesh, your conscience becomes defiled and condemns you. God never condemns you because you are His child, and He loves you unconditionally; but your conscience will condemn you. In your earthly life, your awareness of God's love is everything. It is the knowledge and confidence of His love that will help you resist temptation to sin and keep a clear conscience and a pure heart.

First John 3:21 says, "Beloved, if our heart condemn us not, then have we confidence toward God." Today, be persuaded that God loves you no matter what! Then you will have confidence to move forward in the life He has for you overcoming sin and succeeding in every area of your life.

The Miracle of the Donkey and the Colt
John 12:14-15

And Jesus, when he had found a young ass, sat thereon; as it is written,
Fear not, daughter of Sion: behold, thy King cometh, sitting on an ass's colt.
John 12:14-15

This is the fulfillment of Zechariah 9:9, and it was fulfilled to the smallest detail. Zechariah prophesied Jesus would not only ride an ass but also a colt or unbroken foal of an ass. He declared that the people would rejoice and shout over the Messiah, which certainly came to pass on this day.

All four Gospels include a triumphal entry, but only Matthew records a donkey with a colt. A simple explanation to a so-called "contradiction" is that Jesus rode the colt while the other donkey went along, and He may have ridden each animal part of the way.

Jesus hadn't been in Jerusalem in quite a while and there is no indication He had made previous arrangements with anyone there to obtain these animals. Knowing where the ass and colt were was supernatural knowledge imparted to Him through the Holy Spirit.

God also worked some kind of miracle in the owner of these animals as well, so he would be willing to release them. Perhaps he was a devoted follower of Jesus who gladly surrendered them when he knew Jesus was the one wanting them. Either way, this whole episode in Jesus' life was miraculously orchestrated by God.

What do you need today? As a child of God and joint-heir with Jesus, all your needs have already been supplied. Just like Jesus, the Holy Spirit will tell you where you need to go and who you need to see to obtain the resources you require to fulfill His call on your life.

The Power of Praise and Worship
Luke 19:29-40

And some of the Pharisees from among the multitude said unto him, Master,
rebuke thy disciples. And he answered and said unto them, I tell you that,
if these should hold their peace, the stones would immediately cry out.
Luke 19:39-40

There is nothing wrong with praising God. It is encouraged and commanded thousands of times in the Scriptures. The reason the Pharisees were so upset was because they didn't accept Jesus as God. Indeed, it would be blasphemy for Jesus to accept worship if He wasn't God. This is another confirmation of His deity.

Only Luke records this account of the Pharisees' objection and Jesus' answer. This was the triumphant entry of Israel's King, what we call Palm Sunday, that had been prophesied and they had anticipated for centuries. The excitement could not be contained. If people refused to praise Him, the creation would have broken out in spontaneous praise. No rock should have to do what God created us to do!

By compiling all of the writers' accounts of what the multitudes were saying, we have this record: "Hosanna to the Son of David" (Matthew only). "Blessed is he" ("the King"- Luke; "the King of Israel"- John) "that cometh in the name of the Lord. Blessed be the kingdom of our father David that cometh in the name of the Lord" (Mark only). "Hosanna in the highest" (Matthew and Mark only). "Peace in heaven, and glory in the highest" (Luke only).

One thing reserved for God alone is worship, and the devil has always sought that. If he can't be the one to receive worship, then he seeks to turn others away from giving true worship to God. This is why the Pharisees, who were Satan's puppets, wanted the people to stop praising Jesus.

If you want to make the devil run in terror today, praise and worship the Lord with all of your heart.

The Meaning of Passover
Luke 22:15-18

For I say unto you, I will not any more eat thereof,
until it be fulfilled in the kingdom of God.
Luke 22:16

The Lord longed to share the Passover meal with His disciples. He was less than twenty-four hours away from fulfilling His mission, and like anyone who can see the finish line, He must have had feelings of relief and excitement. The Passover meal commemorated the Jews' deliverance from slavery in Egypt (Ex. 13:3-10), but it also had a much deeper spiritual application that would be fulfilled through His death.

On the night of the original Passover, the Lord passed through the land of Egypt and judged the land by slaying all the firstborn men and beasts. To avoid this judgment, each Jewish family had to slay a spotless lamb, take its blood, and apply it to the doorposts of their homes. They were commanded to remain indoors, under the covering of this blood, until morning. When the Lord passed through the land at midnight to execute His judgment, He passed over the homes that had the lamb's blood on their doors.

This is a perfect picture of the redemption that Jesus provides for us through His blood. Jesus was sacrificed on the fourteenth day of the first month of the Jewish year—the exact day and time that the Passover lambs were being slain at the Temple. Truly, "Christ our Passover is sacrificed for us" (1 Cor. 5:7).

Today you deserve judgment for your sins, but when you confessed Jesus as your Lord and Savior, you applied His blood to your heart. Now you no longer need be afraid of the Day of Judgment, because your sins are forgiven and washed away. You are no longer under judgment. You are under the grace and mercy of God.

His Emotional Pain
Luke 22:43-44

And being in an agony he prayed more earnestly: and his sweat was as it were great drops of blood falling down to the ground.
Luke 22:44

It is interesting that Luke is the only one of the gospel writers to mention that Jesus' sweat was "great drops of blood." This is probably because Luke was a physician (Col. 4:14), and this fact had special significance to him. There have been documented medical cases of people actually sweating drops of blood under extreme emotional pressure.

Luke also is the only writer to mention that an angel strengthened Jesus. The other time this happened was when Jesus fasted for forty days in the wilderness, and the devil tempted Him. The Bible says that angels ministered unto Him. (Mark 1:13.) Here, too, He needed supernatural strength to endure His sufferings.

The use of the words "as it were" might also mean that the sweat of Jesus was only comparable to blood in consistency or size, but it certainly underscores the effect Jesus' agony had on His physical body. His sufferings for us were more than just physical. In the garden, He suffered emotionally, almost to the point of death. As Luke records, an angel had to come and give Him strength or the emotional struggle alone would have killed Him.

Living in this world is not easy, and I am sure you have had some difficult and maybe even some tragic times in your life. However, have you ever been so emotionally stressed that you actually started sweating blood? This is what Jesus went through for you. He took all your emotional pain and distress so that you could be free. If you have any doubt that He wants you to be happy and free of cares today, remember the blood He shed for you in the garden.

The Power of His Name
John 18:5-9

As soon then as he had said unto them, I am he, they went backward, and fell to the ground.
John 18:6

I t is evident that it was the power of God that made all these men fall backward to the ground, but why did it happen when He said, "I am he"?

In this verse and also in verse eight, the word *he* is italicized. That means the word *he* was not in the original text but was added by the translators to make the sentence grammatically correct. This serves a useful purpose and is very helpful in most cases. However, in this case the translators could have left the text as is.

Jesus literally said, "I am." Every Jew knew that when Moses had asked God who He was, God had said He was "I AM" (Ex. 3:14). They knew that was God's name. All Jesus did was declare who He was, and He released the power of His glory. No wonder it knocked the men to the ground!

In the moments in which He was arrested, Jesus miraculously healed the guard's ear (after Peter cut it off) and then knocked everyone to the ground at the sound of His name. Why did He do these things? This graphically illustrates how He could have easily defended Himself against any size army that would come to take His life. He was demonstrating what He had said in John 10:18, that no man takes His life; He lays it down of His own free will.

You can be totally secure in the knowledge that you are in Christ, He is in you, and the name of Jesus has been given for you to use with the same power and authority Jesus used the day they came to arrest Him. Today you can walk in His power.

His Silence Spoke Volumes
Luke 22:63-64

And the men that held Jesus mocked him, and smote him. And when they
had blindfolded him, they struck him on the face, and asked him, saying,
Prophesy, who is it that smote thee?
Luke 22:63-64

This is the account of God's creation mocking and insulting His Son without Him intervening. The pain this must have caused the Father defies description. Those who struck Jesus and told Him to prophesy must have taken Jesus' silence as proof that He was not who He claimed to be. The natural mind could not conceive that Almighty God would take this kind of abuse from His creation. But this was the plan of God.

Isaiah prophesied, "as a lamb to the slaughter, and as a sheep before her shearers is dumb, so he openeth not his mouth. (Isa. 53:7.) Jesus did not open His mouth. Isaiah also mentioned that Jesus "was taken from prison and from judgment" referring to Jesus not getting a fair trial. (Isa. 53:8.) Isaiah went on to prophesy in Isaiah 53:9 that Jesus would make "his grave with the wicked, and with the rich in his death." This was fulfilled when Jesus was crucified between two thieves and buried in a rich man's tomb.

The truth is, Jesus' silence spoke volumes. It spoke of His unfathomable love for His Father and for you and me. It spoke of His total trust in His Father's promise to raise Him from the dead. It spoke of the source of His strength to endure the Cross, which was the joy set before Him. And it spoke the words Satan had longed to hear for centuries: The Messiah is in your hands.

However, Jesus' silence also spoke something the devil didn't hear: He was not murdering the Messiah; he was sacrificing the Lamb of God who would take away the sin of the world and thus strip him of all authority! First Corinthians 2:8 says that if Satan had known what the death of Jesus would accomplish, he never would have crucified him.

Today when you wonder how God could possibly get you out of your dilemma—how He could change your heart, your circumstances, or anyone else's heart or circumstances—remember how He even got the devil to do His will!

Pilate Washes His Hands
Matthew 27:19-24

When Pilate saw that he could prevail nothing, but that rather a tumult was made,
he took water, and washed his hands before the multitude, saying,
I am innocent of the blood of this just person: see ye to it.
Matthew 27:24

When Pilate washed his hands, he was performing a symbolic custom of the day that declared his innocence in the matter, but he was also performing a ritual prescribed in the Jewish law. (Deut. 21:6,7; Ps. 26:6.) Matthew is the only writer to record that Pilate washed his hands of any guilt over Jesus' death. He was also the only writer to record that Pilate's wife came to him with the details of a dream she had had about Jesus. She begged him not to have anything to do with Him. Secular accounts record her name as Claudia, and she was the only person who spoke for Jesus during His trial.

Claudia's dream came from God since Claudia would have had to have dreamt it before she knew that Jesus had been brought before Pilate. Not only did the Lord bare witness in Pilate's heart to the innocence of Jesus, but He also gave Pilate's wife a very clear message through this dream. Pilate was not innocent in this matter. Together, these instances underscore that Pilate did not innocently condemn Jesus to death. Pilate will be trying to wash the blood of Jesus off his hands throughout eternity.

If God was faithful to show Pilate and his wife, two unbelievers, the truth in this situation, you can be assured that He will reveal to you–His precious child–the truth about any situation you are facing today. All you need to do is ask, and He will give you the wisdom you need. (James 1:5.)

Relationship Not Religion
John 19:28-30

When Jesus therefore had received the vinegar, he said, It is finished:
and he bowed his head, and gave up the ghost.
John 19:30

When Jesus cried, "It is finished," He was not referring to the whole plan of salvation. He still had to descend into the lower parts of the earth and lead the captives out (Eph. 4:8,9), come back from the dead, and ascend to the Father. (Heb. 7:25.) Paul made it very clear in 1 Corinthians 15:14 and 17, that if Jesus did not rise from the dead, our faith is in vain, and we are still doomed to everlasting hell in our sins.

Why is the resurrection so important? We are saved by believing God raised Jesus from the dead (Rom. 10:9) because the resurrection proved the debt for our sin had been paid. Legally, God could not have raised Jesus up if He had died in any personal sin. When Jesus was resurrected, it proved He had been qualified to take all our sin and satisfy the demands of the Law against us. The Law is what He finished on the Cross.

The Law could only point to our sin and condemn us, so Jesus fulfilled it and took all our transgressions against it on Himself. (Eph. 2:15.) He fulfilled the Law for us, satisfied divine justice by paying the price for our sins against God's Law, obtained God's forgiveness for us, and gave us the opportunity to live by God's grace. Instead of trying to keep religious ordinances to please God and making the specified sacrifices when we could not, we now have a living, intimate relationship with the Father and walk according to His Spirit.

The resurrection of Jesus makes Christianity different from all religions because you are dealing with a real, live person, not laws and rules. Your faith is lived in fellowship with Jesus, who is alive and communicates freely with you. Talk with Him as you go about your day today.

Why Seek the Living Among the Dead?

Luke 24:1-9

And as they were afraid, and bowed down their faces to the earth,
they said unto them, Why seek ye the living among the dead?
Luke 24:5

The angel asked the women at the tomb, "Why seek ye the living among the dead?" That's a great question! The women who came to the tomb that resurrection morning were seeking Jesus, but they weren't seeking a living, victorious Christ. They were grieving because the Jesus they were seeking was dead.

Likewise, we often seek a dead God. We don't phrase it that way, of course, but that's what it amounts to. We pray and talk about how big and impossible our problems are, just as if God was dead. We forget or don't believe that Jesus overcame all the problems of this life. We say things like, "The doctor told me I'm going to die." What does this mean to the One who has already conquered death? A doctor's report is nothing to Him. If we pray to the risen Christ, then death won't overwhelm us either.

It doesn't glorify the Lord to fall apart like a two-dollar suitcase every time something bad happens. We have access to Him, who has all power in heaven and earth. We need to come to the risen Christ and expect resurrection power to flow into our situations.

When the women at the tomb believed Jesus was alive, all their sadness turned to joy. That's the way it will be with you, too, when you turn to your risen Savior, who has put all your enemies under His feet and therefore your feet. Recognize that Jesus is alive and Almighty God is working in your life today, and let true joy arise in your heart.

Denying the Resurrection
Matthew 28:1-15

Now when they were going, behold, some of the watch came into the city,
and shewed unto the chief priests all the things that were done.
Matthew 28:11

In the Jews' efforts to prevent anything from happening that would cause people to believe Jesus was resurrected, they gave one of the greatest proofs of it. They sealed the tomb after He was buried, and Pilate agreed to send his guards to watch the tomb so that the disciples could not steal Jesus' body and claim He had risen from the dead. (Matt. 27:64-66.) In the end, what they did removed any doubt that Jesus had been supernaturally resurrected.

In order for the disciples to steal the body, they would have had to kill the Roman guards on duty, break the seal, and roll the stone away. In the morning, there would have been dead guards to prove their deception. Instead, the guards were completely shaken by what they had witnessed. They had been frozen "as dead men" when the angel appeared, rolled away the stone, and announced that Jesus had risen. (vv. 2-6.) They then fled to tell the chief priests what had happened. That was when the Jews bribed the Roman guard to say that the followers of Jesus stole His body.

Anyone who knew the code of honor of a Roman soldier would highly suspect their story. They were to give their lives to carry out the will of their commander, and Pilate had commanded them not to let the disciples steal Jesus' body. If their story was true, they should have been dead!

In this way, the enemies of Jesus became a historical witness that Jesus literally rose from the dead. The very ones the Jews had secured to guarantee there would be no rumors of Jesus being raised became the first witnesses and heralds of the resurrection. This is just another of many examples where God took Satan's plans and used them in His plan. He can do the same for you today.

Valuable and Precious
Luke 8:11-15

Now the parable is this: The seed is the word of God.
Luke 8:11

Y ou have the fullness of Christ in you, but how do you walk in it? How do you come to know it? Revelation and understanding come through reading the Word of God and the enlightenment of the Holy Spirit.

You may not know what a privilege it is to have God's Word in your own language. Six hundred years ago there was no English translation of the Bible available to believers. Most of the manuscripts were in Latin, and only the clergy had access to them. However, thanks to the efforts of John Wycliffe (1384) and William Tyndale (1523), today we are able to read the writings of the prophets and apostles for ourselves. These men gave their lives to bring English-speaking believers God's Word, and we should see our Bibles as valuable and precious.

The piece of armor known as the "sword of the Spirit" is the only piece that has the ability to cut, wound, and hurt our enemy. It's not the Bible lying on your coffee table that makes the enemy flee, but it is the Word of God hidden in your heart, activated by the power of the Holy Spirit, and spoken in an appropriate situation. It's similar to what was spoken by Jesus in John 6:63, "The words that I speak unto you, they are spirit and they are life." The Word by itself doesn't make us free. It is the Word we know and speak that will deliver us. (John 8:32.)

Why is the Word so effective? It's because it is God's Word. His Word carries His sovereign authority, which supersedes all authority of the church, of human reason and intellect, and certainly of Satan and demonic power. When you speak God's Word in faith, the Holy Spirit goes into action to perform it. Today you must avail yourself of God's Word by placing it in your heart, guarding it as the most precious and valuable possession He has given you, and living by it. In this way you will experience the fullness of Christ.

God's Word: Use As Directed
Luke 8:4-11

Now the parable is this: The seed is the word of God.
Luke 8:11

In the parable of the sower, Jesus taught that the seed was God's Word, but it had to be planted in our hearts and allowed to germinate before it released God's power. He said the seed of the Word was planted into one of four types of ground, which were the four conditions of people's hearts. The Word is always the same, but the results are different because the condition of each person's heart is different. The variable in this parable is the condition of the heart, not God's Word. Like a seed planted in good soil, the Word will always grow and bear fruit if it is planted in a good heart.

How do you have a heart in which the seed of God's Word will grow and flourish? Good ground doesn't just happen; it must be cultivated. This is the reason why only one out of four people in Jesus' parable brought forth fruit. It takes a lot of time, effort, and diligence to be a fruitful Christian. The Christian life is not like a 100-yard dash but rather a 26.2-mile marathon, and any farmer will tell you that it is quicker and easier to raise weeds than it is to raise tomatoes or corn!

In this whole parable, it was the Word that produced the fruit. The ground simply gave it a good place to grow. If we will simply put God's Word in our hearts, protect it, and give it priority in our lives, the Word will produce fruit of itself. Satan has deceived many people into thinking they don't have the talents or abilities to be fruitful Christians, but they are not the ones who bring forth fruit; it's God's Word in them that brings joy and success to their lives.

Today, meditate on and live according to the Word you sow in your heart. If you protect and stand upon the Word sown in your heart, the Word will do the rest.

Understanding God's Word
Luke 8:4-13

Those by the way side are they that hear; then cometh the devil, and taketh away the word out of their hearts, lest they should believe and be saved.
Luke 8:12

In the parable of the sower, the first kind of person Jesus describes was someone who does not understand God's Word. (Matt. 13:19.) Before God's Word can penetrate your heart, you have to have some comprehension of what it is saying. You must relate to it and embrace it as your own. If you don't get it at all, it will be scattered (the wayside) because it doesn't mean anything to you. Then birds will eat the seed, and there will be no fruit.

Mark 4:15 and Luke 8:12 make it clear that the birds represent Satan, and Mark says that the devil comes immediately to steal the Word. Satan did not have direct access to the Word in any of the other heart-types that Jesus described. Satan cannot steal the Word from us if we hide it in our hearts. (Ps. 119:11.) This first type of person simply hears the Word, but does not receive it. They never apply it to their lives, so they lose it.

Notice that Luke links belief and salvation with the Word being sown in our hearts in the same way Paul described in Romans 10:14-17. If there is no Word, there cannot be any belief or salvation. (1 Pet. 1:23.) We must preach the Word—not just morality or social issues—for people to be saved.

Luke's use of the word *saved* could include but is not necessarily limited to being born again. This verse could describe a person who does not receive the Word and is never saved, or it could be describing a Christian who does not receive the Word in a certain area of their life and therefore does not experience the deliverance, healing, or victory Jesus provided for them.

If you are not experiencing the abundant life Jesus died to give you, perhaps you need to plant the Word in your heart, embrace it, and allow it to direct your life. Then you will begin to see the fruit of the Holy Spirit and victory come forth.

No Distractions Please
Mark 4:13-20

And these are they likewise which are sown on stony ground; who,
when they have heard the word, immediately receive it with gladness.
Mark 4:16

The second type of person Jesus describes in the parable of the sower is one who does receive the Word with great joy, but their commitment to the Word is shallow. The Word does not take root in their heart. Just as a plant must establish a strong root system to sustain its growth, we must become rooted and grounded in God's Word.

A seed planted in shallow earth will germinate and grow faster than a seed planted in deep soil because it has nowhere to grow but up. However, the seed in deep soil will put all of its energy toward developing the roots first. The plant in shallow soil will look like it is far ahead of the other seed for a while, but that will not last. It soon withers and dies, while the seed with roots grows strong and brings forth fruit.

Notice that afflictions, persecutions, and tribulations are instruments of the devil used to stop God's Word from bearing fruit in our lives. They are not good things that God brings our way to improve us. They are instruments of Satan to take our attention off of God's Word, thereby stopping the Word from taking root in us. It's like the runner who spends all of his time in the grandstands arguing with the hecklers over the way he's running the race. He may win an argument, but he will lose the race.

Too much attention on visible growth will cause you to become impatient and not take the time to become firmly established in the truths of God's Word. This will always result in fruitlessness. You must not let anything distract you from meditating on God's Word day and night; for only then will you make your way prosperous and have good success. (Josh. 1:8.) By consistently putting God's Word first in every area of your life, you will let that Word become so rooted in you that nothing can remove it.

Worldly Cares Are Thorns
Luke 8:5-14

And that which fell among thorns are they, which, when they have heard,
go forth, and are choked with cares and riches and pleasures of this life,
and bring no fruit to perfection.
Luke 8:14

The third type of ground Jesus taught about in the parable of the sower is characteristic of a large part of the body of Christ today. These are believers who have received God's Word and have the commitment to remain faithful in persecution, but they become preoccupied with the affairs of this life. The Word sown in their hearts is choked and no fruit is produced. Just as weeds in a garden will steal all of the nutrients and starve the plants, so both the worries and the pleasures of this life stop the Word from bearing fruit because they have become consumed with the fears and desires of everyday life.

Throughout history the church has always grown in size and strength during persecution. This is because during persecution we get our priorities straight. We realize that our lives are in Jesus (John 14:6), not in things (Luke 12:15), and we focus all of our attention on Him. Prosperity has been far more damaging to the body of Christ for the exact reason stated here in this verse. God wants to bless His children with material wealth (Ps. 35:27; Matt. 6:33), but a preoccupation with these things will choke God's Word and make it unfruitful.

Jesus said no fruit in this person was brought to perfection. They exhibited some fruit, but it was always small and short of what it could have been. Do you feel frustrated because you are just getting by and are not really experiencing the abundance Jesus has for you? Examine your lifestyle and look for thorns! See if worries or pleasures of this life are choking God's Word. If you follow His formula for prosperity found in Matthew 6:19-34, seeking His kingdom first in every area of life, your heart will be good soil. The Word will bring forth fruit, and you will enjoy all the blessings God wants to give you.

The Good Heart
2 Kings 4:8-37

Let us make a little chamber, I pray thee, on the wall; and let us set for him
there a bed, and a table, and a stool, and a candlestick: and it shall be,
when he cometh to us, that he shall turn in thither.
2 Kings 4:10

Jesus taught that God's miracle-producing power flows through those who give (Luke 6:38), and there are many examples of this in the Old Testament. This story in 2 Kings is one of the greatest miracles recorded in the Bible. Every believer would love to see God's power displayed in their lives like this! Yet miracles don't just happen; there are reasons why some people receive them and others do not.

If it was up to God alone, all of us would experience miracles. He loves every person and extends His grace to all. The reason few people experience His miraculous power is because few cooperate with Him. Electricity doesn't flow through wood, and miracles don't flow through hearts and minds that are hard toward God and His people. Miracles flow through the lives of those whose hearts are fully God's and full of His compassion for others.

This woman built an extra room on her house just for Elisha. He appreciated it and wanted to bless her back, offering her favor with the king or the top general in the land; but she didn't accept it. This says volumes. She didn't bless Elisha to get something from God. She didn't give to get. The motive behind her gift was totally unselfish. She gave expecting nothing in return. There's a lesson for all of us here.

Later when Elisha said God wanted to bless her with a son, she accepted His gift joyfully because she never doubted His love and faithfulness. She had a heart that Jesus called "good soil," and her good heart brought forth good fruit in her life. How is your heart today? Are you doing a good job for your employer? Do you go out of your way to help a friend? Are you kind to those who don't treat you well? God is watching, and what you give will come back to you in the miracles you need.

Shut the Door and Go in Faith!

2 Kings 4:8-37

And she went up, and laid him on the bed of the man of God,
and shut the door upon him, and went out.
2 Kings 4:21

The woman in this story had a heart after God and had blessed Elisha, so after years of being barren, God had given her a son. Then one day her young son died a tragic death. Maybe you have experienced enough tragedy that you know how she felt. What do you do in a crisis like that?

Sadly, most of us tend to nurse our hurt and problems. We indulge grief and rehearse the tragedy over and over in our minds. We don't let go and cast our care and pain on the Lord. (1 Peter 5:7.) We become dominated by our affliction. But this mother carried her dead son to the man of God's room and left him there. She shut the door. She put him in the hands of the One who had given him to her. That's hard to do! But sitting there holding him wouldn't have changed anything. She did what she had to do to continue receiving miracles from God: she trusted Him alone and went to get His prophet.

When Elisha saw her, he asked how it was with her, her husband, and her son. She replied, "It is well." That's awesome. She refused to let grief swallow her because she hadn't accepted it as being final. Her faith in God gave her a different perspective on her problem. She was not in denial of the facts; she lived in the reality that God can change the facts.

Elisha came to her home and raised her boy from the dead because this woman shut the door on death and grief and released her faith in a life-giving God. Have you shut the door on your pain and problems by giving them to the Lord? Are you speaking words of faith in Him to heal and deliver? All you have to do is look into His Word to see all He has promised and wants to give you. Believe Him and trust Him. Just shut the door and go in faith.

Tares Among the Wheat
Matthew 13:24-30

But while men slept, his enemy came and sowed tares among the wheat,
and went his way.
Matthew 13:25

The tares Jesus is talking about refer to the Old World variety of darnel, which is poisonous. Virtually all grains are almost indistinguishable from tares when they send up the first blade from the ground. By the time the tares become distinguishable, they are so well rooted that uprooting them would mean uprooting the productive grain next to them. Therefore, in verse thirty Jesus admonishes us to let both wheat and tares grow together until the harvest. By that time the tares are long and black in contrast to the wheat and are easily separated out.

Of course, Jesus used this as an example of how some people will say they are Christians, but as time passes you will see they have produced no godly fruit. In fact, their presence has caused nothing but strife and division. Satan secretly infiltrates the church with some of his followers for the purpose of hindering the influence of the church. This has been a more effective strategy than direct opposition.

There also will be those who are deceived and unaware that they are not born again. Jesus warns us against trying to root them out especially since it is not always possible to discern other people's hearts. In an effort to destroy these tares, we might offend one of Christ's "little ones" and cause their profession of faith to waver.

It is important to be aware that the children of Satan are placed among the children of God. The best strategy is to preach the Word of God without watering it down. False brethren will not endure sound doctrine. They will either be convicted and completely surrender their hearts and lives to Jesus, or they will leave.

King of Hearts
Mark 4:30-34

And he said, Whereunto shall we liken the kingdom of God?
or with what comparison shall we compare it?
Mark 4:30

The word *kingdom* means "the realm over which a king rules." When applied to God, this could refer to all creation, since "his kingdom ruleth over all" (Ps. 103:19); but God's kingdom more often applies to His rule in and through people who are submitted to Him. "The kingdom of God" more specifically refers to Christ living and ruling in our hearts. Praying "thy kingdom come" is praying for the expansion and influence of God's rule in the hearts of people everywhere, and ultimately the establishment of His physical kingdom here on earth at the second coming of Jesus. (Rev. 11:15; 20:4.)

Throughout Jesus' earthly ministry, the Jews kept looking for Him to establish a political kingdom here on earth and deliver them from the oppression of the Romans. Although during the Millennium, the kingdom of God will physically rule over the nations of the earth, Jesus' kingdom is spiritually established by His Word and not by carnal weapons. (2 Cor. 10:3-5.) Jesus said, "The kingdom of God cometh not with observation...behold, the kingdom of God is within you" (Luke 17:20,21).

Paul said we are already in the kingdom of God. (Col. 1:13.) Therefore, the kingdom of God is Christ's invisible church—His body. The kingdom began during His earthly ministry and is still ruling the hearts of believers today. The new birth ushers us into His kingdom, which is infinitely greater in wonder and benefits than our finite minds can comprehend.

To the degree that you understand how God's kingdom works and apply that to your life, you will experience heaven here on earth. Today, ask the Holy Spirit to reveal to you all you are and have in Christ Jesus. Then pray for His kingdom in you—all that you are and have in Him—to be released into the natural realm.

God's Hidden Treasure
Matthew 13:44-50

Again, the kingdom of heaven is like unto treasure hid in a field;
the which when a man hath found, he hideth, and for joy thereof
goeth and selleth all that he hath, and buyeth that field.
Matthew 13:44

The field is the world, the man buying the treasure is God, and the treasure is you! The price He paid for you was the life of His Son. Furthermore, in foreknowledge Jesus saw you would receive Him as Lord and Savior, and "for the joy that was set before him" He endured the Cross (Heb. 12:2). He purchased you for Himself with His own blood. (Acts 20:28.) He purchased the whole world, but not everyone will receive Him. Therefore, you and His church are hidden in the world today, like an extremely valuable and exquisite treasure in the middle of a wild field.

Father God had the plan of salvation worked out before He even created the world. Most of us would not have created the world and mankind if we had known the heartache and terrible sacrifice this act would cost, but God is not a human being. In His judgment (which is always correct), the prize was worth the cost. He knew in advance who would accept His offer of salvation. The Scriptures teach that we believers were chosen in Christ before the foundation of the world. (Eph. 1:4.) That's how infinite His understanding is. We are holy and without blame because He sees us in Christ.

God knew before He even made Adam and Eve that you would become His child. He fully accepts you and loves you. He would no more reject you than He would reject Jesus because you are accepted by the Father in Him. The world may not recognize or understand who you are, but today you can live boldly in the reality that you are redeemed and forgiven and truly blessed of your Father God.

Joint-Heirs With Christ
Matthew 12:46-50

For whosoever shall do the will of my Father which is in heaven,
the same is my brother, and sister, and mother.
Matthew 12:50

We are not just heirs; we are joint-heirs with Christ. (Rom. 8:17.) It would be wonderful to inherit any amount of God's glory and power, but the idea that we share equally with the one who has inherited everything God is and has is beyond comprehension. This is an awesome blessing, but it also places a tremendous responsibility on us.

In the same way in which a check made out to two people cannot be cashed without the endorsement of both parties, so our joint-heirship with Jesus cannot function without our cooperation. Unaware of this, many Christians think Jesus will do everything. All they need to do is ask Him. They are acutely aware they can do nothing without Him, but they don't realize He will do nothing without them. Ephesians 3:20 says, "Now to him who is able to do immeasurably more than all we ask or imagine, according to his power that is at work within us." God displays His awesome power through us.

The idea that God will do exceedingly abundantly above all that we ask or think—period—is not true. He has absolute power and ultimate authority, but He also does things according to His Word. He has given us dominion on this earth (Gen. 1:26), and He works with us and through us. The exceeding greatness of His power works according to the faith we exercise in Him and His Word. It was this principle that Paul referred to when he declared, "I can do all things through Christ which strengtheneth me" (Phil. 4:13).

The way you endorse your heavenly check for everything pertaining to life and godliness (2 Peter 1:3) is to believe what God promised in His Word and act on it as if it were true. It is! Jesus has already signed His name to every promise in the Word, and you are His joint-heir. You aren't waiting for Him; He is waiting for you.

Peace in the Midst of the Storm
Matthew 8:23-27; Mark 3:31-35; 4:35-41; Luke 8:19-26

And there arose a great storm of wind, and the waves beat into the ship so that it
was now full. And he was in the hinder part of the ship, asleep on a pillow: and
they awake him, and say unto him, Master carest thou not that we perish?
Mark 4:37,38

Considering the boat was filled with water, it is amazing the disciples had to awaken Jesus. This was not a large ship with cabins below deck, but rather a small, open boat. Jesus was probably soaked to the bone. What this reveals is how tired He must have been to be sleeping that deeply. Medical science has discovered that the deeper we sleep, the more rest we get. This is a clue as to how Jesus could maintain His grueling pace, many times praying all night and ministering all day. He obviously received the maximum benefit from His sleep.

How could Jesus sleep so soundly in a boat filled with water? The answer is found in what He said before He got into the boat. He did not say, "Let us go out into the midst of the sea and drown in a storm." He said, "Let us go to the other side." He was going to the other side. This shows that the disciples still didn't understand Jesus' authority. They were committed to Him as their Messiah, but they hadn't yet realized that He was Lord even over the physical elements.

Jesus had peace because He believed His Word. He rested in His Word. He also understood that the benefits of being a child of God were both spiritual and physical, encompassing every area of life. If you are in a storm today, what you say and what you believe will determine whether you cross over to the other side or sink. Know that Jesus is not asleep concerning the things you face in this life; He's right there in your ship, resting and giving you peace to get where you need to go. His peace is yours if you will just believe His Word and rest in His love.

What Manner of Man Is He?
Mark 4:35-41

Whosoever will be great among you, let him be your minister; And whosoever will be chief among you, let him be your servant: Even as the Son of man came not to be ministered unto, but to minister, and to give his life a ransom for many.
Matthew 20:26-28

When Jesus told the winds and the waves to be still, the disciples asked, "What manner of man is this?" To fully understand what manner of "man" Jesus is, we have to go back to the beginning. God created this physical world and then Adam and Eve, He gave mankind authority to rule and subdue His creation. (Gen. 1:26.) Although He still owned the universe and all that was in it, He gave control of the earth to human beings. When Adam sinned, he and many of his descendants often used this power against God's wishes, which was to their own destruction.

God did not ordain all the terrible things that have happened throughout human history, yet He did not take back our dominion on the earth. Instead, He became a man and birthed a new race of people who were filled with His Spirit and carried out His will in the earth. After His resurrection in Matthew 28:18, Jesus said, "All power is given unto me in heaven and in earth," and then He gave His power and authority to His disciples.

Jesus became flesh to regain all power and authority in heaven and in earth for God and His righteous ones. Jesus was a "God-man." As stated in 1 Timothy 3:16, He was God manifested in the flesh, which is a great mystery. He came in the power and authority of His Father to point men to the Father. He existed as God and was equal with God, yet He humbled Himself and became a servant while here on earth. (Phil. 2:6-8.) He did not come to promote Himself but to give Himself as the way to the Father.

This is radically different from the "great men" of secular human history. The Caesar of Jesus' day proclaimed he was god and demanded to be worshipped. He and lesser leaders ruled by exalting themselves over the people and oppressing them to increase their own wealth and power. The disciples had never seen a man like Jesus!

You may be in a position of authority as a parent, a leader in your church or school, an employer, or a community leader. If all you lead is your dog, you are still a leader. What manner of leader are you? Today, be like Jesus. Stay humble. Listen. Seek His wisdom and understanding. You will discover that the weight of responsibility becomes light and joyful when you carry it out with Jesus.

It's Your Turn
Mark 4:35-41

And he was in the hinder part of the ship, asleep on a pillow: and they awake him,
and say unto him, Master, carest thou not that we perish?
Mark 4:38

This was not just a question on the disciples' part. It was a criticism and a complaint. These disciples were fighting for their lives, and Jesus wasn't doing a thing. It's not like He didn't know what was happening. This was a small open boat that was full of water. (v. 37.) Jesus had to be aware of the situation. Yet, He was doing nothing. They wanted Him to do something—bail water, row, something!

We, too, sometimes think the Lord isn't doing His part. We're fighting to survive, yet it seems like our prayers go unanswered. "Where's Jesus? I thought He was never going to leave me or forsake me. Doesn't He care?" The answer is always *yes.*

Jesus has already done His part for us, and He had given the disciples everything they needed to conquer their situation. He had just taught ten parables on how the Word works when we believe. Then He told them, "Let us pass over unto the other side" (v. 35). This storm was like their pop quiz on what He had just taught them. He said they were going over, not under. Would they believe His Word or be overcome by the circumstances?

Jesus did His part when He gave them the Word that would take them over to the other side. Their part was to believe that Word and in faith command the storm to stop or the boat to stay afloat. Instead, they panicked and blamed Jesus.

Today Jesus has already done His part for you. He paid the price for your sin, forgave you, and gave you His Spirit and His Word to walk in. Now you must believe and put the Word to work in your life. It's our turn to believe God's promises and conquer our impossible situations.

How Determined Are You?
Mark 5:25-34

When she had heard of Jesus, came in the press behind, and touched his garment.
Mark 5:27

One of the ingredients of faith is *determination*, which is defined as "the power to make choices, set goals, and to act upon them firmly in spite of opposition or difficulty." This woman was determined. She had already spent years and all of her money on doctors, yet nothing had helped. She was actually worse. Most people would have just given up, but this was one determined lady. She heard of Jesus and knew that she would receive her healing through Him; but when she found him, she encountered yet another obstacle: a multitude thronged Him.

Jesus was hemmed in on all sides by a crowd of people that were pressing in on Him. She was a frail, sickly woman. How could she ever make it through that crowd? On top of all this, the woman's issue of blood made her unclean. She wasn't supposed to be in public because she would defile them. If someone recognized her and revealed her uncleanness, Jewish law allowed the crowd to stone her to death. But she would not be deterred.

She crawled through the crowd and touched the hem of Jesus' garment. Crawling was the only way she could have done this. In a crowd that dense, she could not have bent over and grabbed the hem of His garment. She had to be on her hands and knees. This woman would have done anything to get her healing!

Most people wouldn't do what this lady did. They wouldn't go to all that trouble. They wouldn't put their lives in jeopardy by being in a crowd that might stone them. They wouldn't get on their hands and knees and crawl through a throng of people. And they probably wouldn't get healed either. Most people lack her determination.

What stands between you and what you need from the Lord today? Make sure it's not your lack of determination.

Learning God's Laws
Mark 5:25-34

And Jesus, immediately knowing in himself that virtue had gone out of him,
turned him about in the press, and said, Who touched my clothes?
Mark 5:30

W as it possible that Jesus really didn't know who touched Him? Certainly it was! Jesus was God manifest in the flesh, but His physical mind had to grow in wisdom. (Luke 2:52.) This means Jesus had limitations to His physical mind just as we do. It was through His Spirit that He was able to draw on the mind of God just as we do. When the woman didn't come forward on her own, Jesus perceived who she was (Luke 8:47), but this happened after she was healed.

The significance of this is that Jesus didn't size this woman up before virtue went out of Him to heal her. That's the way most people feel God does things. They bring their requests before Him and believe He then evaluates whether or not they have enough faith or are holy enough to receive His blessing. If they pass the test, God blesses them. If they don't, their requests are denied. That's not scriptural.

God's power is governed by laws. He doesn't make a case-by-case determination of who receives what. He's provided all we need, and if we put His laws in motion, His power flows. That's what the woman with the issue of blood did. She was determined (Luke 11:5-13; 18:1-8) and spoke in faith saying, "If I may touch but his clothes, I shall be whole" (Mark 5:28; 11:23-24). She acted on her faith, and the power of God healed her. (James 2:17.)

If you grab a live electrical wire, the electric company doesn't send a special jolt of electricity out to shock you. The electricity was already there, and you just operated in natural laws that caused you to be shocked. It's not personal. Likewise, there are laws that govern the flow of God's power. Today, make a determination that you are going to learn from His Word what they are, and then start receiving all you need and all He wants to give you.

Financial Prosperity Is in Christ's Atonement
2 Corinthians 8:1-15

For ye know the grace of our Lord Jesus Christ, that, though he was rich, yet
for your sakes he became poor, that ye through his poverty might be rich.
2 Corinthians 8:9

This verse couldn't be any clearer. It's a part of Christ's atonement for us to be financially rich. Yet many Christians persist in their belief that God delights in His children being stuck in poverty. The way many people have gotten around the obvious truth of this verse is to say that Jesus came to make us rich spiritually, not materially. But the whole context of this verse deals with money. Jesus died to produce financial prosperity for us. He would no more make us poor than He would make us sin. He died to free us from both sin and poverty. We need to get the same attitude toward poverty that we have toward sin.

There is no doubt that many people have learned lessons as the result of their sins. People have been broken and have come to the end of themselves because of their own disobedience. But does that mean the Lord led them into sin? Did God want them to commit adultery so they could learn the value of the mate He had given them? Certainly not! Likewise, people can learn things through poverty. They can learn the value of things that money can't buy. But poverty itself is a killer. We should seek to overcome poverty the same way we seek to overcome sin.

God put poverty in the same category as sin and redeemed you from it. Now you should agree with Him. If you haven't already, today begin to take advantage of the prosperity He has provided through the atonement of Christ. Release your faith in His declaration that Jesus became poor so that you could be rich in all respects.

Worship Is Warfare

Matthew 8:28-34; Mark 5:1-17; Luke 8:27-39

But when he saw Jesus afar off, he ran and worshipped him.
Mark 5:6

The word *worshipped* is translated from the Greek word *proskuneo*, which means "to prostrate oneself in homage to; do reverence to; adore." The man who ran to worship Jesus was a very famous, demon-possessed man. That this tormented person ran to Him and not away from Him indicates that even demon-possessed people have free will, and Satan cannot control people without their consent.

Many battles have been fought over whether a Christian can be demon possessed. The Greek word translated *possessed* literally means "to be demonized." The Bible makes no clear distinction between degrees of demon activity, such as oppressed, depressed, and possessed. The Word simply refers to people as being "demonized." What we do know is that we all fight evil spirits, and if we don't put on the whole armor of God, Satan and demons can certainly affect us or even control us.

The best way to administer deliverance from demons is through God's Word. As we receive the Word, it sets us free and also helps guard our hearts and minds when the demon tries to come back into our lives with seven other spirits. In severe cases of being demonized, an individual needs the help of a believer, and that's the reason Jesus equipped all believers with authority over evil spirits.

Anointed praise and worship will also drive off evil spirits. One thing reserved for God alone is worship, so the devil has always sought it. If he can't be worshipped, then he will try to turn others away from worshipping God. Praising and worshipping our Father is such a powerful tool against all demonic forces!

If you feel at all oppressed, depressed, or just stressed today, praise the Lord and meditate on His Word. Worship Him in spirit and in truth. The Father is just waiting to lift all that pressure and darkness off of you.

Passive and Active Faith
Mark 5:24-34; John 5:1-9

And he said unto her, Daughter, thy faith hath made thee whole; go in peace,
and be whole of thy plague.
Mark 5:34

There's a dramatic contrast between the faith of the woman who had the issue of blood and the man who was lame at the pool of Bethesda. Both desperately wanted to be healed. The man at Bethesda was feeling hopeless because he didn't have anyone to help him into the pool. He had faith, but it was passive, based on someone else doing something. However, the woman had an active faith that reached out and took God's healing. She acted while the man sat and waited. Both were healed, but there was a big difference.

Jesus told the woman that her faith had made her whole. That's an amazing statement! Her faith, not Jesus' faith, produced her miracle. This woman was able to receive when Jesus wasn't physically there because her faith was active. However, the man didn't have the kind of faith that produced on its own. He was passive and Jesus had to encourage him to believe and then tell him, "Rise, take up thy bed, and walk" (John 5:8). If the man had not believed and acted in faith, someone else would have had to come along and do what Jesus did all over again.

An active faith is full of energy and felt so strongly that it compels the individual to act. A passive faith is one that only acts on the encouragement of others. The believer with an active faith depends on God; the believer with a passive faith depends on the faith and encouragement of other believers. While the first won't be denied what God has promised, the other can be easily discouraged and let go of what's theirs in Christ.

Which kind of faith would you rather have? Both of these individuals were in hopeless situations, but they had totally different responses. Choose to stir up your faith today so that it's active instead of passive.

Faith Is the Antidote for Fear
Mark 4:35-41

And he said unto them, Why are ye so fearful? how is it that ye have no faith?
Mark 4:40

Most people accept fear as a normal part of life, but Jesus rebuked His disciples for being afraid. He didn't accept it as normal. Also, we know He would never reprove them for something beyond their control, so fear is a choice. We don't have to be afraid, and Jesus told us how. We can overcome fear by having faith.

We don't need to be insensitive to those who are experiencing fear, nor do we need to be ashamed if we feel afraid. Since fear torments (1 John 4:18), we should have compassion on others—and ourselves. However, in our efforts to comfort, we don't need to embrace and promote fear as normal. That's not what Jesus did. The "normal" Christian today would have said to the disciples, "That's okay, boys, I know just how you're feeling."

But Jesus said, "What's the matter with you? Why don't you have any faith?"

The difference between Jesus' attitude toward fear and today's average Christian's attitude toward fear is why so many of us are living far below what Jesus sacrificed Himself to give us. He died so we could be delivered from fear of all evil, and that includes poverty, sickness, death, and even being lonely. To Him, anything but a happy and victorious Christian life is abnormal. He wants us to live free from fear.

Jesus made it clear that faith is the antidote to fear. Faith and fear cannot coexist. They are enemies and opposing forces. If faith is strong, it will cast out all fear. So we must always be building and strengthening our faith by reading and studying God's Word. (Rom. 10:17.)

Your faith in the goodness and faithfulness of God (Gal. 5:6) will overcome whatever you are afraid of today.

Watch Your Words
Matthew 12:31-37

*But I say unto you, That every idle word that men shall speak, they shall
give account thereof in the day of judgment.*
Matthew 12:36

My wife and I were trying to go to sleep in a Denver hotel room when a couple checked in to the room next to us. The walls were so thin, you could have heard them talking in sign language! The wife was griping and calling her husband every name you could imagine. He seldom said anything. She wouldn't let him. This went on for nearly an hour until they fell asleep. When they woke up in the morning, she picked up where she left off. The first words out of her mouth were poison. This continued until the man just left the room.

I couldn't restrain myself. I knocked on their door, and the woman came to answer. I told her I didn't mean to listen, but I couldn't help it. We had heard every word she'd said. I told her I'd been praying for her and just wanted her to know that Jesus loved her and could take her anger away. She started crying and told me she was already a Christian. She didn't know why she was acting that way. She said she needed help.

I had to go because I was appearing on a television program, but I told her to watch the show and I would share how to overcome strife. On the air, I told her story without using her name and explained how to stop the hatred. I never heard from her, but I've often wondered what happened. One thing's for sure: That woman learned that her words weren't as private as she thought.

Imagine what it'll be like on judgment day when every idle word will have to be accounted for. It's to your advantage to watch your words today, knowing that someday they will be made known. Since you have to eat your words, you might as well make them sweet.

Look Up!
Mark 6:35-44

And when he had taken the five loaves and the two fishes, he looked up to heaven,
and blessed, and brake the loaves, and gave them to his disciples to set before them;
and the two fishes divided he among them all.
Mark 6:41

Jesus faced an impossible task. There were five thousand men, and many of them with families, who needed to be fed. All He had were five loaves of bread and two small fish. Although Jesus was God, He was also a man. This situation was more than His sinless natural mind could comprehend. He had to look beyond the natural and tap into His Father's supernatural ability. That's why He looked up!

Jesus took His eyes off the natural realm and looked into the spiritual realm. The Greek word translated *looked up* means "to look up; by implication, to recover sight." This word is also translated *receive* seven times and *received* seven times in reference to blind eyes being opened. When Jesus looked up, His spiritual eyes were opened to the power of God. That was more than enough to multiply what He had in His hands and accomplish this miracle.

There's a spiritual answer to every physical problem you face. The answer is just as real as the natural impossibility, and God's supply is infinitely greater than your lack! In order to appropriate that supply, you need to look up and receive spiritual sight. If you are blind spiritually, you have just as much difficulty in the spiritual realm as a physically blind person has in the natural realm, but you don't have to stay that way. All you need to do is see with your faith.

Can you see by faith what God wants you to have? If you can see it on the inside, you can have it on the outside.

What Do You Need?
John 6:66-69

Then said Jesus unto the twelve, Will ye also go away?
John 6:67

A friend of mine married a woman who had been verbally and physically abused in her first marriage. Therefore, she clung to her new godly husband as if her life depended on it. She became co-dependent and smothered him. If he would have left her, her whole world would have collapsed. That's not healthy!

A real breakthrough came one day when he told her how much he loved her and reassured her of his commitment to both her and the marriage. Then he said, "But I don't need you." He wasn't rejecting her. He was just trying to make her understand that he was complete in Christ—with or without her. He loved her and wanted her, but he could make it without her because his foundation was Jesus. That's how it should be.

This was what Jesus was doing with His disciples. He loved them, wanted them to be with Him, and had chosen each one individually; but when the multitudes left, He asked His disciples if they wanted to leave too. Jesus wasn't encouraging them to go, but He wouldn't have fallen apart if they had. He didn't need them in the sense that He couldn't do without them. His total security was in His relationship with His Father.

Unknowingly, we have allowed ourselves to become dependent on many things other than the Lord for our stability and security. They may be good things like mates and children. In fact, some would even argue that it is correct to be that way. However, Jesus Christ is the only foundation that will always support us through the pressures of life. Everyone and everything else can fail us.

What must you have to be satisfied? The only things that can let you down are those you lean on, so make sure you are leaning on the One who will never let you down.

The Gospel Is the Power of God
Matthew 9:35-38; 13:53-58; Mark 6:1-6

Pray ye therefore the Lord of the harvest, that he will send forth
labourers into his harvest.
Matthew 9:38

People are born again through the power of the Word of God, not through prayer. Prayer is very important, but it is not a substitute for the Gospel. Many people petition God for someone to be saved and can't understand why it doesn't happen. They don't have to ask the Lord to save anyone. He isn't willing that anyone should perish (2 Peter 3:9) and has made provision for everyone's salvation. So what do we pray? Jesus said to pray that God would send laborers across their path. They need to hear the Word. Also, we should bind the influence of the god of this world, Satan, who tries to blind them to spiritual truth. (2 Cor. 4:4.)

God is more motivated to save our loved ones than we are. All we have to do is look at the Cross to see how motivated He is! We don't need to plead with Him, but rather we need to become a channel for Him to flow through to reach that person. We do that by sharing the Good News with them and/or praying for others to come across their path who will do the same.

The Gospel is the power of God that releases the effects of salvation in our lives. (Rom. 1:16.) If a person needs healing, it's in the Gospel. If deliverance is needed, it's in the Gospel. Prosperity, answered prayer, joy, peace, love—they are all found through understanding and believing the Gospel of Jesus Christ.

The Gospel is the Good News. You have every motivation within you to share this Good News with the people you meet and know and love today. If you are unable to share the Gospel with them, then pray for the Father to send others. Release your faith for Him to send just the right person at the right time to every lost person—and remember, sometimes that will be you.

Godly Sorrow Leads to Repentance
Mark 6:7-12

And they went out, and preached that men should repent.
Mark 6:12

Repent comes from the Greek word *metanoeo* and literally means to have another mind. It is a necessary part of salvation. Repentance may include godly sorrow, but sorrow does not always include repentance because repentance is a change of mind accompanied by corresponding actions. If someone is truly repentant, you will see a godly difference in their attitude and actions.

There is a godly type of sorrow and an ungodly type of sorrow. Godly sorrow leads to a change of heart that will manifest in outward behavior. Ungodly sorrow, or the sorrow of this world, just destroys and kills. Some believe sorrow of any kind is a negative emotion, and in general our culture has rejected all negative emotions; but God gave us the capacity for them, and there is a proper use for them. Ecclesiastes 7:3 says, "Sorrow is better than laughter: for by the sadness of the countenance the heart is made better."

People should feel bad about sin! There should be sorrow over moral failures. However, this sorrow should lead to repentance toward God and anyone who has been harmed. Then, when forgiveness is received from God, the sorrow can be cast upon Him. (Isa. 53:4.)

On the other hand, the sorrow experienced by those who do not turn to God to repent and to be forgiven produces death. They grieve over their situations because they cannot cast their care on the Lord. Christians should only have sorrow until they repent. Once repentance has come, we need to appropriate the forgiveness and cleansing that are already ours through Christ. (1 John 1:9.)

Godly sorrow that produces repentance leaves you with no regrets because God's love and forgiveness melt away all guilt and shame. Today, let the negatives in your life become positives through Jesus. If you have said or done something wrong, go immediately to Him, repent, and be cleansed.

About Persecution
Matthew 10:16-26

But when they persecute you in this city, flee ye into another: for verily I say unto you, Ye shall not have gone over the cities of Israel, till the Son of man be come.
Matthew 10:23

Persecution is an inevitable part of the Christian life. It is from Satan and is designed to uproot God's Word from our hearts by taking our eyes off Jesus. We should not think it is strange to be persecuted. "All that will live godly in Christ Jesus shall suffer persecution" (2 Tim. 3:12). We can actually rejoice because we are being persecuted for Jesus' sake, knowing that He will be with us in the midst of it and there will be more than ample reward when we stand before Him. (Heb. 11:26.)

Persecution is an indication that the ones doing the persecuting are under conviction. They realize they are not living what our words or actions are advocating; therefore, in defense of self, they attack the ones whom they perceive to be the source of their conviction. If this is understood, it makes persecution much easier to take. They aren't just mad at you; they are convicted. When the Gospel is presented in the power of the Holy Spirit, there will always be either a revival or a riot—never indifference.

There are many forms of persecution. Having your life threatened because of your faith in Jesus is one way you can be persecuted, but history shows that the church flourishes during these times. During intense, life-threatening persecution, believers come together in unity and return to their first love. (Rev. 2:4.)

You may not be suffering life-threatening persecution today, but make sure Jesus is your first love, and pray for your brothers and sisters around the world who are being persecuted, tortured, imprisoned, and sentenced to death because of their faith.

Degrees of Denial
Matthew 10:32-33

But whosoever shall deny me before men, him will I also deny before
my Father which is in heaven.
Matthew 10:33

This word *deny* can mean a variety of things from "to assert the contrary of" to "to disavow; disown." For example, we can see that it must have been the lesser type of denial that was committed by Peter because God certainly forgave Peter's sin and continued using him. In Hebrews 6:4-6, however, the Word states there is no repentance from total denial of the Lord. (Heb. 10:29.) Therefore, even though Peter denied (asserted he did not know) the Lord, he did not disown or disavow the Lord.

No believer desires to deny their Lord, but failing to pursue spiritual health is the first step in that direction. Remembering this will help motivate us to seek the Lord as we know we should. It takes more than desire; it takes effort. We have all been taught how to rely on ourselves, but we have to learn how to be strong in Him and in the power of His might. (Eph. 6:10.) To keep our physical bodies strong and healthy, we have to exercise them; in the same way, we have to exercise ourselves unto godliness. (1 Tim. 4:7.) Then we will be spiritually strong to stand for the Lord when the time comes.

Maybe you have been tormented by fear, thinking you have denied the Lord because of some type of sin in your life. Rest assured God knows your heart. (1 Sam. 16:7.) Regardless of how offensive your actions or words might have been, if you still honor Him in your heart and are truly repentant, He will not deny you. (2 Tim. 2:12-13.) He will forgive you, cleanse you, and you can begin anew!

Opposition to the Gospel
Matthew 10:34-42

Think not that I am come to send peace on earth: I came not to send peace, but a sword.
Matthew 10:34

This statement seems to contradict the Old Testament prophecies like Isaiah 9:6, which said Jesus would be the Prince of Peace. There are also Jesus' other statements concerning peace, and much of what was written of Him in the New Testament epistles. However, the peace Jesus purchased with His blood was peace between God and people. Through Him any person can now have peace with God. (Rom. 5:1.) We are exhorted to take this peace and extend it to everyone, but it is also made very clear that not everybody will receive it.

Peace can only come when we relate to God on the basis of faith in what He did for us instead of what we do for Him. People who believe they must live up to some standard to be accepted by God will have no peace because the burden of their salvation is on their shoulders, and they can't bear that load. When these people are confronted by the true peace and joy of a believer who knows they are saved by grace through faith (Eph. 2:8), they often attack the believer in order to defend their own self-righteousness. This is the "sword" Jesus refers to in Matthew 10:34.

The Gospel will always produce opposition from those who don't receive it. This sword of division, even among family members and friends, is not from God but from the enemy. Satan stirs up pride in people to oppose anything that goes against their being able to please God in their own efforts and abilities. Opposition will inevitably come to all believers, so Jesus was simply preparing His disciples for it.

As much as you would like everyone you love to be saved the moment you tell them the Gospel, you must not think it is strange when they don't receive the truth as you have. Jesus was rejected by His own, and you will be also. Today, remain faithful to continue preaching the Good News, for there are others who will receive; and never lose your faith and hope for your family and friends to be saved.

No Peace for the Wicked
Matthew 14:1-12; Mark 6:14-29; Luke 9:7-9

Now Herod the tetrarch heard of all that was done by him: and he was perplexed,
because that it was said of some, that John was risen from the dead.
Luke 9:7

O thers may have thought Jesus was John the Baptist risen from the dead, but as can be clearly seen by looking at Matthew's account and especially Mark's record, Herod was convinced of this. He was under conviction of the sin John had rebuked him for his sin of beheading John, and he was afraid of John and the God he represented. Overall, you could say Herod was obsessed with John because of his guilt.

As revealed in Mark 6:20, at one time Herod listened gladly to John. It is certain that John was preaching his favorite message of, "Repent ye: for the kingdom of heaven is at hand." For Herod to hear him gladly, he must have been under deep conviction from God. But Herod feared his wife and the opinions of others more than he feared God. He was not like Festus, who told Paul he was mad for speaking of the resurrection from the dead. He knew the truth and was sorrowful—but not with godly sorrow. In the end he chose death—John the Baptist's physical death and his own spiritual death.

In these verses above, Herod had no peace. He had chosen to be wicked, and he was haunted and tormented the rest of his life. According to the world's mentality, peace is the absence of problems; but getting rid of John didn't solve Herod's problems!

Your peace is not dependent on circumstances; it is dependent only on Jesus, who is the same yesterday, today, and forever. (Heb. 13:8.) Today you can have great peace even in the midst of terrible problems because your faith is in Him. "Thou wilt keep him in perfect peace, whose mind is stayed on thee: because he trusteth in thee" (Isa. 26:3). Trust Him alone, and let His peace rule in your heart.

You Are the Christ
Mark 8:27-30

And he saith unto them, But whom say ye that I am? And Peter answereth
and saith unto him, Thou art the Christ.
Mark 8:29

People often think how wonderful it would have been to be one of Jesus' disciples. They speculate that if they had seen Him perform all those miracles, it would have been easy to believe. Not so! I once dreamed I was one of Jesus' disciples. I saw Him raise Jairus' daughter from the dead. I saw blind eyes see and deaf ears hear. I walked down a road with all the disciples, and we talked about the incredible things we had seen when Jesus walked right up to me and asked, "But who do you say I am?"

I was torn with emotion. Everything I'd witnessed and all my heart wanted to say, "You are the Christ," but how could I? As I looked at Jesus, He appeared like any other man. There was nothing special about His looks. There was no halo like you see in some pictures. All my sensory knowledge screamed that He was just a man. That's when I realized just how hard it was for Jesus' disciples to believe.

Finally, I gave Peter's reply; but to say, "You are the Christ," took all the faith I could muster. I had to look past His physical body and see who He was on the inside. Now I understand how in some ways it is actually easier for us who are removed from the scene to believe. The disciples were constantly battling the logic of how God could be in a human body. We just read the Word about all the miraculous things Jesus did, about His death and resurrection, and envision Him seated on the throne in heaven. Knowing all that, it is easy for us to believe.

You can believe in Jesus just as strongly as those who walked with Him during his physical ministry. Choose to believe and follow Him today, being fully persuaded that His love and power will manifest fully in your life and all the lives you touch.

Gratitude Glorifies God
Luke 17:12-19

There are not found that returned to give glory to God, save this stranger.
Luke 17:18

Jesus healed ten lepers and told them to show themselves to the priests as Moses commanded. As they obeyed Him, they were healed; yet only one returned to thank Jesus. Verse sixteen says this man fell at Jesus' feet and gave Him thanks. Then in verse eighteen, Jesus said this man glorified God. Therefore, giving thanks to God is glorifying Him.

Thanking and praising God means you acknowledge Him as the fountain of your blessings. You are humbling yourself and proclaiming it was His ability, not yours, that raised you up. Ingratitude is like a child whose parents paid all the expenses to put them through college, but they just go out and brag on what they did without mentioning their parents' generosity. We would think that young person was self-centered and spoiled, and we'd be right! Likewise, it is self-centered and arrogant to fail to thank God.

Our gratitude glorifies God. A very simple yet profound theology is, "There's only one God, and I am not Him." We didn't make ourselves. (Ps. 100:3.) God is our Source, and we must glorify Him accordingly. We do that by being thankful for all He has so graciously done for us. As the doxology, which many of us were raised with, says, "Praise God from whom all blessings flow."

When you express your gratitude to God in everything you accomplish and for every blessing, large and small, you are someone who glorifies Him with your life. You won't have a hard heart. You will never dethrone Him and place yourself on the throne of your heart. So you see, keeping an attitude of gratitude glorifies God and keeps you safely in His hands.

Healed or Whole?
Luke 17:12-19

And he said unto him, Arise, go thy way: thy faith hath made thee whole.
Luke 17:19

Ten lepers cried out to Jesus for healing. He told them to act healed by showing themselves to the priests and asking them to declare they were clean. They obeyed, and all were healed; yet only one came back to thank Jesus–and I'm sure He noticed that 90 percent of the lepers did not return. There is no indication that their lack of gratitude caused Jesus to withdraw the healing He had given. That's not the way God is. The Lord "maketh his sun to rise on the evil and on the good, and sendeth rain on the just and on the unjust" (Matt. 5:45).

Jesus did do something special for the leper who gave thanks, and it is interesting that he was a Samaritan. Normally, Jews and Samaritans did not go near one another, but as we saw with Jesus and the woman at the well in John 4:9, He is no respecter of persons.

As you may know, leprosy causes parts of the body to decay and fall off. Lepers often lose fingers or toes. All these men were healed, which meant that the leprosy was no longer in their bodies and no longer doing any damage. However, Jesus told the man who returned that he was made whole. This implied that not only did the leprosy depart, but any damage the disease had done was repaired. It's possible that at that moment his fingers and toes grew back. Praise the Lord!

Which would you rather have, healing or wholeness? Of course, everyone would rather be whole. Only the leper who returned to give thanks was made whole. Why settle for less than God's best? Today, be thankful for all God does for you, and you will see the greater miracles in your life.

How Far Are You Willing to Go?

Mark 8:22-26

And he took the blind man by the hand, and led him out of the town; and when
he had spit on his eyes, and put his hands upon him, he asked him if he saw ought.
Mark 8:23

We usually focus on the miracle this blind man received, but for a moment, think about the faith he exhibited. Jesus took him by the hand and led him out of town. Remember, this man was blind. He didn't know where he was going, and he was putting himself at risk. If Jesus decided to just leave him, what would he do? He couldn't find his way back on his own—he couldn't see! This man was committed. He was expecting to be healed. He made no arrangements for anyone to take care of him in case he wound up stranded and still blind.

What if this man would have decided to stop following Jesus as soon as he discerned he was getting out of his familiar territory? After all, if he remained blind, he would be in trouble. It's probable that thoughts of unbelief like that could have stopped him from receiving his healing. He had to go all the way with Jesus. So do we.

There's no record that Jesus explained where He was taking this man or how far away it was. He just told him to hold onto His hand and follow Him. Isn't that enough? We often don't know exactly where the Lord is leading us or how things will go if we don't receive our miracle. But as long as we're holding His hand, we should feel safe.

How far are you willing to go with the Lord? Jesus didn't fail this blind man, and He won't fail you either. You can feel His hand as you fellowship with Him today. You don't need a Plan B or Plan C in case Jesus doesn't work. No backups are necessary. He's more than enough.

Money Is the Entry Level
of Faithfulness
Luke 16:1-13

He that is faithful in that which is least is faithful also in much: and he that
is unjust in the least is unjust also in much.
Luke 16:10

This was an amazing statement from Jesus, and it has many applications. In context, however, Jesus was speaking about money. The whole parable about the unjust steward is talking about his unfaithfulness with money. Jesus repeats this truth in the very next verse and substitutes the words *unrighteous mammon* for *that which is least.* The Word of God leaves no doubt that money is the lowest level of stewardship.

This brings up some serious questions. If money is least and we can't trust God with our finances, how can we trust Him in greater things like our eternal destiny? How can a person say, "Oh yes, I know I'm going to heaven, but I can't trust God to tithe to my church." If we don't have enough faith to trust God to give, then how can that faith get us to heaven?

Jesus used this same reasoning to minister to the rich young ruler. (Mark 10.) This man had an outward show of devotion, and he professed that he had done everything right. But Jesus saw his heart and told him to sell everything he had and give it to the poor. Jesus could tell by his response how truly committed to God this man was.

Did you know that your use of money says volumes about your faith in God? No one can profess true faith in God if they aren't faithful to Him with their money. Money is the entry level of faithfulness. Financial stewardship is the very least expression of faithfulness to God. It's like the bottom rung of a ladder. You can't go any higher if you don't take that first step. Be faithful with your giving today, and God will move you up the ladder to greater things tomorrow.

Rest and Re-Fire
Matthew 14:13-21; Mark 6:30-44; Luke 9:10-17; John 6:1-14

And he said unto them, Come ye yourselves apart into a desert place, and rest a while: for there were many coming and going, and they had no leisure so much as to eat.
Mark 6:31

Jesus often separated Himself from others so He could spend time with the Father. Here, we see Jesus calling His disciples apart for rest and leisure. Many zealous Christians have neglected the needs of their physical bodies and have cut their ministries short through death or severe illness. Likewise, many have failed to take the time to be still and know God. (Ps. 46:10.) This will also cut your ministry short through non-effectiveness. One of Satan's deadliest weapons against those involved in ministry is busyness. We must balance our time ministering to others with our time being ministered to by our Father. If the devil can't stop you from getting on fire for God, then he'll try to get you burned out.

The reason Jesus and His disciples went to this remote place was to get away from the multitude and rest. Rest was not optional but rather a necessity. Jesus and His disciples were taking a much needed vacation. However, the multitude followed them and their vacation ended even before it began. Surely, they were just as disappointed as you or I would have been, but instead of getting angry or bitter, Jesus was moved with compassion and ministered to them.

Later on in the evening, Jesus went up onto a mountain and prayed until the fourth watch (3 AM to 6 AM). The Lord intends for us to take care of our physical bodies, as can be seen by His actions in taking His disciples aside for rest, but we also see how He gave priority to His spirit and stayed up all night praying and getting the spiritual rest He needed.

Today, follow Jesus' example. Get the physical rest you need and respect the needs of your physical body, but make your time alone with the Father your first priority.

God's Options Or Ours?
Matthew 14:22-33

But straightway Jesus spake unto them, saying, Be of good cheer;
it is I; be not afraid. And Peter answered him and said, Lord,
if it be thou, bid me come unto thee on the water.
Matthew 14:27-28

It is important to analyze Peter's statement. Peter was overwhelmed when he saw Jesus walking on the water, and he also wanted to walk on the water. While there is really nothing wrong with his desire, the request he put before Jesus was totally wrong. He didn't ask the Lord if He wanted him to walk on the water, nor did he ask Him if his faith was up to it. Instead he said, "If it be thou, bid me come unto thee on the water." What was Jesus going to say?

"It isn't Me. Don't come."

There are no other examples of someone walking on water in the Word of God. Jesus had a definite reason for walking on the water; however, Peter simply wanted to see if he could do it. This story shows us that God will permit us to do things that are not His perfect will for us.

Many times we hinder our own prayers by the way we ask God for things. We say, "Do you want me to do A or B?" The Lord may not want us to do either one. We should offer Him a third choice—C, none of the above. Or better still, we should simply put the entire situation in His hands and ask Him what He desires for us to do.

Today, I encourage you to trust God's wisdom and allow Him to select the options you choose. It may keep you from sinking!

About Humility
John 6:15

*When Jesus therefore perceived that they would come and take him by force,
to make him a king, he departed again into a mountain himself alone.*
John 6:15

Jesus "was in all points tempted like as we are, yet without sin" (Heb. 4:15). The temptation for Him to submit to the crowd and exalt Himself must have been there, but He didn't respond to it. He came to do the Father's will and not His own will (John 6:38), so He immediately withdrew from everyone and spent all night in prayer with His Father. Prolonged prayer is an antidote for the temptation of pride and will work a God-type of humility in your life.

In Galatians 2:20, Paul taught about dying to self, and it is very important to notice how this death takes place. Paul said he was dead through what Jesus did. He experienced this death by simply reckoning what had already happened through Christ to be so. (Rom. 6:11.)

Some believers today have taken the dying-to-self doctrine to an extreme, and instead of being free of self, they are totally self-centered. They constantly think of self. It may be in negative terms, but it is still self-centered. A truly humble person is one who is Christ-centered. Dying to self is not a hatred of self but rather a love for Christ more than self.

There are false religions that preach a denial of self. We need to be not just dead to self but alive to God. A focus on the denial of self without the enthronement of Christ leads to legalism. True humility is not a debasing of self or a hatred of self or our accomplishments. Humility is simply an awareness that all that we have and are is a gift from God. Therefore, only a person who acknowledges God can operate in true humility.

You can be humble like Jesus today if you lose yourself in Him. Be consumed with what He desires to do, how He wants to minister to others through you, and what He is saying and feeling. Then you will just naturally walk in His humility.

The Power of One Word
Matthew 14:29

And he said, Come. And when Peter was come down out of the ship,
he walked on the water, to go to Jesus.
Matthew 14:29

One word, "Come," was spoken by the One who made all things (John 1:3), and that one word had just as much power in it as the words that were spoken at creation. Peter walked over those waves on the power of one word from the Lord. Likewise, any word spoken to us by God carries in itself the anointing and power it takes to fulfill that word if we will release it by believing it and acting on it.

We need to not only know God's power but the greatness of God's power and then the exceeding greatness of God's power. (Eph. 1:19.) This exceeding greatness of God's power is toward us. That means that it is for us and our benefit. Some people get glimpses of God's power, but very few have the revelation that it is for us and at our disposal. It doesn't do us any good to believe that God has power if we don't believe it will work for us. The exceedingly great power of God is effectual only for those who believe. We must believe to receive, for if we doubt, we do without.

Despite all the criticism Peter may have received, he did walk on the water. Although the eleven other disciples in the boat saw Jesus and Peter walking on the water, they did not participate. One of the important steps in receiving a miracle from God is to leave the security of your natural resources (get out of your boat) and put yourself in the position where there has to be a miracle from God to hold you up.

God is no respecter of persons. (Rom. 2:11.) Any of the disciples could have walked on the water if they would have asked and gotten out of the boat. Are you hiding in a boat, afraid to step out and walk in the exceeding greatness of God's power, power that is toward you? Today is your day to make that step of faith and trust Him for the miracles you need.

Enter Doubt, Exit Faith

Matthew 14:30-31

But when he saw the wind boisterous, he was afraid; and beginning to sink,
he cried, saying, Lord, save me.
Matthew 14:30

The reason Peter began to sink was because of his fear. In verse thirty-one, Jesus used the word *doubt* in reference to Peter's fear. Fear is simply negative faith or faith in evil instead of God's love and goodness. Where did this fear come from? Second Timothy 1:7 says, "For God hath not given us the spirit of fear; but of power and of love, and of a sound mind." It didn't come from God. This fear was able to come upon Peter because he took his attention off Jesus and put it on his situation.

Fear or doubt cannot just overcome us; we have to let it in. If Peter had kept his attention on Jesus, the Author and Finisher of his faith (Heb. 12:2), he wouldn't have feared. In the same way that faith comes by hearing the Word of God (Rom. 10:17), fear comes by hearing or seeing something contrary to God's Word. We would not be tempted with fear or doubt if we didn't dwell on what Satan does to cause fear and doubt. The wind and waves didn't really have anything to do with Peter walking on the water. He couldn't have walked on the water apart from Jesus even if it had been calm. The circumstances simply took Peter's attention off of his Master and led him back into carnal thinking. Likewise, Satan tries to distract us with thinking about our problems.

Peter's faith didn't fail him all at once because the Bible says he only "began" to sink. If there had been no faith present, he would have sunk all at once and not gradually. This illustrates that the entrance of fear and the exit of faith do not happen instantly. There are always signs that this is happening.

If you will turn your attention fully on Jesus, He will save you from drowning in all your problems today. No problem is too big for Him, and He wants to see you do well and be happy.

Sensitivity to the Right Things
Mark 6:45-52; John 6:15-21

For they considered not the miracle of the loaves: for their heart was hardened.
Mark 6:52

Most of the time we think of a person with a hard heart as being someone who is in terrible rebellion to God. While it is true that a rebellious person does have a hard heart, in this verse the Word is referring to the disciples' hearts being hardened. They were, "sore amazed in themselves beyond measure, and wondered" at Jesus walking on the water because they forgot that He had just miraculously fed over five thousand people.

The word *hardened* as used here, means "to make calloused, unyielding or cold in spirit, or insensitive to." The disciples were not God haters, but rather they had become so sensitive to the natural world and its limitations that they were overwhelmed to see Jesus supersede these laws. Therefore, they had hard hearts.

If they had kept in mind the miracle they had just seen Jesus perform (the feeding of over five thousand people), they wouldn't have been amazed to see Jesus walking on the water. After all, He had constrained them to get into the ship and was therefore responsible for them. He was just a short distance away from them and was in the same storm Himself, so they knew He was aware of their situation. They should have expected Him to save them, even if He had to walk on the water to do it.

Are you more prone to fear and doubt the truths of God's Word? Perhaps you have thought more about things that minister fear and doubt. You can turn this around today and actually harden your heart to doubt by considering only God's Word! It is a possible and obtainable goal to become just as sensitive to God and faith as you were to Satan and doubt. Meditate on God's Word today.

Salvation: A Relationship
Mark 6:53-56

And when they were come out of the ship, straightway they knew him.
Mark 6:54

The word *know* can mean many things, from as little as "to perceive with the senses or the mind," to a much deeper meaning of "a thorough experience with." This knowing, then, is not just intellectual but a personal, intimate understanding. Jesus defines eternal life as knowing God the Father through Him. Eternal life is having an intimate, personal relationship with God the Father and Jesus the Son. This intimacy with God is what salvation is all about.

Forgiveness of our sins was not the goal of salvation; it was the means to achieve the goal, which was intimacy with the Father. Jesus died to purchase forgiveness for our sins because unforgiven sins keep us from a close relationship with the Father. Sin was an obstacle that stood between God and us. Jesus had to deal with it. Anyone who views salvation as only forgiveness of sins and going to heaven is missing out on eternal life with God.

Scripture presents salvation as the way sinful people come back into peace and harmony with God. Instead, it has often been presented as the way to escape the problems of this life and later the judgment of hell. It is possible to get born again with that kind of thinking, and people who get saved with that view only see the Lord as Someone to help them through times of crisis. They never enter into the daily joy of knowing Him intimately.

Jesus died for you because He loved you (John 3:16)—a love that longed to have intimate communion with you. Explore your relationship with Him today, and then tell your unbelieving friends about Him. Most likely they are fed up with religion and have not been satisfied by what the world offers either. Tell them you know firsthand that only an intimate relationship with the Father can give them what they need for this life and the life to come.

Self-Seeking or God-Seeking
Matthew 14:34-36; Mark 6:53-56; John 6:22-39

Jesus answered them and said, Verily, verily, I say unto you, Ye seek me, not because ye saw the miracles, but because ye did eat of the loaves, and were filled.
John 6:26

Jesus knew the hearts of all men; therefore, He did not commit Himself to this crowd. Just the day before these same people tried to take Him by force and make Him their king, but He withdrew and spent the night in prayer.

This crowd looked like they were seeking Jesus, but they were actually trying to use Jesus to seek their own end. It is true that there are many personal benefits from serving the Lord, but the benefits are never to become our goal or desire. In all things, Christ must have the preeminence. (Col. 1:18.)

Jesus exposed the true intentions of the people's hearts by preaching a strong message of commitment. Those who were self-centered were offended and left, while those who were willing to lay down their lives to experience God's abundant life remained. Commitment to God Himself (not what He can produce) is what always separates the true worshippers of God from the false worshippers.

When Jesus declared that He was the only way to the Father (John 14:6), the people grew angry. It always angers our proud, carnal nature to think that all our righteous acts can't save us! But Jesus made it clear that our only part in salvation is to believe. Believe what? Believe on Him and His sacrifice—not ours. Salvation is a gift and cannot be purchased. (Rom. 10:2,3.)

Do you find yourself getting so intent on seeking God in one area that you forget the greatest miracle of all, which is the love and redemption given to you from God through His Son. Today, remember His sacrifice and how much He loves you. That truth will put everything else in proper perspective.

Dead Works
John 6:24-29

Then said they unto him, What shall we do, that we might work the works of God?
John 6:28

Throughout history, mankind has been seeking ways to do the works of God. All people have the knowledge of the reality of God within them (Rom. 1:18-20), as well as a desire to be right with Him. However, just as with these Jews, few agree with the Lord on how to do it. These Jews were willing to do something to obtain salvation, but they were not willing to surrender their lives to Jesus as Lord and accept His gift of salvation.

This is one of the major differences between Christianity and the religions of the world. Religion is willing to make sacrifices to obtain right standing with God, but Christianity recognizes our complete inability to ever do enough to save ourselves and calls for total faith and reliance on what Jesus did for us.

You do not deserve to be saved because no one deserves to be saved! You cannot earn it by what the Bible calls "dead works." (Heb. 6:1; 9:14.) Dead works include all religious activities, good deeds, or charity you might do as a means of justifying yourself to God. Only your faith in what Jesus has done to save you will justify you, so your part is simple—just believe it. Today you can rest in the truth that your salvation is fully His work, not yours.

Bread of Heaven
John 6:31-35

Then said they unto him, Lord, evermore give us this bread.
John 6:34

It is probable these Jews expected Jesus to rain down manna on them the way God did for their ancestors in the wilderness. After all, anyone who could feed five thousand men with one small lunch should be able to produce manna. They were still thinking of physical food.

The word *manna* means "what is it?" The children of Israel said, "It is manna: for they wist (knew) not what it was" (Ex. 16:15, insert mine). Manna was a nutritious food that appeared on the ground every morning shortly after the children of Israel left Egypt and began their forty-year wandering in the wilderness. Moses called it, "Bread which the Lord hath given you to eat" (Ex. 16:15).

Manna was small and round, like coriander seed, and was white or yellowish, like bdellium. It was gathered every morning and had to be used that day or it would stink and have worms. The exception was on the sixth day when it could be gathered for the Sabbath and wouldn't spoil. (Ex. 16:22-26.)

"And Jesus said unto them, I am the bread of life" (John 6:35). The people were looking for pieces of bread to materialize, which would have been a great miracle; but that would have been insignificant compared to the miracle being manifested before them. They were talking to the greatest miracle God had ever performed, but they were blind to it. All they could see was what they needed and what Jesus could give them.

Many times, we get so intent on seeking God in one area that we forget the greatest miracle of all, which is the love and redemption given to us from God through His Son. Today, consider what life would have been like without Jesus and how your life has been transformed because He is your Lord and Savior.

Be Taught of God
John 6:40-45

It is written in the prophets, And they shall be all taught of God. Every man therefore that hath heard, and hath learned of the Father, cometh unto me.
John 6:45

The Old Testament prophets prophesied of a New Covenant in which we would all be taught of God. They were speaking of revelation knowledge coming from within through our spirits. Under the Old Covenant, God dealt with His people through the outer man. He did this because those who were not born again could not perceive the spiritual truths revealed in the New Covenant by the Spirit. (1 Cor. 2:14.)

Old Testament believers were like children in their ability to grasp spiritual truth. It is impossible to explain spiritual truth to a young child, yet they must be restrained from submitting to evil. Therefore, the Word of God taught parents to use the "rod of correction." (Prov. 13:24; 19:18; 22:15.) The child might not understand resisting the devil, but when the devil tempted them to steal, they would say no because they feared the rod. Likewise, Old Testament saints were restrained from sin by a fear of the wrath and punishment of God. This curbed sin, but it also hindered them from receiving the goodness and love of God. (1 John 4:18.)

In John 6:45, Jesus was speaking of the New Covenant in which the punishment for your sins was laid on Him. You no longer serve God out of fear of punishment. Now you serve Him out of love because He has sent the Spirit of His Son into your heart making you His son or daughter. You serve Him because your nature has been changed through the new birth. Now you are like Him. Today, let the Holy Spirit inside your spirit lead you and teach you.

The Spirit and the Word Are One
John 6:40-71; 7:1

*It is the spirit that quickeneth; the flesh profiteth nothing: the words that
I speak unto you, they are spirit, and they are life.*
John 6:63

Jesus was stating that life originates and comes from your spirit, not your flesh. These people were so dominated by their physical lives that they were missing all the spiritual significance of His words. Although God's Word does benefit our physical bodies, the Word is spiritual and must be understood through our spirits. God's Word is spirit, and the Holy Spirit in our spirits illuminates God's truth to our minds.

The Word of God is not just paper and ink. Jesus is the Word, and He existed in spiritual form long before any words were inspired by the Holy Ghost to be written down. The Bible is simply a physical representation of Jesus and spiritual truth. It is inspired of God and totally accurate and reliable, yet until we receive the Holy Spirit in our spirits, the Bible will not profit us. This is why many people who have read and even memorized the Word are not reaping its benefits. They have never been born again and do not have the spiritual Teacher (John 14:26) living inside them.

Just as the physical part of us receives life from the food we eat, our spirits receive life as we partake of Jesus, the "bread of life." (John 6:48.) Jesus plainly stated that the words He spoke were spiritual—not physical. If we want to know what spiritual truth is, we must believe the Bible, for it is spirit and life. If we want to be led by the Spirit, then we must follow God's Word. If we want to hear from the Spirit of God, then we must listen to what God says in His Word. The Spirit (Holy Spirit) and the Word (Jesus) are One. (John 1:1.)

Today you can find peace in every decision you make by making those decisions as the Holy Spirit leads you in God's Word. The Spirit and the Word always agree, and when you come into agreement with them, you will know you are moving in the right direction and doing the right thing.

The Law Is Not of Faith

Mark 7:1-7

And when they saw some of his disciples eat bread with defiled, that is to say,
with unwashen, hands, they found fault.
Mark 7:2

In this verse the Pharisees were concerned with what religious people are concerned about, the outward appearance; while Jesus was concerned with the heart. (1 Sam. 16:7.) The Old Testament laws concerning washing served a secondary purpose of hygiene, but as stated in Colossians 2:16-17 and Hebrews 9:1,9-10, their real purpose was to shadow or illustrate spiritual truth. Defiled food may hurt our bodies, but it cannot reach our spirits. (John 3:6.)

The scribes and Pharisees missed the principle of spiritual purity taught by the Old Testament ordinances and became completely corrupt in the spiritual realm. The apostle Paul also dealt with this in Galatians 3:12, which says, "The law is not of faith." Combined with Romans 14:23, which says, "Whatsoever is not of faith is sin," the idea of living by faith and not the law was blasphemy to the legalistic Jews, just as it is to legalistic Christians today. But God gave the Law to reveal sin, not to make us righteous by it. (Gal. 3:24.)

It is sin for the New Testament believer to try to relate to God by attempting to keep the Old Testament Law. The Law itself is not sin (Rom. 7:7), but it is sin to try to keep the Law to justify yourself to God. The purpose of the Law is to reveal that you can't save yourself. Only putting your faith in the redemptive work of Jesus Christ will save you.

Under the Law, you get what you deserve. Through faith in Jesus, you receive God's grace because of what He did for you. Any departure from faith, especially a departure back to the Old Testament Law, voids the work of Christ (Gal. 2:21) and is the worst sin of all. Only faith in Jesus Christ unlocks the door to the Law's harsh imprisonment of guilt and condemnation. Jesus purchased your freedom at great personal price, so put your faith in Him for everything today. Then you will do the right thing and enjoy His life.

Take Off the Mask
Mark 7:6-9

He answered and said unto them, Well hath Esaias prophesied of you hypocrites, as it is written, This people honoureth me with their lips, but their heart is far from me.
Mark 7:6

A biblical definition of a hypocrite is someone whose words and heart-actions don't agree. Hypocrites act the part of a Christian or believe God's Word, but they won't do both. Either they do not act on what they know is true, or they don't believe in their hearts what they say and do—they just do it to appear righteous and holy. Only when both their confession and what they do from their heart are consistent with God's Word are they truly saved. (Rom. 10:9,10.)

The word *hypocrite* comes from the Greek word *hupokrites,* meaning, "the playing of a part on the stage; an actor." It was a custom for Greek and Roman actors to use large masks when acting to disguise their true identity. Hence, *hypocrisy* became "the feigning of beliefs, feelings, or virtues that one does not hold or possess; insecurity."

It has become customary in our society to conceal our real feelings behind a hypocritical mask. Although we should be tactful and not purposely say things to offend people, there is a time and a place for speaking the truth, even if it isn't popular. In Leviticus 19:17, the Lord said, "Thou shalt not hate thy brother in thine heart: thou shalt in any wise rebuke thy neighbour, and not suffer sin upon him." This verse is saying that if we fail to rebuke our brother when we see sin approaching, then we hate him.

Many people have concealed their true feelings about evil under the pretense of, "I just love them too much to hurt their feelings." The truth is, they just love themselves too much to run the risk of being rejected. That's hypocrisy. Motives, not actions, are usually what make a person a hypocrite. Let God's love be your motivation today and everyday.

Tradition Neutralizes
Mark 7:1-13

Making the word of God of none effect through your tradition,
which ye have delivered: and many such like things do ye.
Mark 7:13

Deuteronomy 4:2 clearly states, "Ye shall not add unto the word which I command you, neither shall ye diminish ought from it." This same thought is repeated in the New Testament in Revelation 22:18-19 with very stiff penalties. Religious people are very swift to observe the part about not diminishing any of God's commandments, but there seems to be an unwritten law that adding to them is okay.

Every denomination has its own set of dos and don'ts that aren't found in Scripture, and like those of the hypocritical Pharisees, their unwritten laws usually have to do with outward appearance. We need to remember that adding to God's commandments is just as bad as taking away from them.

The commandments of God and the traditions of men must always be clearly separated. Any attempt to place them on the same level will always result in making the Word of God ineffectual in your life. You have to either lay aside the commandment of God to keep the traditions of men, or you have to lay aside the traditions of men to keep the commandments of God. (Ex. 20:3.) You neutralize the positive power of God's Word in you by elevating man's traditions above God's Word.

The Word will not profit anyone who doesn't believe it, but God's Word never loses its power. Today, take a good look at why you do the spiritual things you do. Are your beliefs and actions based on God's Word or a tradition of your church or denomination? Remember that only the Word has the power to save you, heal you, prosper you, and give you peace and joy!

What Really Defiles You
Matthew 15:1-20; Mark 7:1-23

There is nothing from without a man, that entering into him can defile him:
but the things which come out of him, those are they that defile the man.
Mark 7:15

The Old Testament dietary laws were shadows of spiritual truths that would become realities in the New Covenant. These Pharisees (as well as many Christians today) missed the spiritual significance of these laws. The real spiritual meaning the dietary laws symbolized was that we were supposed to be holy (separated) unto God in everything—even in what we eat. Under the Law it was forbidden to eat or even to touch certain animals not because there was anything wrong with the animals but to illustrate the point of being separated unto God. The practice of these laws served as a constant reminder of this separation.

Under the New Testament, we don't need dietary laws to remind us we are holy and separated unto God because His Spirit lives inside us and His Word says we are righteous and holy through the blood of Jesus Christ. Jesus' statements in this passage of Scripture refer to what really defiles a person. We cannot interpret this to mean that any type of abuse to our bodies, such as gluttony or drug abuse, is okay, but He is saying it is not what goes into our mouths that can defile us; it is what comes out of our mouths that defiles us.

Jesus knew that we speak what is in our hearts, and if our hearts are corrupt with sin, we will speak evil. He knows whatever comes out of our mouths comes from a defiled heart. On the other hand, if we are born again and have a new heart, a heart after God, then we will speak words that are right and holy. God looks on our hearts and what our mouths speak from our hearts as pure and clean.

Today, think about the condition of your heart. The words you speak will tell you whether your heart has been tainted by the world, deceived by the enemy, and overcome by your flesh. If so, all you have to do is repent and be cleansed. (1 John 1:9.) Then you can rejoice that you are a child of God and have a great day with Him.

Know What Is Yours
Mark 7:17-23

For from within, out of the heart of men, proceed evil thoughts,
adulteries, fornications, murders.
Mark 7:21

These verses (vv. 21-23) further establish the truth that our hearts include more than just our spirits. Even Christians still struggle with things like pride and foolishness, which Jesus said come out of the heart. It's certain that our born-again spirits are not the source of these sins; therefore, the heart encompasses more than the spirit.

The word *spirit* is used in different ways in Scripture. The most frequent usage refers to either the Spirit of God or the spirit of man. It either denotes the person of the Holy Spirit or the spiritual part of our three-part being. (1 Thess. 5:23.) The word *spirit* can also describe a mental disposition. In Ephesians 1:17, Paul prayed that what was already true in our spirits would become our "mental dispositions." He prayed for a release into our soul of what was already present in our spirit.

The Christian life is not an attempt to get more faith, more anointing, or to get closer to the Lord. We already have these things in their fullness. We just need a revelation of what is already ours. Understanding this takes a lot of frustration and doubt away. It's much easier to release something you already have than to try and get something you don't have. Why would anyone doubt whether they could receive what they already have?

Through Christ, you are already blessed with all spiritual blessings. (Eph. 1:3.) All you have to do is appropriate what is already yours, and you do that by renewing your mind with God's Word. His Word tells you who you are and what you have. Once you know what is yours, then your spirit and soul will form a majority, and your flesh will experience the life of God that has been deposited in your spirit.

Jesus Tried Her Faith
Matthew 15:21-39; Mark 7:24-37; 8:1-10

But Jesus said unto her, Let the children first be filled: for it is not meet to take the children's bread, and to cast it unto the dogs.
Mark 7:27

Although Jesus came to fulfill God's promise of a Messiah to the Jews, He also came to offer salvation to the Gentiles. Jesus certainly knew this and had already ministered to numerous Gentiles without any disdain. Here in Mark, however, He is very rude to the Syrophenician woman. Jesus could not be forced into ministering to this woman's daughter if it was not His will to do so; therefore, His silence and rough answer to this woman must have been designed to accomplish a godly result.

Humility is an important ingredient of faith. This woman was a stranger to the covenants of promise and had no right to demand anything. Although she fell at His feet, He knew what was really in her heart. Jesus' silence and then comparison of her to a dog would certainly have offended an arrogant person, and it is possible that for this very reason Jesus tried her faith. He didn't need to do this with the centurion in Luke 7:6-7. The centurion didn't fall at His feet, but Jesus knew he was humble in his heart.

No doubt this woman needed to have her faith tried to bring her heart to a place of humility. Only in this way would she truly know that the miracle she received had nothing to do with her and was solely due to the grace of God shown her. It took great humility to put her and her daughter in the same class as dogs, and it proved to Jesus that she knew she was a sinner in need of a savior.

The truth is that without Jesus, you, too, were just a dog, trying to please and gain affection from a Master you couldn't really communicate with or understand. All you could do was beg for whatever you needed and hope He blessed you. But today you can celebrate the truth that you are His very own child. You can communicate with Him, understand Him, and you know He has already provided everything you need through the blood of His Son. Hallelujah!

The Ministry of the Holy Spirit
Mark 8:11-13

And he sighed deeply in his spirit, and saith, Why doth this generation seek after a sign? verily I say unto you, There shall no sign be given unto this generation.
Mark 8:12

The Greek word used here for *sighed deeply* means "an intense grieving, inaudible prayer, or groan." This is intercession of the Holy Spirit, with groanings that cannot be uttered. (Rom. 8:26.) Some Spirit-filled Christians believe this means groanings that cannot be uttered in normal speech and that this refers to speaking in tongues. However, this actually refers to a type of intercession different than speaking in tongues.

In John 11:33 and 38, Jesus groaned in the Spirit twice, and in those cases there were no words uttered. It was exactly as the Scripture states, a groaning in the Spirit. Everyone who has the indwelling presence of the Holy Spirit has or will have this happen to them. Paul was referring to this in Galatians 4:19 when he spoke of travailing in birth for the Galatians. This groaning of the Holy Spirit is not just grief but a groan of anger and resistance against Satan's devices in our lives. Many times Christians don't discern this because they think it is just their own grief over the situation; however, this is the Holy Spirit desiring to intercede with us against our problems.

Jesus drew on this ministry of the Holy Spirit. John 11:33 and 38 say that Jesus groaned in the Spirit twice when He raised Lazarus from the dead. What infirmity did Jesus have that He needed this ministry of the Holy Spirit? Jesus had no sin, but He did have an infirmity. It was His physical mind. Even a sinless human mind could not comprehend raising a man from the grave after four days.

If Jesus needed the Holy Spirit to help Him when He didn't know how to pray, then this should certainly be an important ministry of the Holy Spirit in your life. Today be mindful of the Spirit's unction inside you to pray and intercede for others. You may be surprised at how He will use you to impact the lives of others.

Jesus Is Always a Threat to Religion
Matthew 16:1-4

The Pharisees also with the Sadducees came, and tempting desired him that
he would shew them a sign from heaven.
Matthew 16:1

The Sadducees were a Jewish sect (Acts 5:17) of both a political and religious nature that opposed the more popular party of the Pharisees over doctrinal and political beliefs. Sadducees rejected the oral tradition of the Pharisees who made a mountain of burdensome legislation and accepted only the written law. We are told they believed there was "no resurrection, nor angel, nor spirit" (Acts 23:8). From Josephus, we learn that the Sadducees believed the soul perishes with the body[1] and can receive neither penalties nor rewards in an afterlife[2].

The most significant mention of the Sadducees in the Gospels concerns their interview with Jesus in Jerusalem. They tried to trap Him with a crafty question concerning the resurrection. In His answer, Jesus accused them of not knowing the Scriptures nor the power of God. (Matt. 22:29.) He then proceeded to quote from the Pentateuch (the first five books of the Bible) out of Exodus 3:6 in support of the doctrine of the resurrection.

The Sadducees became alarmed and decided to take action (John 11:47), especially after the episode in which Jesus had cleansed the temple in Mark 11:15-18. They were able to unite with their traditional enemies, the Pharisees, for the purpose of disposing of Jesus. Both parties worked together for His arrest and trial by the Sanhedrin. Obviously, these religious leaders were so caught up in external actions that they missed the sinful condition of their hearts.

Jesus will always pose a threat to religion because religion is dead and powerless, but Jesus is the way, the truth, and the life. He is the only way to the Father, and He takes us by way of our hearts. Today, be grateful that you have the life of God in you through Jesus Christ!

[1] The Antiquities of the Jews, Book 18, Chapter 1, Section 4.
[2] The War of the Jews, Book 2, Chapter 8, Section 14.

Petition Not Repetition
Matthew 16:13-15; Mark 8:11-25; Luke 9:18-20

And he looked up, and said, I see men as trees, walking. After that he put his
hands again upon his eyes, and made him look up: and he was restored,
and saw every man clearly.
Mark 8:24-25

I t was unusual for Jesus to inquire about the results of His ministry as He did in verse twenty-three. It was even more unusual that Jesus laid hands on this man a second time. This is the only example in the New Testament where Jesus had to minister to any need more than once to manifest a total healing.

Many people request things from God and then look at their circumstances to see if God answered their prayers. That is walking by sight and not by faith. If they can't see God's answer in the natural realm, they pray again. This is not the way Jesus taught us to pray and receive. We can be certain Jesus didn't lay hands on this man a second time because He thought His Father hadn't heard Him the first time. Since the man received partial sight, it is evident that God's healing power was at work in him. Jesus was not petitioning His Father again for healing.

Through His spirit, Jesus knew that unbelief was hindering a perfect manifestation of God's power in this man, and He simply gave him another dose of the anointing of God. Satan may hinder, but he cannot prevail over someone who continues resisting him.

Today, believe that you receive when you pray and then continue to apply the power of God no matter what your physical senses tell you. Press in to such a degree that you can confront anything that is contrary to what you have asked and overcome it. Perseverance in prayer is the key to overcoming Satan, not persuading God. God was persuaded the moment you prayed His will and Word in faith!

Your Cross

Matthew 16:16-26; Mark 8:30-37; Luke 9:21-27

And he said to them all, If any man will come after me, let him deny himself,
and take up his cross daily, and follow me.
Luke 9:23

Self-denial is an important part of the Christian life. Jesus sacrificed His life for us, and He demands that we die to ourselves to experience the new life He has provided. We do this by first recognizing that we can't save ourselves by our own efforts and then by trusting God, not ourselves, for salvation. Daily, we need to deny our own wisdom and seek God's wisdom and direction for our lives.

Self-denial is only good when we are denying ourselves for the singular purpose of exalting Jesus and His will for us in some area of our lives. Some have made a religion out of self-denial and find pleasure in their denial—not in Jesus' lordship. This leads to legalism and bondage, which Paul condemned as "will worship" (Col. 2:23). We are told not only to deny ourselves, but to deny ourselves, take up our cross, and follow Jesus.

The Cross is what Jesus died on. Your cross consists of the circumstances and difficulties of life that give you the opportunity to die to yourself each day. These are not things like sickness and poverty, for which Jesus' atonement provided redemption, but rather things like persecution and the constant battle between your flesh and your born-again spirit. The cross you bear today is to take God's Word (which is His will) and exalt it above your own will in each situation you face.

A Willing Sacrifice
Genesis 22:1-18

*And they came to the place which God had told him of; and Abraham built
an altar there, and laid the wood in order, and bound Isaac his son,
and laid him on the altar upon the wood.*
Genesis 22:9

In Luke 18:8 Jesus said, "When the Son of man cometh, shall he find faith on the earth?" He is looking for faith in believers, and our faith ought to be even greater than that of Old Testament believers who weren't born again. This amazing account of Abraham offering his son Isaac to God as a sacrifice has inspired faith in many people through the ages. Yet Abraham wasn't the only one to express amazing faith and faithfulness. Isaac's actions were pretty awesome too.

Most scholars believe Isaac was about seventeen years old at this time, which means Abraham was 117. Isaac probably could have overpowered Abraham. Certainly he could have outrun dear old dad, but he allowed his father to bind him and place him on the altar, knowing full well that he was his father's sacrifice. There is no indication that Isaac screamed for help or resisted in any way. Isaac had complete trust in God, his father, or both.

This is a perfect picture of how God sacrificed His Son Jesus for us. It was an astonishing act of love for us on God's part, but it was equally wonderful what Jesus did. Jesus could have called for legions of angels to deliver Him, but He didn't. (Matt. 26:53.) He yielded Himself to His Father just as Isaac did, even unto death.

Such love and sacrifice had great purpose—to redeem and reveal God's great love for you and Jesus' loving sacrifice for you. Now that is something you can have faith in! Today you can look to Jesus, who willingly and lovingly gave Himself for you, and willingly and lovingly give yourself for Him in everything you do. Then, when He looks down on the earth, He will find your faith.

What Are You Thinking?
Genesis 22:1-18

I and the lad will go yonder and worship, and come again to you.
Genesis 22:5

I t is hard for most of us to relate to the story of Abraham offering his son, Isaac, to God as a sacrifice. Much of the reason is because we incorrectly imagine how hard this must have been on Abraham.

One movie about this incident depicts Abraham hitting his fist against a stone wall and crying out, "No, God! Anything but Isaac!" It portrays Abraham wrestling with God all night and finally grudgingly complying with His demand. But that's not what the Bible states. There is no hint of any resistance on Abraham's part. In fact, verse three shows Abraham rising early the next morning and heading to the place of sacrifice. He told his servants, "We will worship and then we will come back to you" (Gen. 22:5 NIV).

In Hebrews 11:19, the Word of God reveals Abraham believed God would raise Isaac from the dead. He never saw Isaac dead and gone because God had promised him that He was going to give him a multitude of children through Isaac, and Isaac hadn't had any children yet. Therefore, Isaac had to live. Abraham wasn't thinking on death; he was thinking about resurrection.

What are you thinking about? Are you looking at the sacrifice or the reward? What you think upon will determine your reaction to God's requests. If you think on the sacrifice, your faith in God will fade; and even if you do obey, you will not expect victory. But if you think on the promise of God, like Abraham you will have faith to sacrifice anything. The choice is yours, and your choice will determine whether you resist or rejoice.

Jesus, the Chief Cornerstone
Matthew 16:13-19

And I say also unto thee, That thou art Peter, and upon this rock I will build my church; and the gates of hell shall not prevail against it,
Matthew 16:18

Some people have mistakenly interpreted this passage to say that Peter was the foundation on which Christ would build His Church; however, that would violate many scriptures that refer to Jesus as the "chief cornerstone." Ephesians 2:20 does mention the apostles as being part of the foundation stones of Christ's church, but it doesn't single Peter out above any of the other apostles. This same Scripture also mentions Jesus as the "chief cornerstone."

There are two different Greek words used for *Peter* and *rock* respectively in verse eighteen. The word translated *Peter* signifies a piece of rock like a pebble. In contrast, the word translated *rock* signifies a massive boulder, which certainly refers to Jesus, the "chief cornerstone." Some have suggested that the foundation rock referred to was a confession Peter made, saying that Jesus was "the Christ, the Son of the living God" (Matt. 16:16). Although it is true that to enter God's kingdom we must confess that Jesus is Lord (Rom. 10:9,10), in light of the Old Testament prophecies and New Testament references to Jesus being the "chief cornerstone," this passage of Scripture must be referring directly to Jesus as the rock upon which He will build His church.

One of the greatest differences between New Testament believers and Old Testament believers is that New Testament saints are the temple of God. God Himself actually dwells in you and me. God does not dwell in a building made by man's hands. He now lives in the hearts of those who have made Jesus their Lord. (Rom. 10:9.)

The cornerstone of your life in God must be an ever-increasing revelation of His Son. When you have a real understanding of the reality of Christ in you (Col. 1:27), it drastically changes your attitudes, emotions, and actions.

Recognize the Real Enemy
Mark 8:30-33

But when he had turned about and looked on his disciples, he rebuked Peter,
saying, Get thee behind me, Satan: for thou savourest not the things that
be of God, but the things that be of men.
Mark 8:33

Jesus was not implying that Peter and Satan were the same person. He was declaring that Satan had inspired Peter's statement. This type of metaphor was used elsewhere in Scripture, such as when God spoke to the serpent in the Garden of Eden (Gen. 3:15) as though addressing Satan. The serpent was merely the vehicle of communication Satan used to tempt Adam and Eve, while Peter was the vehicle Satan used to tempt Jesus.

Jesus recognized that Peter's reaction to His prophecy about His death was motivated by His enemy, Satan, so He went right to the source. We must do the same. Ephesians 6:12 reveals that our warfare isn't with people but against the evil spiritual powers who inspire and use them. Every Christian is at war. There is a perpetual struggle against Satan and his kingdom from which there are no "leaves" or "discharges." Our enemy goes about as a roaring lion, seeking whom he may devour (1 Pet. 5:8), but those who resist the devil will see him flee. (James 4:7.)

Some of us believe that anger will put others in their place. But "the wrath of man does not work the righteousness of God" (James 1:20). Anger against people makes us play right into the hand of the devil. The way to overcome the spiritual powers that come against us through people is to forgive and turn the other cheek. (Matt. 5:39.) This makes the demons flee in terror! Some believe the higher echelons of the devil's kingdom take more power to rebuke or remove. That's not true. There is no demonic power, including the devil himself, that will not flee when the name of Jesus is spoken in faith.

You cannot win a spiritual battle with carnal weapons. You must realize who your real enemy is and fight with the spiritual weapons the Lord has given you. Today when you encounter someone who is being used by the enemy, pray for them and rebuke the enemy in Jesus' name. What a wonderful name.

The Hope of His Calling
Ephesians 1:15-23

The eyes of your understanding being enlightened; that ye may know what is the hope of his calling, and what the riches of the glory of his inheritance in the saints.
Ephesians 1:18

Paul prayed that we would know the "hope of His calling." We are carrying out the call of Jesus, not our own. Great peace, hope, and faith are the results of knowing that we are fulfilling His call and not just doing our own thing. I found that out in 1969 when an Army recruiter came to my home to show me all the advantages of volunteering for the Army, rather than being drafted.

I told the recruiter I could save him a lot of time if he would listen to me. I explained that the reason I was 1-A was because I had quit school. He agreed. Then I shared how the Lord specifically directed me to leave the university, and that I was in His hands. If God wanted me drafted, I would be; and if He didn't, I wouldn't be.

The recruiter started laughing and said, "Boy, I can guarantee that you'll be drafted!" That really made me mad. I told him that if it was God's will for me to stay at home, then neither he, the United States government, nor all the demons in hell could draft me. He thought I was crazy. Sure enough, I received a draft notice in the next day's mail.

When I went to Vietnam, however, I knew in my heart that I was there because of my obedience to the Lord. It was His calling, not mine. This gave me a confidence and a hope others didn't have. I knew the Lord was responsible for my safety and my life.

Today, live your life in the hope of His calling, and you will have perfect peace that wherever His calling takes you, you will be safely and securely in His all-powerful, loving hands.

Wrapped in God's Love
Matthew 24:1-13

And because iniquity shall abound, the love of many shall wax cold.
Matthew 24:12

I went through some trying times in Vietnam. Aside from the pressures every soldier experiences in war, I was fighting a war of another kind. I had lived a very sheltered life and suddenly was thrust into the midst of a world full of temptation and sin I never knew existed. Iniquity truly abounded.

Although my situation was an all-time low, my love for Jesus was at an all-time high. The abundance of iniquity doesn't have to make our love for the Lord cool off. I was being driven closer to Him because of choices I made. In every situation, I chose to follow Him instead of my flesh.

One night, while on bunker guard, I was shivering because of the cold. I was wet and chilled to the bone. As soon as my watch was over, I went inside the bunker, wrapped up in a blanket, and began to feel the warmth come back into my body. It was a wonderful feeling that I still remember.

I also remember praying a prayer. I compared the chill to the sin that was all around me. Without protection, anyone would get cold, but if the Lord would wrap me in His love like I was wrapped in that blanket, I knew I could make it.

Iniquity is sending a chill through our society today as never before. Unprotected, your love for the Lord will grow cold, but that doesn't have to happen. You can dress for the weather. A little extra time in the arms of the Lord will warm your heart so that instead of your love growing cold, His love in you will melt the hardened hearts of those around you.

No One Has an Excuse
Romans 1:18-20

For the invisible things of him from the creation of the world are clearly seen,
being understood by the things that are made, even his eternal power
and Godhead; so that they are without excuse.
Romans 1:20

When I was in Vietnam, I often drove past an ancient temple that always caught my attention. The jungle was beginning to overtake it as trees grew out of the bricks in the top and sides of the structure. The thing that intrigued me was that this temple was three separate buildings, yet one. Each building was about three-stories high and separated by only a few inches.

I asked around and found out that that temple was for a deity that was one god manifested in three personalities. Amazing! And this temple predated the introduction of Christianity to Vietnam by nearly five hundred years. This temple was a vivid illustration of the above Scripture.

The Lord put an intuitive knowledge of Himself inside every person who has ever walked on the earth. Even His Godhead is known by His creation. That's what this temple reflected. In the following verses of Romans 1, Paul speaks of how mankind perverted this knowledge and went into idolatry and other perversions. I'm not saying that these people were worshipping the one true God that we know, but it does verify that they had a kernel of truth that could only have come from Him.

The Bible says that those who have never heard a clear presentation of the Gospel of Jesus Christ aren't off the hook. Although they won't be held accountable for what they don't know, they have a built-in homing device for God and will have to give an account of what they did with that knowledge. As you minister to others today, remember that God has already shown them the truth in their hearts.

Faith Is a Heart Issue
Romans 10:8-17

For with the heart man believeth unto righteousness.
Romans 10:10

I encountered a few people in Vietnam who claimed to be atheists. They argued with me that they had no doubt in their hearts about their beliefs. They felt no conviction from God. They were sure there was no God. Yet when the bullets started flying, these same men cried out to God at the top of their lungs. Truly, there are no atheists in foxholes.

It's only a mind game that some people get into that embraces the concept of atheism or agnosticism. No one truly believes in their heart that there is no God. The Scripture proves this in Romans 1:18-20. Therefore, when witnessing to a professed atheist, there's no need to discuss the existence of God. They know better. Just speak the Word as the Holy Spirit leads, and He will bear witness to the truth and put them under conviction.

You may think, *But they don't believe in God or the Bible.* That doesn't matter. You don't have to believe in a sword to get killed by one. The Word is a sword (Eph. 6:17), and it will work regardless of what they say they believe if your will speak it in faith. Have faith in the Lord to deal with their hearts.

It's with the heart that a person believes. Faith is not a head issue; faith is a heart issue. If we get sidetracked from speaking to a person's heart, we lose the convicting power of the Holy Spirit. That doesn't mean that faith doesn't make sense! Faith in God is the ultimate wisdom. However, faith will always be a heart issue.

God called you to be a witness, not a judge or a jury. Today, just tell people what Jesus has done for you, and let the Holy Spirit do His job. He will draw them to Jesus by working in their hearts just like He did you.

The Power of an Experience
John 9:1-28

He answered and said, Whether he be a sinner or no, I know not:
one thing I know, that, whereas I was blind, now I see.
John 9:25

In Vietnam I held a Bible study with about seven or eight men. Everything was going well until a man who claimed to be an atheist showed up. He was a Princeton intellectual who tore me to shreds. He made me look like a fool for believing in God. The whole group left with him as they laughed at me.

Thirty minutes later I was still sitting there wondering what I could have done differently when this same atheist walked back into the chapel and sat down. I prayed and asked the Lord to give me another chance. To my amazement, he came over and gave me the shock of my life. He told me he wanted what I had. I couldn't believe it!

I said, "You out-argued me. You made me look like a fool, yet you want what I have?" He explained that his whole life was based on an argument. If someone would have out-argued him the way he did me, he would have killed himself. He saw that I had something stronger than an argument. I had faith that came from a personal experience with God. He wanted that.

That day I learned firsthand that a man with an experience is never at the mercy of a man with an argument. The blind man whom Jesus healed didn't have any theological training, yet his experience with Jesus gave him a better understanding of God than the Pharisees had. He didn't know everything, but he couldn't be talked out of what he did know, and his assurance convicted all the theologians who were present.

If you have experienced the love of God, you are an expert. Regardless of what arguments others may offer, your relationship with Jesus is a stronger witness. Be bold today and show others the way.

Alive Unto God
Matthew 17:1-8; Mark 9:1-8; Luke 9:28-36

And was transfigured before them: and his face did shine as the sun, and his raiment
was white as the light.
Matthew 17:2

It is interesting to compare Jesus' transfiguration with that of Moses'. Jesus' face shone as the sun, and His garment was as white as the light. This certainly exceeded what Moses experienced, yet Jesus' face did not continue to shine when He came down from the mountain as Moses' face did.

Moses' face reflected the glory of God, but Jesus was the glory of God. (John 1:14; Heb. 1:3.) Moses put a veil over his face to conceal the glory of God (Ex. 34:29-35) so that the people would not be afraid to come near him. Jesus' body was His veil that concealed His true glory within. During His transfiguration, He pulled back the veil of His flesh, and the disciples caught a glimpse of His glory that He had with the Father before the world was. (John 17:5.) At Jesus' death, the veil of His body was "rent in two" giving us direct access to the glory of God. (Heb. 10:19,20.)

We need to be conformed to the death and resurrection of Christ. We can't just focus on our death to sin, and either omit or make secondary being alive unto God. It is assumed that if we will just die to sin, then life in Christ will come automatically. That's no more true than physical death automatically producing physical resurrection. We must be alive unto God in order to die to sin.

God wants you to be alive in Him today. He needs you to know who you are in Christ and walk in the victory that the risen Christ is actually living through you. There are over a hundred scriptural references to the indwelling presence of the Lord in you. Look into the Word, and see what God has to say about you!

Fasting Casts Out Unbelief
Mark 9:28-29

And he said unto them, This kind can come forth by nothing, but by prayer and fasting.
Mark 9:29

Prayer and fasting do not drive demons out. If the name of Jesus and faith in His name won't do the job, then fasting and praying won't either. Jesus is saying that fasting and praying are the only ways of casting out this type of unbelief.

Unbelief that is due to ignorance can be done away with by receiving the truth of God's Word. (Rom. 10:17; 2 Peter 1:4.) However, the unbelief that hindered the disciples in this case was a natural type of unbelief. They had been taught all of their lives to believe what their five senses told them. They were simply dominated by this natural input more than by God's Word. The only way to overcome the unbelief that comes through our senses is to deny our senses through prayer and fasting.

Fasting accomplishes many things. One of the greatest benefits of fasting is that through denying the lusts of the flesh, the spirit man gains ascendancy. Fasting was always used as a means of seeking God to the exclusion of all else. It does not cast out demons, but rather it casts out unbelief. Fasting is beneficial in every aspect of the Christian life—not only in casting out devils.

The real virtue of a fast is in humbling yourself through self-denial (Ps. 35:13; 69:10), and that can be accomplished through ways other than total abstinence. Partial fasts can be beneficial, as well as, fasts of your time or pleasures. However, because appetite for food is one of your strongest drives, fasting from food seems to get the job done the quickest.

If you have never fasted, pray about doing one. Ask the Lord to show you what you should fast, how long you should fast, and for what reason. Fasting should be an important part of seeking God in your life.

One Hundred Times Zero
Matthew 17:24-27

Notwithstanding, lest we should offend them, go thou to the sea, and cast an hook,
and take up the fish that first cometh up; and when thou hast opened his mouth,
thou shalt find a piece of money: that take, and give unto them for me and thee.
Matthew 17:27

The disciples were concerned that they needed money to pay their taxes, so Jesus gave them the above instructions. This was quite a miracle. Not only was the money supplied for their taxes, but also it was the exact amount needed; and it was from the first fish that was caught.

Although this sets the precedent that God can supply our needs in a miraculous way, it is important to remember that God doesn't counterfeit money. He didn't create money in the fish, but rather he had the fish miraculously find and swallow the exact Roman coin the disciples needed. It is a mistake to pray and wait on God to rain the money down from heaven. As Luke 6:38 says, God uses people to give finances to us. He can do it in a very unexpected, supernatural way, but it will involve people and existing currency. We need to believe that the Lord hears and answers our prayers, and then pray for the people He's going to use to deliver the answer. This could be our employer, the person who buys our goods, or any number of people.

The Lord also blesses what you set your hands to do. When in need, seek His direction for something to set your hands to, and trust Him to bless it and multiply the results of your work. One hundred times zero is zero. Don't miss your miracle because you never took the first step of faith and used what you have! God can give you a creative idea today that will bless you enough to meet all of your needs—and give you the opportunity to be a blessing to others.

Humble Like a Child

Matthew 18:1-5; Mark 9:30-37; Luke 9:46-48

Whosoever therefore shall humble himself as this little child, the same is greatest
in the kingdom of heaven.
Matthew 18:4

It is interesting that Jesus used a little child to illustrate humility. Although it is true that little children have a purity and are teachable, unlike most adults they certainly are not selfless. Babies come into the world totally self-centered, wanting what they want when they want it. Parents are to train children out of this self-centeredness.

Jesus chose these children as an example of humility because humility's dominant characteristic is God-dependency instead of self-sufficiency, and children are completely dependent upon their parents for everything. They look to them for love, wisdom, provision, protection, and all the blessings of life. The humility of being completely in the hands of God was what Jesus was talking about here.

The path of humility could not possibly work if there was no God. We would simply be trampled underfoot by those who would take advantage of us. But humility is a step of faith—faith that God is the Judge and that promotion comes from Him. (Ps. 75:6,7.) He resists the proud and gives grace unto the humble. (1 Pet. 5:5.) When we trust Him and step out in faith, He provides everything we need.

Humility is having faith in God instead of yourself. This is why it is easy to be humble when you have failed and hard to be humble when you have achieved success. Today, as you pursue what God is calling you to do and operate in the gifts He has given you, remember who called you and gave you those gifts. As you walk in humility, completely trusting in Him for everything, He will impart to you all the love, wisdom, and strength you need; and He will provide for you, protect you, and bless you in ways you never dreamed of.

Angelic Protection
Matthew 18:10-11

Take heed that ye despise not one of these little ones; for I say unto you, That in heaven their angels do always behold the face of my Father which is in heaven.
Matthew 18:10

We have angels assigned to us. Hebrews 1:14 further reveals that their purpose is to minister to us or on our behalf. In the Old Testament, Psalm 91 teaches on the ministry of angels to God's people. Some have realized this truth and have taken it even further to say that we are supposed to speak to our angels and they will obey our commands. There is no instruction in Scripture to do this, nor is there any example of it being done. Many of the angels' protective duties described in Psalm 91 are preventative, and we certainly could not effectively command these activities.

Angels are dispatched exactly as this verse describes—by looking at the Father's face. God Almighty controls them for us; however, we do have a part to play. In Psalm 91 it is those who dwell in the secret place of the Most High that benefit from angelic activity. (v. 1.) Verse two further instructs us to say that the Lord is our refuge and fortress and that we trust in Him.

It is the combination of our faith in God and His faithfulness to us that releases the angels on our behalf. If it was solely up to God, His provision would be the same for everyone because of His mercy and grace. However, we have to receive God's grace by faith. (Eph. 2:8.)

Today you can rest in the knowledge that God's angels were created to minister to you. As you speak words of faith and praise, beholding your Father's face, He will send His angels on your behalf.

God Loves You
Matthew 18:12-14

Even so it is not the will of your Father which is in heaven,
that one of these little ones should perish.
Matthew 18:14

One of the greatest truths of the Bible, and also one of the hardest to comprehend, is that we are the objects of God's love. God didn't just pity us or feel some sense of moral obligation to save us. He saved us because of His infinite love for us. (John 3:16.) He loves people. He even loves those who have gone astray. As Jesus said in a similar parable (Luke 15:7), "I say unto you that, likewise joy shall be in heaven over one sinner that repenteth, more than over ninety and nine just persons, which need no repentance."

Once we experience the life-changing power of Christ, there is a tendency to become harsh and impatient with others who continue to live their lives without Him. We sometimes forget that it was the love and goodness of God that brought us to repentance (Rom. 2:4), and we become condemning and judgmental toward the lost. This is not the attitude Jesus had, nor is it the attitude He wants us to have.

"Even when we were spiritually dead because of our sins, God's forbearance was working on our behalf. He was tolerant, patient and kind towards us. God abounded in excessive proportion with good will, compassion, and desire to help us. His disposition was kind, compassionate, and forgiving in His treatment of us. He wanted in abundant supply to alleviate our distress and bring relief from our sins. He did this by giving us life in place of death. It was with Christ that this salvation was secured. By grace, kindness, and favor we are saved. All of this was the result of God's extremely large degree of love wherewith He loved us, always seeking the welfare and betterment of us. God likes us" (Eph. 5:2, paraphrased).

Whatever happens to you today, remember how much God loves you!

Discipline Brings Life
Matthew 18:15-19

Verily I say unto you, Whatsoever ye shall bind on earth shall be bound in heaven:
and whatsoever ye shall loose on earth shall be loosed in heaven. Again I say
unto you, That if two of you shall agree on earth as touching any thing that
they shall ask, it shall be done for them of my Father which is in heaven.
Matthew 18:18-19

Verses 18 and 19 have many applications, but taken in context they are specifically referring to church discipline. Some might think that church discipline is only symbolic and carries no real weight; however, Jesus is making it clear that in the spiritual realm, discipline that is directed by the Holy Spirit has much power.

The scriptural commands concerning church discipline are designed to help restore the brother or sister who is in sin just as much as they are designed to protect other members of the body from that sin. If the person being disciplined repents, the objective has been achieved, and no further action should be taken. Church discipline is two-fold. It consists of withdrawing both our fellowship and our intercession.

Proper intercession can actually keep Satan at bay from an individual who is living in sin. This is good if the person uses this freedom from the consequences of their sin to repent and come back to God. On the other hand, if they use this freedom from the wages of sin to commit more sin, there comes a time when intercession ceases to be beneficial. In that case, intercession against Satan's attacks should be withdrawn, and we should actually bind that person's sins to them so they can no longer get by without experiencing the death that sin brings. (Rom. 6:23.) As they start reaping what they have sown, hopefully it will cause them to turn back to the goodness of God they once enjoyed.

This is the binding and loosing being referred to in this verse. Heaven and earth are affected by your binding and loosing. As you intercede for those you know that are backslidden today, be led of the Holy Spirit whether you are to bind their sin to them or loose it from them.

Unlimited Forgiveness
Matthew 18:21-35

Shouldest not thou also have had compassion on thy fellowservant,
even as I had pity on thee?
Matthew 18:33

Peter thought he was being very generous by offering to forgive his brother 7 times in one day, but Jesus said he should forgive him 490 times in one day. Of course, it would be impossible for someone to sin against you 490 times in one day. Jesus was actually saying there should be no limit to forgiveness.

When we are offended or hurt, we often feel justified in holding a grudge. The Old Testament law expressed this when it stated, "Eye for eye, tooth for tooth" (Ex. 21:23-25). Until the offense was paid, people did not feel free to forgive; however, God dealt with all offenses by placing sin upon the perfect Savior, who was judged in our place. To be so forgiven by God and then demand that others earn our forgiveness is not like Christ. He died for every person's sins, extending forgiveness to us while we were yet sinners, and we should do the same.

The main thrust of this parable is that when people wrong us, we should remember the great mercy God has shown to us and respond likewise. Any debt that could be owed to us is insignificant compared to the debt for which He forgave us. We should have compassion on others as He had on us.

You have been given unlimited forgiveness from God through the shed blood of Jesus. Let the reality of this truth resonate in your heart today, and if anyone offends you or hurts you, that truth will enable you to forgive them quickly. This is one of the major ways you will grow up in God and become a mature witness for Jesus Christ. By forgiving those who cause you harm in any way, you are allowing the love of Jesus to flow freely through you to them.

A Matter of the Heart
John 7:21-24

Moses therefore gave unto you circumcision; (not because it is of Moses,
but of the fathers;) and ye on the sabbath day circumcise a man.
John 7:22

The covenant of circumcision was given to Abram in Genesis 17:9-14. God said that any man who did not carry this sign of the covenant in his flesh was to be killed. This placed a great importance on the act of circumcision. Paul says in Romans 4:3-13 that Abraham had already been justified by faith before he was circumcised. Abram's faith in God and His promise saved him at least thirteen years before He commanded Abram to be circumcised.

Through the centuries, the Jews turned their focus to the outward act of circumcision instead of the inward act of faith as the reason for salvation. This was a source of contention between Jesus and the religious leaders too. They emphasized all the outward acts the Lord had commanded and were totally disregarding the condition of their hearts. Jesus said that if an individual would cleanse their heart, their actions would inevitably change too.

The condition of a person's flesh is not the important thing. It doesn't matter if that flesh is circumcised or not. It is the condition of the heart that matters to God. Today the act of circumcision is not the issue, but we get hung up on the doctrine of water baptism, church membership, and other outward acts that some preach are necessary for salvation.

Your faith in the love of God, as expressed through Jesus on the Cross and in His resurrection, is the only thing God demands for your justification. Religious rites mean nothing when it comes to being saved. You can rejoice today that the only thing that counts with God is your faith in Jesus Christ as your Lord and Savior.

Effortless Fruit
John 7:37-41

He that believeth on me, as the scripture hath said, out of his belly shall flow
rivers of living water.
John 7:38

These "rivers of living water" are referring to the Holy Spirit and the effects He produces in the life of a believer. Galatians 5:22-23 says, "The fruit of the spirit is love, joy, peace, longsuffering, gentleness, goodness, faith, meekness, temperance." These qualities should flow out of us like an artesian well. They should not have to be pumped. They will flow as we conform our thinking to God's Word.

Jesus speaks of bearing fruit in John 15 and declares, "Without me ye can do nothing" (v. 5). This fruit is the product of the Holy Spirit, not our efforts. However, since, "He that is joined unto the Lord is one spirit" (1 Cor. 6:17), this fruit of the Spirit is also what our born-again spirits produce. Our spirits always have these attributes regardless of what we feel in our emotions.

Failure to understand this truth has caused many Christians to think they would be hypocrites to express joy when they feel depressed. However, it is only our soulish part that gets depressed. Our spirits are always bearing the fruit of the spirit. A person who seeks to walk in the spirit is a hypocrite when they allow their soulish emotions to dominate their spiritual emotions. Those who understand this have the choice of letting their souls depress them or letting the Holy Spirit, through their born-again spirits, release His joy and peace.

Your fruit is not produced by you; it is produced by the Holy Spirit in you. Your part is to yield to Him and show His emotion, not yours. Do this today, and you will live in union with Him, producing much fruit!

The Measure of Faith
Romans 12:1-12

For I say, through the grace given unto me, to every man that is among you,
not to think of himself more highly than he ought to think; but to think soberly,
according as God hath dealt to every man the measure of faith.
Romans 12:3

If someone was serving different people soup out of a large pot with just one ladle, the ladle would be *the* measure, and everyone would receive the same amount of soup. Likewise, the Lord doesn't give us different amounts of faith. He's given every believer *the* measure of faith" (italics mine).

What about the places in Scripture where Jesus speaks of great faith (Matt. 8:10) and little faith? (Matt. 8:26.) He's saying that we can use and manifest great faith or little faith, but this doesn't affect the amount we have been given. We are all given the measure of faith.

Paul said the faith he used was "*the* faith *of* the Son of God" (Gal. 2:20, italics mine). Also, he didn't say "faith *in* the Son of God," but "*the* faith *of* the Son of God." We have been given Jesus' faith! And if we all have the same measure of faith, and Paul's measure was the same as Jesus', then ours is too. There isn't a shortage of faith. There's just a shortage of people who use the faith God gave them.

There are many things you can do to release the God-given faith in you, but before you can do any of them, you must believe the faith is there, that it is His faith, and that His faith can change and overcome anything. Instead of acknowledging your lack and shortcomings today, acknowledge the faith of Jesus you have in your heart. This is the first step toward making your faith effective (Philem. 1:6) and manifesting great faith in your life.

Avoid Evil Communication
1 Corinthians 15:32-34

Be not deceived: evil communications corrupt good manners.
1 Corinthians 15:33

Have you ever noticed that it's easier to gain weight than to lose it? It's also easier to destroy things than to build them, to get sick than to stay well, and to ruin a relationship than to maintain one. It seems that the things we desire are harder to come by than the things we wish to avoid. It's the same way with what we hear.

Values and attitudes that take a long time to build can be easily destroyed by just a few words. Certainly, everyone has had their enthusiasm quenched by the disapproving words of someone else. Our words are important but so are the words of every person we hear. To succeed in the kingdom of God, we not only have to watch what we say, but also we must guard what we hear.

In our day and age, Christians are exposed to the negative words of this world as never before. Most of us pipe those words right into our homes and automobiles. In seconds we are aware of all the terrible things going on around the world. Some people even listen for entertainment to songs that wail about the miseries and sorrows of mankind. Yet these words have power—evil power. They have the ability to depress us and cause us to be afraid. We don't need that! We are to be a people of faith and hope.

Think about the words you hear today. Do you really need or want what you're seeing and hearing? Choose life instead of death. (Deut. 30:19.) If a word spoken to you does not increase your faith and draw you to Jesus, rebuke it and reject it. Then turn your thoughts to His Word and be glad.

The Blessed Hope
Titus 2:11-15

*Looking for that blessed hope, and the glorious appearing of the great
God and our Saviour Jesus Christ.*
Titus 2:13

The promise of the second coming of our Lord Jesus Christ is a great comfort. Regardless of how bad things get in this life, we have the promise that our Lord is coming again in total triumph and power.

While in basic training before I went to Vietnam, I was often overwhelmed with all the ungodliness around me. My drill sergeants delighted in mocking God. They started every training session by having me stand in front of the company while someone blasphemed God, told a filthy joke, or shared what he had done with a local prostitute the night before. They did this to embarrass me and to try to provoke me. I remember the sergeant saying, "Preacher, I love to see you blush!"

At times, this all seemed too much. I longed for the Lord to come and just wipe them all out, but I knew that wasn't right. Then one evening as we were forced to march and my body and emotions were screaming, I looked up and saw one of the most gorgeous sunsets I've ever seen. This displayed the awesome power of God in such a way that all the corruption around me just vanished. The cursing of the vilest men couldn't stop God from showing His glory. Jesus was still the same and on His throne, and there would come a day of reckoning. (Matt. 12:36.)

This is the hope that the second coming of our Lord produces. He's not deaf or blind as some people's actions suggest. He's just patient and waiting for the full harvest of souls to come in before He reveals Himself. At that time, every tongue will confess that Jesus is Lord, and the righteous will shine as the sun in its brightness. Our victory is nearer than we think. Hold on to that blessed hope today.

Forgiveness Brings Miracles
2 Kings 5:1-14

And the Syrians had gone out by companies, and had brought away captive
out of the land of Israel a little maid; and she waited on Naaman's wife.
2 Kings 5:2

Jesus came to obtain forgiveness for our sins and transform our hearts into forgiving hearts like His, and there is no better demonstration of the fruit of forgiveness than the healing of Naaman's leprosy. This was one of the greatest miracles the Lord did through Elisha; yet it never would have happened if it hadn't been for a young servant girl who chose to forgive.

This maid informed Naaman's wife about God's healing power. If she had not spoken up, no miracle would have taken place. This is especially meaningful when you realize this young girl was an Israelite who had been captured during a Syrian raid and taken back to Syria as a slave. The Hebrew word used for *maid* in this verse means "a young girl from the age of infancy to adolescence." This means she certainly wasn't out on her own yet. She was taken from her parents! It is possible her parents were killed by the Syrians or made slaves themselves. She easily could have been bitter and could have chosen not to tell her mistress about her God who healed.

Leprosy in those days was considered by many to be God's judgment on sin. She could have thought, *It serves him right!* She even could have prayed for his death. Instead, she showed concern and compassion for her master. Apparently, she had forgiven him and overcome any bitterness. This allowed God to use her as an instrument to touch the highest-ranking general in the Syrian army. No doubt, many Syrians came to faith in the Lord because she decided to forgive and serve God where she was.

You cannot change your past, but you can decide your future and how you will affect others. Regardless of what situation you find yourself in, bloom where you are planted. It's possible that the very ones you have grievances with would respond to the touch of God if you reach out to them. Show someone God's love today.

Go All the Way
2 Kings 5:1-14

*Then went he down, and dipped himself seven times in Jordan, according to
the saying of the man of God: and his flesh came again like unto the flesh
of a little child, and he was clean.*
2 Kings 5:14

When someone came to Jesus to be healed, He always was willing and healed them immediately. In light of that, Elisha's actions and instructions to Naaman were strange. What was he trying to accomplish by telling Naaman to go dip himself in the dirty Jordan River seven times?

For one thing, Naaman hadn't really humbled himself before the Lord yet, which is a very important part of faith. Jesus said that no one can believe who is seeking the honor that comes from men more than the honor that comes from God. (John 5:44.) Naaman was too impressed with himself. That's why Elisha didn't even bother to go out and see him. He sent his servant to deliver his instructions to Naaman.

This incensed Naaman. He headed back to Syria in a rage. Elisha hadn't responded to him as his position deserved. Besides, he thought any Syrian river was better than the Jordan in Israel. Naaman definitely had a pride issue, but his servants prevailed on him to give the prophet's instructions a try. Need often drives people to do things they wouldn't otherwise do, and so Naaman humbled himself and dipped in the Jordan River.

Nothing happened the first or the second time. His healing didn't come gradually. He was still a leper after dipping six times in the Jordan. But on the seventh time, his flesh was completely restored. Just think: Naaman's pride almost caused him to miss his miracle!

Are there issues of pride in your life that have kept you from doing what God has told you to do? If so, humble yourself and obey. Don't do it halfheartedly. Your deliverance will come when you go all the way.

Tempted Like You
Hebrews 4:15

For we have not an high priest which cannot be touched with the feeling of our infirmities; but was in all points tempted like as we are, yet without sin.
Hebrews 4:15

Have you ever pondered the temptations of Jesus? How could He really have suffered the temptations that come with marriage when He was never married? How could he have suffered the temptation of drug addiction when He never encountered cocaine? There are many pressures we battle that seemingly He never did. However, God's Word plainly says He was tempted in all points just like we are. This underscores the truth that our actions are not where temptation actually takes place. It's in our beliefs that we are tempted.

Jesus was tempted to not believe God just as we are, but He kept believing and stood strong. The material things and pleasures Satan tempts us with aren't the true temptation. All of his devices are simply bait to get us to bite the hook of unbelief—that God will not or cannot supply everything we need and desire in life.

Too often the church argues against sin on the basis of the physical consequences it produces. For instance, they say homosexuality is wrong because it produces disease. What if they find a cure for AIDS? Would that mean homosexuality would no longer be a sin? Of course not! As bad as the consequences of our actions are, the real root of sin is the rejection of God's Word. This is the temptation that takes place in our hearts long before we act it out. A person is tempted to not believe the biblical truth that God created male and female for marriage, period. When they give in to that temptation and reject God's Word, they inevitably sin. The root of all sin is rejecting God's truth. That is the real temptation.

Today, make it a point to choose to believe God and His Word no matter what people say or do to tempt you to not believe. Your faith in Him will bring joy and peace regardless of the situations you face.

Don't Look Back
Hebrews 11:1-15

And truly, if they had been mindful of that country from whence they came out,
they might have had opportunity to have returned.
Hebrews 11:15

If Abraham and Sarah had been mindful of the country they left, they would have been tempted to return. However, since they weren't mindful of that country, they weren't even tempted to return. What a revelation! Their temptation was linked to their thoughts. You can't be tempted with something you don't think about. Therefore, control your thinking, and you can avoid temptation. We can be powerful in God if we avoid being tempted. By controlling our thinking, we can do just that.

Many believers try to control their actions but don't realize that actions are a direct result of the way they think. They allow themselves the luxury of pondering things they shouldn't, and then when temptation comes, they struggle to remain faithful to God. They often wonder why they are tempted all the time. It's because of what they are thinking about.

God has called all of us to leave things behind. It may not be a country but it may be a lifestyle or certain friends. Maybe there are habits or hobbies He has asked us to lay down. The secret to walking away from them is not dwelling on them. Thinking, *What if?* is always a faith killer! We don't need to be looking back; we need to look forward to what God has promised us and called us to.

Today, turn your thoughts from what you have left behind to what you have to look forward to in your life in Jesus Christ. Take a look ahead through faith at what God is calling you to do and all the wonderful brothers and sisters you will be doing that with. You'll find that your positive thoughts will bring you hope instead of temptation.

Replacing Evil Thoughts
Hebrews 11:1-16

But now they desire a better country.
Hebrews 11:16

Y ou can't get rid of negative thoughts by rebuking them. Unwanted thoughts must be replaced with new ones.

Think of an apple. Now quit thinking of an apple. Rebuke thoughts of an apple. Don't think of an apple in Jesus' name. Refuse to think about apples. Are you still thinking about apples? Of course you are! Trying to not think about something only causes you to think about it more.

Instead of thinking about apples, turn your attention to strawberries. See a beautiful, plump, red strawberry. Think how sweet it would taste. Imagine a whole strawberry patch with all the delicious berries just begging to be picked. Or think about bananas. See a whole bunch of them. Imagine going to some tropical island and picking them yourself. Wouldn't that be great?

If you continue that line of thought, in just a short time you will have forgotten about apples altogether. You can only get rid of thoughts by replacing them with other thoughts. Any effort to resist negative or sinful thoughts actually strengthens their hold on you. The better way is to replace them with God thoughts from His Word. As you read His Word, His thoughts begin to dominate your thinking, and soon the negative thoughts are gone.

Abraham found something better to think about than what he left behind. He desired a better country. God has given you a new life in Christ Jesus. I'm sure you have something wonderful to think about today.

What Do You Doubt?

Genesis 3:1-13

For God doth know that in the day ye eat thereof, then your eyes shall be opened,
and ye shall be as gods, knowing good and evil.
Genesis 3:5

Adam and Eve's sin was unbelief. Eating the forbidden fruit was just the action that expressed the unbelief that was already present in their hearts. What did they doubt? There were two things the serpent seduced them into doubting about God.

First, they doubted God's Word. They did not believe what He said about the consequences of eating from the tree of the knowledge of good and evil. He said they would die. Obviously, they chose to eat of the fruit because they no longer believed that. They doubted God's Word, and the first sin was committed.

Even more important, Adam and Eve doubted God's love for them. Satan accused God of not wanting what was best for them. He said God was denying them something that would make them wiser. This was a direct attack on God's love and integrity. He had been wonderful to them, providing everything they needed and even visiting with them every day. However, Adam and Eve chose to doubt His love. They took the word of a talking snake over the Word of God.

When you think about it, it is illogical to ever doubt God's love when you consider Jesus' death on the Cross and His resurrection. You have a revelation of just how far God's love extends, and yet you may still worry about whether your needs will be met and your body healed. You try to justify these worries by saying everyone has them. "They're just normal." They are only normal for people who don't know God's great love! When you receive a full revelation of God's love, your doubts will vanish.

If you have any doubt about God's love and infinite care for you today, then open up your Bible and being reading and believing what He says about you. Dispel all your doubts by choosing to believe what He says, and your faith in Him will allow His blessings to flow freely in every area of your life.

Faith Brings Understanding
Hebrews 11:1-3

Through faith we understand that the worlds were framed by the word of God,
so that things which are seen were not made of things which do appear.
Hebrews 11:3

In the Dark Ages, the church demanded acceptance of all its commandments and beliefs without any explanation or justification. The infallibility of the pope left no room for error. This led to terrible situations both inside and outside the church. Science was despised, and many scientists were persecuted.

Then came the Reformation, the Renaissance, and the Age of Enlightenment. The world was found to be round instead of flat. Many things that the church had pronounced as plagues from God were found to be the result of viruses and unsanitary living conditions. Many "God-imposed" limitations were found to be only limitations placed on people due to ignorance.

This caused a total shift in people's thinking. They went from an unquestioned, blind faith in religion to the Age of Reason when they scoffed at faith. No doubt, this liberated people from many of the misconceptions and errors of false religion, but it also left modern man void of simple faith.

The author of Hebrews says that some things can only be understood through faith. God did not deem it necessary to explain everything to us. He is greater and more complex than we can understand with our peanut brains. It's impossible to figure out Him and His ways completely. We must have faith in God.

In this day of technology, your need for faith is greater than ever before—not a blind faith that leads to superstition but an educated faith that is schooled in God's Word and based on your experience with the Holy Spirit. Faith is not mindless; it just acknowledges that there is a spiritual reality that you cannot examine in a test tube.

Amazing Grace
John 8:1-11

They say unto him, Master, this woman was taken in adultery, in the very act. Now
Moses in the law commanded us, that such should be stoned: but what sayest thou?
John 8:4,5

This was potentially the most damaging temptation the scribes and Pharisees ever presented to Jesus. Much of His widespread popularity was because of His teaching about God's mercy and forgiveness toward sinners. This was received with great enthusiasm by a people who before this time had been presented with only a harsh, legalistic, judgmental picture of God.

The scribes and Pharisees often tried to portray Jesus as condoning or practicing sin because of His association with sinners and His ministry to them, especially when it violated Jewish traditions such as the Sabbath. However, Jesus had successfully turned every attack into a victory for God's grace and mercy.

This time the Jews believed they had cornered Jesus. If He held to His teaching of forgiveness and refused to stone this woman, He would be in direct rebellion to the law of Moses. This would give these Jews legal grounds to kill Him. On the other hand, if He stoned the woman as the law declared, the people would forsake Him. It looked like they had Him trapped either way He went.

As always, the foolishness of God is wiser than men, and Jesus rose to the occasion. He did not condone the sin nor disregard the law of Moses. He simply told the one who was without sin to cast the first stone. As the Holy Ghost began to convict them of their own sin, they all had to leave; therefore, they could not fault Jesus for not stoning the woman.

As you go about your day, you will probably have opportunities to be angry, hurt, or offended with those who sin against you or someone else. Whenever that happens, remember how Jesus treated this woman and practice His amazing grace.

Mystery of the Trinity
John 8:12-27

Then said they unto him, Where is thy Father? Jesus answered, Ye neither know me,
nor my Father: if ye had known me, ye should have known my Father also.
John 8:19

Jesus talked about being one with His Father, especially in John 17. This oneness was more than singleness of purpose. Both Old and New Testaments say that there is one God. (Mal. 2:10; 1 Tim. 2:5.) This truth is so well established in Scripture that some people make no distinction between the Father, the Son, and the Holy Spirit; they believe they are simply one God expressing Himself in three different ways. However, in John 8 above, Jesus makes a distinction between Him and His Father. He and His Father are two witnesses, which fulfills the requirement of Deuteronomy 17:6. Jesus would have been deceiving these Jews if there was no distinction between His Father and Himself, yet they are one. (John 10:30; 1 John 5:7.) This is a great mystery!

Deuteronomy 6:4 says, "The Lord our God is one Lord." We do not have three Gods, but one God, clearly identifiable as three persons. This is a great mystery that has not been adequately explained. Scriptures reveal the truth of the Trinity but make no attempt to explain it. We simply accept this revelation as it is. One day we will know all things, even as we are known. (1 Cor. 13:12.)

Jesus said that the witness of His Father was the greatest testimony of who He was. He said that to know Him was to know the Father. Whenever you wonder if you really know the voice and the ways of your Father in heaven, just look at Jesus. Jesus is just like the Father. Whatever Jesus feels, believes, and does; the Father feels, believes, and does. For every question or problem you face today, Jesus is the key to understanding the Father.

Jesus Was Lifted Up for You
John 8:12-30

Then said Jesus unto them, When ye have lifted up the Son of man, then shall ye know that I am he, and that I do nothing of myself; but as my Father hath taught me, I speak these things.
John 8:28

This is the second of three times that Jesus spoke of Himself being "lifted up," the first time in John 3:14 and the third time in John 12:32-33. As the Bible explains in John 12:33, this was a reference to crucifixion. The term Jesus used is referring to being lifted up from the earth and suspended on a cross in crucifixion. The Jews understood Jesus was speaking of His death when He said He would be lifted up.

The crucifixion didn't just happen. God planned for it; however, it does not mean that He bears all responsibility for it, and those who were instrumental in the rejection and crucifixion of Jesus are not guilty. Jesus came to earth to die in our place and thereby purchase redemption for us. That was God's plan, but He didn't force anyone to fulfill it. Jesus' ministry and message placed Him in direct opposition to the devil and his followers. Their hatred for Him caused them to crucify Jesus of their own free will. God, in all His wisdom, simply knew what they would do, and He determined to use their rejection of His Son to accomplish His plan of redemption. He never controls our will to accomplish His.

If you truly understand the message of the Cross, you understand real love and grace. Jesus didn't just make a token sacrifice for you; He was lifted up for you. He paid your debt in full so that you could be fully His.

Sonship or Slavery
John 8:34-36

Jesus answered them, Verily, verily, I say unto you, Whosoever committeth sin is the servant of sin.
John 8:34

The devil has been deceiving the world about sin since the Garden of Eden when he told Eve that through sin she would be like God. Time has proven, not only to Eve but to each one of us, that this is not true. Sin brings death—not life. Jesus also makes it clear that sin enslaves. We become slaves not only to the sin itself but to the author of sin: the devil. We are either servants of God through obedience or servants of the devil through sin.

Jesus is likening the bondage that sin produces to slavery and the freedom that comes by serving God to being a beloved son. No one would doubt that being a son is better than being a slave! Likewise, obeying God is better than yielding to sin. True freedom is found only in serving God. Nevertheless, people continue to fall for Satan's lie that sin is true freedom. He has deceived all of us at one time or another into thinking God is a tyrant who really doesn't want us to enjoy life and consequently tells us not to do certain things. Because we believe this lie, we disobey God (i.e. we sin) in the name of freedom. But it is a false and fleeting freedom with terrible consequences.

The Word of God and personal experience conclusively prove that the wages of sin is death. (Rom. 6:23.) Jesus is stripping sin of any glamour with which the devil may disguise it. Sin brings bondage. The only true freedom is found in Jesus. He not only dealt with the original sin that contaminated the human race, but He also dealt with each individual act of sin.

Today, if you are born again, you are walking in true freedom. You have God's nature to do right and His love that causes you to desire to do right. Be thankful that you are a son or daughter of God and no longer a slave to the devil and sin.

Abraham's Children
John 8:33-38

*I know that ye are Abraham's seed; but ye seek to kill me, because my word
hath no place in you.*
John 8:37

The Jewish people were direct physical descendants of Abraham. However, as with so many biblical truths, there was much more to the Abrahamic covenant than what a casual glimpse would reveal. In truth, some Jews were not the spiritual children of Abraham.

The Holy Spirit revealed through the apostle Paul in Galatians 3:16 and 29 that God's covenant was to Abraham and his "seed" or one descendant, which was Jesus. No one ever became an heir of God's promises through their natural birth. Before Jesus gave Himself as an offering for our sins, the Old Testament saints were justified by faith in God's promises concerning the Messiah who was yet to come. After Jesus' death and resurrection, New Testament saints are justified by faith in what Jesus has already accomplished. No one has ever been saved because of who their parents were.

Those who have been born again through faith in Jesus have been circumcised in their hearts (Col. 2:11,12) and are the true Jews. They aren't Jews in nationality or religion, but they are the true people of God. Gentiles who are united with Christ in the new birth are now God's people. Anyone who is saved through faith in Jesus is now Abraham's seed and an heir according to the promise. (Gal. 3:16, 22, 26-29.)

This leaves no doubt that the church is now God's chosen people on earth. This does not mean God has forsaken the physical descendants of Abraham. There are still prophecies that apply to the nation of Israel that will be fulfilled. However, the New Testament church, composed of Jews and Gentiles, is now God's kingdom on earth. We are all His.

Today you can ponder the fact that as a born-again believer in Jesus Christ you are a true Jew and an heir to all God promised Abraham.

What Pleases God
John 8:53-56

Your father Abraham rejoiced to see my day: and he saw it, and was glad.
John 8:56

Jesus was referring to the day when men would be justified by putting their faith in God and not in their own works. God revealed this truth to Abraham (Rom. 4:13), and when he believed it, he was justified by his faith. (Rom. 4:3,4,9.) Hebrews 11:6 says, "But without faith it is impossible to please him." It was Abraham's faith that pleased God.

There are many reasons we know it must have been Abraham's faith and his faith alone that pleased God. When we gather all the facts concerning Abraham's life, there was more to displease Him than please Him! According to Leviticus 18:9 and 26, it was an abomination for a man to marry a half sister. Sarah, Abraham's wife, was his half sister. (Gen. 20:12.) Therefore, Abraham's marriage to Sarah was not what pleased God.

Abraham lied, saying that Sarah was not his wife, to save his own neck. He was willing to let a man commit adultery with her rather than tell the truth and risk being killed by the man who might want her. And yet, immediately after this incident the Lord counted Abraham's faith in Him for righteousness. (Gen. 15:6.) Abraham tried to accomplish God's will in the flesh with Hagar (Gen. 16), and then repeated the terrible sin of denying that Sarah was his wife again. (Gen. 20.)

Anyone who really studies the life of Abraham and the favor he found with God would have to conclude that it was Abraham's faith that pleased God. So whatever you have said or done that you know displeased God, today just receive His forgiveness and move forward with complete faith in Him. Then you will be truly blessed.

God Made Flesh
John 8:57-59

Jesus said unto them, Verily, verily, I say unto you, Before Abraham was, I am.
John 8:58

Here Jesus made a new statement. He said those who didn't believe He was God in the flesh (1 Tim. 3:16) could not possibly understand what He was talking about. "Before Abraham was, I am" not only declared that He existed before Abraham, but also associated Himself with the great "I AM" statement of Exodus 3:14. This statement could leave no doubt that Jesus was claiming to be God.

Jesus proclaimed, "I am." This is how Jehovah identified Himself to Moses in Exodus 3:14. When spoken under the anointing power of God, Jesus' pronouncement: "I am he," knocked all of those who came to arrest Him backward to the ground. (John 18:5,6.) Jesus was the great "I AM THAT I AM" of Exodus 3:14 manifest in the flesh.

When the Jewish authorities heard Jesus call God His Father, they immediately understood that Jesus claimed for Himself deity in the highest possible sense. That claim was either blasphemy to be punished by death, or Jesus was who He claimed to be.

The purpose of John's gospel is clearly stated, "That ye might believe that Jesus is the Christ, the Son of God; and that believing ye might have life through his name" (John 20:31). Today you have His life because you believe in His name. Don't let the enemy, the world, or your flesh deceive you into thinking Jesus was anything less than God made flesh.

Physical Healing
Isaiah 53:1-5; Matthew 8:16-17

Surely he hath borne our griefs, and carried our sorrows:
yet we did esteem him stricken, smitten of God, and afflicted.
Isaiah 53:4

Physical healing is so prominent in Scripture—especially the New Testament—that there should be no debate about it, but there is. Many people interpret the promises concerning our healing to apply only in a spiritual sense. They believe verses such as Isaiah 53:4-5 are speaking of being healed spiritually.

The best way to interpret Scripture is by Scripture. If a particular passage is quoted and applied in another passage, then we have a very clear understanding of exactly what the Lord is saying. This happened with Isaiah's prophecy concerning the Messiah bringing us healing.

In Matthew 8:16, multitudes came to Jesus for healing, and He physically healed every one of them. Then in verse seventeen, Matthew said this happened "that it might be fulfilled which was spoken by Esaias the prophet, saying, Himself took our infirmities, and bare our sicknesses." This emphatically states that Isaiah's promise of healing was for our physical bodies. Praise the Lord!

Healing is just as much a part of Christ's atonement as is the forgiveness of sin. The Greek word used for *salvation* hundreds of times in the New Testament is *sozo*. It's also translated in reference to physical healing in Matthew 9:22, Mark 5:34, Luke 8:48, and James 5:15.

Your faith for physical healing has to begin at the place of believing that it is God's will to heal you. The truth that this was part of the atoning work of Christ, as prophesied in Scripture, provides you with that foundation.

It's a Done Deal!

1 Peter 2:21-25

Who his own self bare our sins in his own body on the tree, that we, being dead to sins,
should live unto righteousness: by whose stripes ye were healed.
1 Peter 2:24

The last phrase of this verse is the same as Isaiah 53:4, with one important exception: It places our healing in the past tense. We have already been healed. This is a hard concept for some people to grasp. They cannot understand how they could already be healed if there is sickness in their bodies. One way to get around this is to say that this is speaking of spiritual healing, but Matthew 8:17 made it very clear that the healing Isaiah was speaking of was physical, not spiritual.

The key to understanding this concept is relating it to the forgiveness of our sins. When were our sins forgiven? According to Scripture, they were forgiven when Christ died, long before we ever received it. Our prayers only enable us to receive what was already accomplished in the spiritual realm and bring it into physical reality. That's the way it is with healing.

Jesus has already accomplished our healing. The same virtue that raised Him from the dead is resident within every believer. (Eph. 1:19,20.) It's a done deal. All we must do is believe and give physical substance (Heb. 11:1) to what's already true in our born-again spirits. It's infinitely easier to release something that we already have than to try to get something that we don't have, and we already have healing.

Start releasing your healing by confessing and acting on your faith instead of trying to use your faith to ask God to heal you. He's already done it.

You Can See Faith
Matthew 9:1-8

And, behold, they brought to him a man sick of the palsy, lying on a bed: and Jesus
seeing their faith said unto the sick of the palsy; Son, be of good cheer;
thy sins be forgiven thee.
Matthew 9:2

What does faith look like? Faith itself is like the wind. You can't see the wind, but you can see the effects of it. You can see things that are being blown by the wind. Likewise, you can't see faith, but by a person's actions you can tell when someone is moving in faith.

For Jesus to see the faith of these men meant that He saw their actions. Specifically, they climbed on the roof, took the roof off, and lowered their sick friend down right in front of Jesus and in the presence of an antagonistic crowd. They were sure to be criticized by the religious leaders and would certainly be in trouble with the owner of the house whose roof they had just removed! They must have believed that what they were going to receive was worth the price. They believed their friend would be healed.

These men could have believed Jesus could heal their friend but then done nothing about it. If they had not acted on their faith, it wouldn't have done their friend any good. Their faith without any action would have produced nothing. Actions are a vital part of faith. Faith without corresponding action is not faith at all. (James 2:17.)

What kind of action would show true biblical faith in your situation today? Is that the way you're acting? If not, why? Is it because you don't have true biblical faith yet? Determine in your heart today to walk in real trust and reliance on God. Then watch your actions change.

Is Your Heart Sick?
Proverbs 13:12

Hope deferred maketh the heart sick: but when the desire cometh, it is a tree of life.
Proverbs 13:12

When I was in the sixth grade, I competed in a spelling bee. I was determined to win that competition, so I diligently studied for weeks. I knew every word in the book by heart. The day of the competition came, and I was ready. I told everyone—including the teachers—that I was going to win. Therefore, they gave me the very first word to spell. It was the word Rhine, as in the Rhine river. I confidently spelled r-h-i-n-e, which was correct, but I failed to capitalize the letter *r*. Therefore, I was the first one eliminated.

I was humiliated and frustrated because I knew every single word they gave and could have easily won that contest—if I had just capitalized the letter *r*. My heart was sick. I lost all desire to excel in spelling. In my sixth-grade mentality, I actually vowed to never study spelling again. Bad idea! I went on to become one of the worst spellers in history. Much later in life, I confronted this episode in my past and began learning how to spell again. It took me thirty years to get over the hurt, bitterness, and anger of that day.

Is your heart sick because of some disappointment? Maybe your hurt is more serious than mine, but the results are the same. You may have lost your will or your hope to try, but don't let it haunt you another day. Go to the Lord and let Him give you new hope and a new joy. Life without hope and joy isn't God's kind of life.

Sickness Is Not From God
John 9:1-4

And his disciples asked him, saying, Master, who did sin, this man, or his parents,
that he was born blind?
John 9:2

The disciples asked a question that still puzzles many people today. Why is a child born with a physical defect? Is it a judgment of God upon the parents for some sin, or is it possibly God's judgment upon the child for sins God knows they will commit? Jesus had previously linked sickness with sin; however, in this instance He said this blindness was not caused by this man's or his parents' sins.

This has led many people to interpret the rest of this verse as saying that God made this man blind just so He could heal him and be glorified thereby. From this thinking, many doctrinal teachings have risen about how sickness and other problems in our lives are actually blessings from God, intended to bring glory to God and correction to us. This reasoning, however, does not line up with the other truths of God's Word.

It was not God who made this beggar blind. This man was not born blind because of any one person's sins, but because sin in general had corrupted the perfect balance that God had created in nature. Therefore, some maladies happen not as a direct result of an individual's sins, but as an indirect result of sin in general.

Deuteronomy 28 settles forever the question of whether sickness, poverty, and oppression are really blessings in disguise. God says that sickness and poverty are curses—not blessings from God. Christ redeemed us from these curses of the law so that now the blessings may come upon us through Him. (Gal. 3:13.)

The curse of all sin and disease was placed on Jesus, and when you accepted Him as your Lord and Savior, all curses were removed from your life. Today you are blessed with health and healing through the atoning blood of Jesus Christ!

It's Who You Know
John 9:28-30

The man answered and said unto them, Why herein is a marvellous thing,
that ye know not from whence he is, and yet he hath opened mine eyes.
John 9:30

The "acid test" of whether or not someone is of God is their actions. Jesus' actions were so miraculous and overwhelmingly consistent with God's Word that any reservations about whether He was of God should have been set aside. But here, as in Mark 7:13, the Pharisees and some of the teachers of the law had exalted their own traditions above God's Word, thereby making the Word of God of no effect in their own lives. Just like them, theologians today are sometimes the last to accept a move of God if it violates their traditional beliefs, but, "The common people heard him gladly" (Mark 12:37).

In spiritual matters, a person can educate himself in theology to the degree that it does more harm than good. It is possible to win a theological battle and yet lose the war for a person's heart because "Knowledge puffeth up, but charity edifieth" (1 Cor. 8:1). Arguments over points of theology often distract from the more important issues. There is no premium on ignorance, but love is infinitely superior to knowledge. We should learn all we can, but we must make our knowledge a servant to love. "The greatest of these is love" (1 Cor. 13:13).

Don't let your quest for knowledge lead you away from knowing God today. What you know is not as important as who you know, especially speaking of the Lord! Your most important goal in life must be to love God and to know Him personally and intimately.

About Those Pharisees
John 9:34

*They answered and said unto him, Thou wast altogether born in sins,
and dost thou teach us? And they cast him out.*
John 9:34

Much of the Pharisees' problem was spiritual pride, as is evident by this statement. They were so blinded by their arrogance that they couldn't believe that anyone who hadn't been through their "seminary" could teach them anything.

The name *Pharisee* comes from a Hebrew word meaning "separate." This term was applied to this sect because of its extreme devotion to the Mosaic Law and their commitment to leading a separated life. Devout Jews formed this sect when they came back to Jerusalem from the Babylonian captivity and saw the pagan customs and influences of the Babylonians everywhere. Not only their religion but their identity as a nation was being threatened.

The Pharisees were patriots as well as religious zealots, who in the beginning served a very needed function in the Jewish nation that was struggling for survival. However, over the centuries the Pharisees wrote their own interpretations of the Law—interpretations they held to be God-inspired and equal to that of the Mosaic Law. In Jesus' day this group was characterized by hypocrisy and self-righteousness. As a whole, they persecuted Jesus and His followers and received the Lord's most stinging rebukes.

The Pharisees, like many people today, were ignorant of achieving right standing (righteousness) with God through the simple act of receiving His forgiveness by faith. They were trying to earn salvation by their own works. No one can fulfill God's commands (Rom. 3:23) except Jesus. (Heb. 4:15.) Therefore, to be righteous, we must put our faith in what He has done for us.

Be sure to put all your trust in Jesus today.

Is Jesus Looking for You?
John 9:35

Jesus heard that they had cast him out; and when he had found him,
he said unto him, Dost thou believe on the Son of God?
John 9:35

It is one thing to seek God; it is quite another thing to have God seek you. Jesus sought this man out when others had forsaken him. The acceptance of Jesus is worth more than everything this world has to offer. This is what enables the believer to endure and even leap for joy amidst persecution. When our sufferings in Christ abound, then the consolation of Christ abounds much more. Jesus did not seek out this man's parents, who knew the truth but refused to share it for fear of persecution. (John 9:22.) They chose the company of the hypocritical scribes and Pharisees, which is exactly what they got.

Even though we are redeemed and delivered from many afflictions that were a result of sin and its power, we are still called to partake in what the Bible calls the "sufferings" or "afflictions of Christ." (2 Cor. 1:5; Col. 1:24.) However, these afflictions are not sickness and poverty but the "fellowship of sufferings" that we will encounter for doing the will of God and being loyal to Jesus Christ. The Good News is, then He is with us in a very special way, just like this man in the Gospel of John.

The apostle Peter reminds us that these trials of our faith will result in praise, honor and glory at the appearing of Jesus Christ. (1 Peter 1:7.) Jesus' comfort, strength, help, and love are ready to overflow into every trial that you face today. When you stand for Him, He will stand with you.

The Life of God
John 10:7-10

The thief cometh not, but for to steal, and to kill, and to destroy: I am come that they might have life, and that they might have it more abundantly.
John 10:10

The Greek word translated life is *zoe*, and it means life in the absolute sense, or life as God has it. Everyone who is breathing has life in the sense of physical existence, but only those who receive Jesus can experience life as God intended it to be. Jesus came to not only save us from the torment of eternal hell but to give us this zoe or God-kind of life in abundance. The life of God is not awaiting us in heaven but is presently possessed by all born-again people in their spirits.

We can experience this zoe life and enjoy it now by surrendering our natural lives and pursuing our supernatural life in Christ. The way we surrender our lives is to deny any thoughts, emotions, or actions that are contrary to the Word of God, which is (zoe) life. (John 6:63.) When we line our thoughts, emotions, and actions up with the instructions of God's Word, then God's zoe life will manifest in our bodies and souls as well.

The Word is spiritual and must be understood through our spirits. (1 Cor. 2:14.) The Bible is simply a written representation of Jesus, who is the Living Word. He embodies all spiritual truth. The Word is inspired of God and, therefore, totally accurate and reliable, yet until we receive the Spirit of these words, the Bible will not profit us. (Heb. 4:2.)

Today you can walk in the abundant life Jesus died to give you by simply abiding in His Word. His Word is spirit and life to you. (John 6:63.)

Grow In Grace
Luke 9:54-56

But he turned, and rebuked them, and said, Ye know not what manner of spirit ye are of.
Luke 9:55

When a Samaritan village rejected Jesus, the disciples said, "Lord, do You want us to command fire to come down from heaven and consume them, just as Elijah did?" (Luke 9:54). This was right in line with the Old Testament, but Jesus rebuked them. He did that because it was not in line with the grace of God He came to bring mankind.

Jesus did not come to destroy people's lives but to save them. (John 3:16; 10:10.) "God was in Christ, reconciling the world unto himself, not imputing their trespasses unto them" (2 Cor. 5:19). He was just in doing this because He bore our sins (Isa. 53:4-6) and the accompanying wrath of God. (Matt. 27:46; Heb. 2:9.) He didn't reject God's judgment against sin; He took it upon Himself. (2 Cor. 5:21.) Therefore, He was able to extend the grace and mercy of God to those who would have been doomed under the Law of Moses. (Acts 13:38,39.)

The Old Testament Law was like a judge passing sentence upon sin. Jesus became our advocate (lawyer). Even more than that, He became our substitute, bearing "our sins in his own body on the tree" (1 Peter 2:24). He didn't destroy God's judgment; He fulfilled it in Himself so that we could go free. This forever changed God's dealings with sinful people.

In light of what Jesus has done in the New Covenant, forgiving us for all our sins, we should never turn around and release God's wrath upon others as was done in the Old Covenant. There is a difference between Old Testament Law and New Testament grace. "For the law was given by Moses, but grace and truth came by Jesus Christ" (John 1:17). Grow in grace today, and forgive and pray for those who do wrong and reject Jesus.

The Cost of Living for Jesus
Matthew 8:18-22; Luke 9:51-62

And Jesus said unto him, Foxes have holes, and birds of the air have nests;
but the Son of man hath not where to lay his head.
Luke 9:58

This verse has often been used to support the misconception that Jesus and His disciples lived in poverty. However, in this instance the reason Jesus had nowhere to lay His head was because of persecution. Because of a religious prejudice, the Samaritans refused Jesus and His disciples hospitality and a place to stay as He journeyed to Jerusalem. Persecution is part of the cost of living a Christian life. Jesus was communicating to this man that not having a place to stay at times was part of that cost.

There are many forms of persecution. Having your life threatened because of your faith in Jesus is one way you can be persecuted, but it is not the most damaging. A far more deadly form of persecution is when the people we admire, love, or seek approval from simply speak evil of us or separate us from their company. This is more deadly because it is more subtle and more personal.

Many believers who would never directly deny the Lord will fall into self-pity or strife because of someone's criticism, especially someone they look up to and want to impress. This will render them just as ineffective as a negative reaction to having one's life threatened.

It helps to recognize that it is not you people are persecuting but rather Christ in you. You are actually becoming a partaker of His sufferings and will share His resurrection power and rewards as a result. With this in mind, you can actually shout and leap for joy when you are rejected for His sake.

Sharing God's Love
Luke 10:1-2

Therefore said he unto them, The harvest truly is great, but the labourers are few: pray ye therefore the Lord of the harvest, that he would send forth labourers into his harvest.
Luke 10:2

It is commonly thought that an evangelist is someone who has a passion to lead people to the Lord, but they are not alone in this call. Every believer should have a passion for souls. When presenting the Gospel, we are not just presenting a theory about God but the factual account of His dealings with mankind as revealed in His Word. The ultimate witness to the truth is the bodily resurrection of Jesus. Our personal witness of the reality of Jesus being alive in our lives brings Him from theory to reality.

The early Christians experienced the love of Jesus in an intimate and life-transforming way. This motivated them to reach their known world with the Gospel more than any generation of Christians since. They didn't have the benefits of our modern technology, but they did have the benefit of being full of the love of Christ. Experiencing the love of Christ causes us to be filled with the fullness of God (Eph. 3:19) and makes us a witness that the world cannot resist. (John 13:35.)

Today, churches emphasize techniques of evangelism or spiritual warfare. We motivate people to witness through guilt or the threat of punishment. Much of our evangelism has become as dead and non-productive as that of the cults who knock on doors and argue people into their way of thinking.

The early Christians had a much greater impact on their world because they were full of and motivated by the love of God. We need that in our churches today! When we can say with Paul that the love of Christ constrains us, then we will impact our world for the Lord too.

You can't give away what you don't possess. You need to personally know the love of Christ in an experiential way before you try to share it with others.

God's Peace
Luke 10:5-6

And into whatsoever house ye enter, first say, Peace be to this house.
Luke 10:5

J esus said that His followers should bring peace and leave peace wherever they went. All Christians have peace first with God through Jesus Christ. (Rom. 5:1.) When we walk into a room, no matter what is going on between people we bring the peace of God to them. Whether or not they receive it, we offer it to them by our presence, our words, and our actions.

Peace is also a fruit of the Spirit that lives in our spirits, so peace is always present in our spirits. Our minds and emotions and bodies can get caught up in the turmoil of this world, but inside us we always can draw upon the peace of God. Peter exhorted us to always cast our cares upon the Lord (1 Peter 5:7) because he knew that cares will keep us from walking in God's peace. When we eliminate the cares, peace flows freely out of our spirits into our mind, emotions, and body.

Many believers ask God to give them peace so that their cares will leave. It doesn't work that way. Through faith we cast our cares on the Lord, and then His peace in our hearts is released into the rest of our being. Christians who are lacking God's peace have not taken their cares to the Lord and left them there.

Human peace is only experienced in the absence of problems, but God's peace is independent of circumstances and is infinitely greater than any problem you could ever have today. God has given you His supernatural peace to enjoy and to bring to others.

Faith in the Name of Jesus
Luke 10:17-18

And the seventy returned again with joy, saying, Lord, even the devils are
subject unto us through thy name.
Luke 10:17

The power in the name of Jesus and the disciples' faith in that name made the demons subject unto them. This truth was demonstrated in Acts 19:13-17, where certain Jews called on the name of Jesus in an effort to cast demons out of a man. They used the name of Jesus, but it didn't work because they had not put their faith in that name.

These Jews were vagabond exorcists who used incantations to bring deliverance to people who were demon possessed. The first-century historian Josephus wrote of an exorcism he witnessed in the presence of Vespasian and many of his soldiers. The exorcist supposedly followed a ritual for deliverance passed down from King Solomon. Throughout history people have tried to resist demonic spirits, but as this example proves, only Jesus and those who have received His life are successful.

Those who relegate demonic spirits to the realm of superstition do not believe in the entire Word of God. The Gospels alone contain over ninety references to the devil or devils (demons). The apostle Paul told the Ephesians, "We wrestle not against flesh and blood, but against principalities, against powers, against the rulers of the darkness of this world, against spiritual wickedness in high places" (Eph. 6:12). The devil and demons do exist, but all believers in Jesus share in His total victory over them.

The name of Jesus is not magic. It does not work like a charm. As Peter said, "His name, through faith in his name" (Acts 3:16), is what brings results. Today you must put your faith in the name of Jesus to be completely victorious over the enemy. As you trust in Him, whenever you do encounter a demonic spirit you can confidently cast it out and set people free.

Focus on Jesus
Luke 10:20-25

Notwithstanding in this rejoice not, that the spirits are subject unto you;
but rather, rejoice, because your names are written in heaven.
Luke 10:20

We were never instructed to have a Ph.D. in demonology; however, some people justify focusing on Satan and his activity to an inordinate degree. This will actually encourage demonic activity and become a device that Satan can use against them. As Paul said, we should not be ignorant of Satan's devices; we need to know the devil and demons exist and to recognize their activities, but we need to keep our focus on the Lord. Some people who are excessive in spiritual warfare actually spend more time talking to the devil each day than they do talking to God. That's not right.

The best defense against the devil is to be so God-centered that we give no place to Satan. People who are very sensitive to the devil's presence usually are not being sensitive to the Lord's presence. David said, "If I make my bed in hell, behold, thou art there" (Ps. 139:8). Any time Satan's oppression is there, God's presence is there too. (Heb. 13:5.) It's just a matter of which one we focus on. Focusing on the devil is a trick of the devil.

Your ability to live the Christian life is found in Jesus Christ. It is not your ability but your availability to Him that makes the difference. Paul said, "For when I am weak, then am I strong" (2 Cor. 12:10). He was saying that when he recognized his inability and relied on the Lord's ability, that was when the Lord's strength flowed through him. Today you can do all things through Christ (Phil. 4:13) by keeping your eyes on Him.

By Grace Through Faith
Luke 10:25-29

And he said unto him, Thou hast answered right: this do, and thou shalt live.
But he, willing to justify himself, said unto Jesus, And who is my neighbour?
Luke 10:28-29

Pride causes many people to resist the truth of justification by faith in the grace of God. This lawyer loved himself and the public recognition his holy acts brought him. He was not willing to love God first and other people ahead of himself. His question was an attempt to shun responsibility for his self-centeredness. He was seeking to be justified in the sight of God through his actions. He knew he had not loved everyone as he loved himself, so he tried to interpret the Scripture (Lev. 19:18) in a way that would apply to his actions, not his heart. He wanted to define "neighbor" as close friends whom he had treated well. Self-justification always produces excuses, while repentance and faith toward God produces surrender and obedience.

The basis of our salvation is grace—that is, God's undeserved, unmerited favor toward us as expressed in providing redemption through Christ Jesus. The way God saves us is through faith. Through faith we accept His free gift of salvation, which was provided by His grace. We are saved "by grace...through faith" (Eph. 2:8) not by grace alone. Faith grants us admission to God's grace. Without faith, God's grace is wasted, and without grace, faith is powerless. Faith in God's grace has to be released to receive what God has provided through Jesus Christ.

Sodium and chloride are poisonous by themselves, and grace or faith used independently of each other are deadly; but when you mix sodium and chloride together you get salt, which you must have to live. Likewise, putting faith in what God has already provided by grace is the key to victorious Christian living.

Who Is Your Neighbor?
Luke 10:29-37

But he, willing to justify himself, said unto Jesus, And who is my neighbour?
Luke 10:29

This question, "Who is my neighbor?" can be used by Satan to deceive us in more than one way. Not only can he deceive us into thinking we have loved our neighbors as ourselves when we haven't, but he will also try to condemn us by making us think we are not doing enough to love and minister Jesus Christ to our neighbors.

We cannot meet the needs of every single person in the world. Jesus did not teach that or live that way. The wounded man in this story in Luke was directly in the path of three men. The priest and the Levite had to walk around him. Jesus was simply teaching that we should take advantage of the opportunities we have. Just because we can't help everyone is no excuse not to help anyone.

In this parable, Jesus defined a neighbor as any fellow human being that crosses our path and is in need of our assistance. The Samaritan went to the full extent of his ability to help the man, but the priest and Levite did nothing. In light of the racial and religious hatred between Jews and Samaritans, having the priest and Levite ignore the injured man and the Samaritan help him was an interesting choice for Jesus! He made it clear that we could not define *neighbor* on the basis of geographic origin or familiarity.

By Jesus' definition, your neighbor is anyone God puts in your path. Remember that today. You will look at the people you encounter in a whole new way.

Jesus' Words to You
Luke 10:38-42

But Martha was cumbered about much serving, and came to him, and said,
Lord dost thou not care that my sister hath left me to serve alone? bid her
therefore that she help me.
Luke 10:40

There are only three instances in Scripture that give us information about Martha. From these accounts, we can see that Martha had a brother named Lazarus, whom Jesus raised from the dead, and a sister named Mary. Martha had misplaced her priorities on this occasion in Luke 10 and was corrected by Jesus. Later, at a supper for Jesus in the home of Simon the leper, Martha was once again serving while Mary, her sister, was worshipping Jesus by anointing His feet with costly perfume.

Martha was also the first one to run to meet Jesus when He came to their home after the death of Lazarus. It was at this time Martha said she knew Jesus could have prevented Lazarus from dying and that, even then, she knew He could raise him from the dead. She made a confession of faith in the deity of Jesus, every bit as strong as Peter's, which received a blessing from Jesus.

Martha was not wrong in serving Jesus and His disciples. Other women ministered to Jesus in this way without being corrected. Serving was a good thing, but Martha had put it in the wrong place. Her problem was priorities—not what she was doing. It was a great honor to have Jesus in her home and to hear His personal words for them. Martha should have given His words the same priority Mary gave them.

Just like Martha, you may be occupied with things that keep you from hearing the words of Jesus throughout your day. It is easy to recognize and turn from things that are obviously sin, but even good things you are involved in must be prioritized so that nothing takes the place of hearing Jesus' words to you.

Are You Hot?
2 Corinthians 4:7-18

For which cause we faint not; but though our outward man perish,
yet the inward man is renewed day by day.
2 Corinthians 4:16

I remember when my sixth grade teacher heated a metal gas can. Once it was very hot, he put the lid on securely, making it airtight, and set the can on his desk. The whole class watched as it began cracking and popping. Then, right in front of our eyes, the can was crushed without anyone touching it!

Hot air occupies more space than cold air. When the air inside the can was hot, it equaled the atmospheric pressure. As it cooled, however, the air condensed and formed a partial vacuum inside the can. That's when the normal atmospheric pressure crushed it. What an awesome illustration of everyday life. We all face pressures from the outside. If our lives are full of the presence of God, these pressures are no problem. It's only when we have a partial vacuum in our hearts that daily pressures can crush us. Those who seem overwhelmed by everyday life have cooled off in their relationship with the Lord.

Life hasn't become worse or more stressful in our modern times as some proclaim. Life has always been tough. Think about those who fought in World War II. What about those whose families were slaves just a few generations ago? What about the Great Depression? Most of us have never experienced hardships like these people did. Yet, it seems there is more depression, suicide, and heartache today than then.

The difference isn't the pressures outside but the vacuum inside. Today don't get out of your bed without being passionately full of the love, faith, and hope of God. Make sure there is no vacuum in your heart for God, and no pressure you encounter will be a problem.

Who Do You Think You Are?
Judges 6:11-24

And the angel of the Lord appeared unto him, and said unto him,
The Lord is with thee, thou mighty man of valour.
Judges 6:12

Gideon was a man mightily used of God. He took three hundred men and defeated an army that numbered in the millions. It was one of the greatest military victories of all time. Yet Gideon didn't start out with any confidence.

The angel of the Lord greeted him with, "The Lord is with thee, thou mighty man of valour," but Gideon responded by saying, "Why then can't I see it?" He didn't see himself as a mighty man of valor at all. He was threshing his wheat in hiding, afraid the Midianites would steal his meager harvest. Gideon didn't see himself the way God saw him.

After the angel visited Gideon, he was so insecure that he gave God a series of tests to convince himself that He was really with him and that He would do what He said He would do. The truth is that Gideon was a mighty man of valor the moment God said he was; it just took him awhile to recognize it. God knew who Gideon really was before he did.

Likewise, God knows who we are and what our capabilities are because He created us. Furthermore, this isn't just limited to our personal talents and abilities. We have the promise that we can do the same works Jesus did. Each one of us has unlimited potential in Christ. Unfortunately, it doesn't matter what our potential is if we do not believe we are who God says we are. Who we think we are is the determining factor.

Are you convinced that you are who God says you are in His Word? If not, you can be convinced by reading, studying, and meditating in God's Word until He alone defines you. When you know what God says about you is true, then you will be used mightily by God too.

Don't Bypass the Altar
Judges 6:25-32

And build an altar unto the Lord thy God upon the top of this rock,
in the ordered place, and take the second bullock, and offer a burnt
sacrifice with the wood of the grove which thou shalt cut down.
Judges 6:26

The same day the angel of the Lord appeared to Gideon, he gave him instructions to tear down the altar his father had built and build a new altar to the Lord. People often skip over this and go straight to Gideon's great victory over the Midianites, but rebuilding the altar to the Lord was a very important detail.

An altar is where we worship. This symbolized Gideon forsaking all other forms of worship and committing himself to God alone. This was no small deal! The townspeople would kill Gideon for it, which is why he built the altar at night. He knew the risk he was taking, and his actions showed a total commitment to the Lord. Gideon was willing to follow God even unto death.

Our faith and victories come out of relationship with the Lord. Failure to maintain intimacy with Him is the biggest reason for defeat in battle. Before God could really use Gideon, He needed him to be committed and focused on Him.

Notice God didn't have Gideon tear down the altar before calling him. God's gifts and callings are independent of our performance. The Lord has never called anyone because they were worthy. But once the call comes, we will never succeed apart from an intimate relationship with our heavenly Father.

Are you trying to bypass the altar and go straight to the battle? That's not God's way. Remove anything that takes away from your devotion to the Lord, and then you will be ready to meet all the challenges of your day.

Do You Have Too Much?

Judges 6:33-7:8

*And the Lord said unto Gideon, The people that are with thee are too many for me
to give the Midianites into their hands, lest Israel vaunt themselves against me,
saying, Mine own hand hath saved me.*
Judges 7:2

Gideon had been struggling with unbelief. That's why he put a fleece before the Lord. Now the Lord was telling him he had too many people in his army. Although they were already grossly outnumbered, the Lord instructed him to thin the ranks. So Gideon told all who were afraid to leave. Twenty-two thousand men went home! That left ten thousand, but the Lord said there were still too many. He directed Gideon to separate the men according to how they drank from the brook, and he chose three hundred because they knelt down on one knee to drink by cupping their hands and bringing the water up to their mouths.

Why did the Lord cut down Gideon's already-small army? He didn't want anyone else to take credit for the victory. He wanted the number of men to be so small that there would be no doubt in anyone's mind that the victory was a miracle of the Lord. He specifically put them in an impossible situation so His people would come to know just how awesome He was.

The Lord didn't bring the Midianites against His people or cause the problem, but when the problem appeared, He specifically led Gideon in such a way that only His supernatural power could deliver them. He wants to do the same for you today. He may lead you to do things that look crazy to your natural mind just so He can reveal Himself to you in a miraculous way. He often spurns conventional wisdom so you will know your deliverance is totally from Him.

Don't Forget!
Psalm 103:1-22

Bless the Lord, O my soul, and forget not all his benefits.
Psalm 103:2

In May, 1991, I was sitting on a church platform just minutes before I was to minister. The final song was "How Great Thou Art." I suddenly had a flashback to May, 1961, when I was a twelve-year-old boy sitting at my father's funeral. That auditorium was packed with over five-hundred people singing that same hymn, which was my father's favorite. I vividly remember what I was thinking then. I wasn't in tears because I really hadn't yet comprehended what had happened, but I knew something had taken place that would alter my life forever.

The minister spoke of victory and hope, which seemed to be so contrary to the situation. That song also appeared to be out of place; yet in my heart it struck a chord. I felt faith arise, so I prayed to the Lord, "If You really are so great, then protect me and direct the rest of my life."

I hadn't thought about that prayer for thirty years, but that song brought it back to my remembrance in an instant. I was overwhelmed with the faithfulness of the Lord to answer such a simple prayer by a twelve-year-old boy. He did exceedingly, abundantly above anything I had asked or even thought! Remembering His faithfulness has been a vital part of my faith. Good memories stir me up (2 Peter 1:13), and the Lord commanded us not to forget because He knows we will if we don't make a deliberate effort to remember.

All of us have uttered prayers—whether spoken requests or just desires—that we have forgotten, but God hasn't. Only eternity will reveal the vastness of His faithfulness, but in the meantime, you can make an effort to remember His goodness toward you. Today, let the Holy Spirit bring back to your remembrance instances of God's faithfulness to you, and be blessed as I was.

Prayer Power
Luke 11:1-4

And it came to pass, that, as he was praying in a certain place, when he ceased, one of his disciples said unto him, Lord, teach us to pray, as John also taught his disciples.
Luke 11:1

When you consider that Jesus was the greatest miracle worker who ever walked the earth and the greatest preacher who ever lived, it is amazing His disciples asked Him to teach them to pray. Why didn't they ask Him to teach them how to work miracles or how to preach and amaze the people with their doctrine? They knew His prayer life was even more powerful than His miracles or His doctrine. Indeed, it was His union with the Father that gave Him the power to work miracles and His authority to speak as no man had ever spoken before.

Jesus told them repeatedly that it was His Father who was doing the miracles through Him and that His doctrine was not His own but the Father's. The same holds true today. Jesus said in John 15:5 that without Him we can do nothing. There are many things we should do in addition to praying, but there is nothing that we can effectively do without prayer. Prayer is one of the main ways of abiding in Him. (John 15:7.)

When the disciples asked Jesus to teach them to pray, He taught them what we call "The Lord's Prayer." Although every believer prays this verbatim, what Jesus gave was actually an outline that covered how to approach the Father and what subjects we could discuss with Him. He doesn't want to hear the same memorized prayer from all of us. He wants to hear what is on our hearts and minds because He wants a relationship in which He can help us and bless us in any way He can.

Today you can pray and expect to receive answers from your Father. He is ready and willing to answer your prayers. How do you know? Jesus said so! Your prayers are the key to living a powerful Christian life.

Be Filled
Luke 11:11-13

If ye then, being evil, know how to give good gifts unto your children: how much more shall your heavenly Father give the Holy Spirit to them that ask him?
Luke 11:13

The Holy Spirit is a gift (Acts 2:38), and God simply wants you to have Him. You cannot be good enough to earn the gift of the Holy Spirit, but you do have to ask for it. This is speaking of the baptism of the Holy Ghost, which is subsequent to the born-again experience.

The Holy Spirit resides in our spirits, and once He comes, He doesn't leave. (John 14:16.) There is an initial filling when the Holy Ghost first comes; however, His control and influence over our souls and bodies does fluctuate proportionally to how well we renew our minds to His will. (Rom. 12:2.) In that sense, we can be more full of the Holy Ghost than at other times, although in our spirits the presence and power of the Holy Spirit does not come and go. Therefore, even after we receive the baptism of the Holy Ghost, there will be times when our souls and bodies stray from the leadership of the Holy Spirit, and we need, once again, to be filled with the Holy Spirit.

In Ephesians 5:18 believers are commanded to "be not drunk with wine…but be filled with the Spirit." Being filled with the Holy Spirit is in the present tense, making it a continual command for the believer. In the book of Acts, the same people who were filled with the Holy Spirit on the Day of Pentecost were filled again. Most people don't get drunk on just one drink. Likewise, being filled with the Holy Spirit is not just a one-time experience. There is an initial filling of the Holy Spirit but also many subsequent fillings.

You know that drunkenness can change a person's personality and make them act totally different. Likewise, being filled with the Holy Spirit can make you act just like Jesus. Be filled with the Spirit today and tomorrow and the next day.

Two Different Mindsets
Luke 11:37-41

And when the Pharisee saw it, he marvelled
that he had not first washed before dinner.
Luke 11:38

A sure sign of the error of legalism is misplaced priorities, as we see here with these Pharisees. It is not recorded in Scripture that the Pharisees marveled at the wonderful works of Jesus. They were too busy looking for something to criticize. (Mark 3:2.) They did marvel at Jesus not washing his hands. This is a classic example of "straining at a gnat and swallowing a camel" (Matt. 23:24).

Those who seek to earn righteousness through keeping the law are consumed with "doing," while those who receive righteousness by faith are simply confessing what has already been done. This is a simple yet profound difference. If we are still "doing" to get God to move in our lives, then we are still operating under a "law" mentality that is not faith. (Gal. 3:12.) When we simply believe and confess what has already been provided through Christ, we grow in grace through our faith.

A person who lives under the Law and a person who lives under grace should have similar acts of holiness, but their motivations are completely opposite. The legalist has their attention on what they must do, while the person living by faith has their attention on what Jesus has already done for them. For instance, the Scriptures teach us to confess with our mouths and believe with our hearts, and we will receive from God. (Mark 11:23.) The legalist thinks, *I can get God to heal me by confessing, "By his stripes I am healed."* The person who understands God's grace will confess, "By his stripes I am healed," because they really believe Jesus has already obtained their healing on the Cross.

Analyzing your mindset is the simplest way of discerning whether you are operating in faith or legalism today. If your motive is to be accepted by God or to get God to do something for you, that's legalism. If you live wholly in faith and gratitude for what God has already done in Christ Jesus, that's grace. Choose to have a mindset of grace because Jesus has supplied everything you need, all things that pertain to living a godly life. (2 Peter 1:3.)

Holiness Is a Fruit
Luke 11:42-44

But woe unto you, Pharisees! for ye tithe mint and rue and all manner of herbs,
and pass over judgement and the love of God: these ought ye to have done,
and not to leave the other undone.
Luke 11:42

When Jesus said, "and not to leave the other undone," He was not arguing against doing what is right. God's Word stresses holiness in our actions. The Pharisees' error that caused Jesus' rebuke was that they believed their actions could produce a right relationship with God, but right relationship with God only comes by humbling ourselves and putting our faith in the Savior, Jesus Christ.

God cleanses our hearts by grace through faith (Eph. 2:8), and then we have our fruit unto holiness. (Rom. 6:22.) Holiness is the fruit, not the root of salvation. In a similar situation in Matthew 23:26, Jesus said, "Thou blind Pharisee, cleanse first that which is within the cup and platter, that the outside of them may be clean also." True Christianity comes from the inside out. A good heart will change a person's actions, but a person's actions cannot change their heart.

One of religion's favorite doctrines is that if you will just act right, you will be right. Nothing could be further from the truth! You must be born again by the Spirit of God, then your actions will be holy because you are holy. You are holy inside, and that holiness manifests more and more on the outside.

This is the heart of the Gospel. Every major religion of the world has a moral standard for salvation except Christianity, which offers salvation through a Savior. Now that you are saved, you have no need to make yourself look holy on the outside.

Today, just allow His holiness inside you to manifest in your thoughts, words, and actions. This will become more and more obvious as you follow the Spirit and renew your mind with God's Word. (Rom. 12:2.) The fruit of holiness will show up in every area of your life.

The Fear of the Lord
Luke 12:4-5

But I will forewarn you whom ye shall fear: Fear him, which after he hath killed hath
power to cast into hell; yea, I say unto you, Fear him.
Luke 12:5

Second Timothy 1:7 says, "God hath not given us the spirit of fear; but of power, and of love, and of a sound mind." First John 4:18 says, "There is no fear in love; but perfect love casteth out fear: because fear hath torment. He that feareth is not made perfect in love." These Scriptures may look like they are contradictions to Jesus' statement here; however, they are not.

There are two kinds of fear. The *American Heritage Dictionary* defines *fear* as "a feeling of alarm or disquiet caused by the expectation of danger, pain, disaster, or the like; terror; dread; apprehension." It also defines *fear* as "extreme reverence or awe, as toward a supreme power." It is reverence or awe that God's Word teaches saints to have toward God. Hebrews 12:28 says that there is a godly fear with which we are supposed to serve God, and thereby implies there is an ungodly fear that is not acceptable in serving God.

Satan has always used this ungodly dread or terror to torment godly people. Those who have been born again should have no dread or terror of God unless they are planning to renounce their faith in Jesus as their Savior. We have a covenant that guarantees us acceptance with God (Eph. 1:6), as long as we hold fast to our profession of faith in the atoning blood of our Savior, Jesus Christ.

For an unbeliever, the fear of the Lord is a great deterrent from sin, but for you who have received the grace of God, it is His goodness that causes you to fear (reverence) Him and depart from sin. The fear of the Lord you walk in today is not a dread or terror but a peace and joy that He is all-powerful and yet your loving Father.

Stewards of God's Grace
Luke 12:42

And the Lord said, Who then is that faithful and wise steward, whom his lord shall make ruler over his household, to give them their portion of meat in due season?
Luke 12:42

A steward is a person who has been entrusted with administering someone else's wealth or affairs. The possessions a steward controls are not their own, and they do not have the freedom to do with them as they wish. They are supposed to carry out the desires of the one who made them a steward.

A banker is a steward. He has been entrusted with other people's money. He is free to invest that money wisely in a way that will benefit his depositors and stockholders, but he would be sent to jail if he took all that money and simply consumed it himself. A banker is accountable (Luke 16:2) to those who give him their money to steward. The money does not belong to him even though it is in his possession.

This parable and other Scriptures (1 Cor. 4:1; Titus 1:7; 1 Pet. 4:10) describe every believer as a steward of God's grace. The wealth, talents, and abilities we possess, as well as the revelation of God's love we have been given, are not our own to do with as we please. We have received these things from God and are therefore accountable to Him for the use or misuse of these gifts. Keeping this in mind is essential for fulfilling our obligation to God as stewards of His "manifold grace."

Be a faithful and wise steward of God's grace today. Show other people the love and forgiveness you have received from Him, and point them to Him in everything you say and do.

No Excuses
Luke 12:45-48

But he that knew not, and did commit things worthy of stripes, shall be beaten with few stripes. For unto whomsoever much is given, of him shall be much required: and to whom men have committed much, of him they will ask the more.
Luke 12:48

This verse speaks of varying degrees of God's judgment based upon the knowledge of the person who committed the sin. The whole fourth chapter of Leviticus is written to deal with sins committed in ignorance. Jesus said in John 9:41, "If ye were blind, ye should have no sin: but now ye say, We see; therefore your sin remaineth." Also, Romans 5:13 says, "Sin is not imputed when there is no law."

Paul said in 1 Timothy 1:13 that he obtained mercy because he had sinned "ignorantly in unbelief." The sin he was speaking of was blasphemy, which Jesus taught was unforgivable if done against the Holy Ghost. Therefore, we see that ignorance in Paul's case entitled him to a second chance. If he had continued to blaspheme after he saw the truth, he surely would have paid the price.

This is not to say that a person who doesn't have a complete revelation of God's will is innocent regardless of their actions. Leviticus 5:17 makes it clear that an individual is still guilty even if they sin in ignorance. Romans 1:18-20 reveals there is an intuitive knowledge of God within all people to recognize and even understand the Godhead. This same chapter goes on to explain that people have rejected and changed this truth, but that God did give it and they are without excuse.

No one will be able to stand before God on Judgment Day and say, "God is not fair." He has given every person who has ever lived, regardless of how remote or isolated they may have been, the opportunity to know Him.

Reconciliation
Luke 12:56-59

When thou goest with thine adversary to the magistrate, as thou art in the way,
give diligence that thou mayest be delivered from him; lest he hale thee to the judge,
and the judge deliver thee to the officer, and the officer cast thee into prison.
Luke 12:58

Jesus had just spoken about relationships before He gave this parable of delivering ourselves from the judge. The warning is clear that we should do everything within our power to avoid strife. (Rom. 12:18.) However, the consequences of failing to settle our differences are more than just physical prison or punishment.

Strife can produce spiritual and emotional prisons. James 3:16 says, "Where envying and strife is, there is confusion and every evil work." Depression, fear, loneliness, bitterness, sickness, financial problems, and many other things can become prisons from which we will not be delivered until we reconcile.

The dictionary states that to reconcile means "to re-establish friendship between; to settle or resolve, as a dispute." The key to reconciliation is effectively dealing with the enmity, ill will, hatred, or hostility that has caused the dispute. There are several approaches to reconciliation that may be applied. For instance, if we've offended someone by an unkind word, we can apologize. If we owe money to someone, we can pay the debt. If we have done something to harm someone, we can make the necessary restitution. In every case, reconciliation lies in dealing effectively with the root cause of the strife.

The strife between God and you was sin, but He took the initiative to remove this barrier through the blood of Jesus Christ, thus leaving you as friends once again. You were reconciled to God by Jesus' death and resurrection. Now you are also a minister of reconciliation. (2 Cor. 5:18.) Today you are anointed by God to reconcile with those you have experienced strife with and to lead others to reconcile with God through Jesus Christ.

You Must Receive
Luke 13:10-17

And ought not this woman, being a daughter of Abraham, whom Satan hath bound,
lo, these eighteen years, be loosed from this bond on the sabbath day?
Luke 13:16

This woman's sickness was the work of Satan—not the work of God. Jesus said it had bound her, not blessed her, for eighteen years. The teaching that says sickness is actually a blessing in disguise because the Lord is working His plan in someone's life is not found in Scripture. As Acts 10:38 says, Jesus "went about doing good, and healing all that were oppressed of the devil." People are oppressed of the devil, not God.

There are seventeen times in the Gospels when Jesus healed all of the sick that were present. There are forty-seven other times when He healed one or two people at a time. Nowhere do we find Jesus refusing to heal anyone. He said He could do nothing of Himself, but only what He saw the Father do. His words and actions are proof enough that it is always God's will to heal!

It is God's will that no one should perish, but many do because of their unbelief. Likewise, it is God's will that we all be healed, but not all are healed because of failure to believe. It is a mistake to assume whatever God wills, will automatically come to pass, and that we don't play a part in receiving from God.

In Hebrews 3:18-19 the children of Israel did not enter into God's rest (salvation, which includes physical healing) because of their unbelief. This is just after verse twelve says, "Take heed, brethren, lest there be in any of you an evil heart of unbelief, in departing from the living God." The Holy Spirit was talking to "brethren." That means you and me.

Today you must believe His Word with regard to healing in order to receive the divine health and healing He wants you to have.

Are You Chasing Your Tail?
Colossians 2:1-12

And ye are complete in him, which is the head of all principality and power.
Colossians 2:10

Most of us have seen a dog chase its tail. It's amusing and puzzling at the same time. Why chase something you already have? I can't speak with authority as to what a dog really thinks, but it appears to me that a dog that chases its tail is the only one who can't see that it's already his.

Amazingly, Christians tend to do the same thing. We ask for joy, faith, healing, wisdom, and all kinds of necessities and blessings, but according to God's Word we already have everything that pertains to life and godliness in Christ Jesus. (2 Peter 1:3.) The Christian life is not a continual process of asking and receiving more from God, it is renewing of our minds to know and appropriate what we already have in Christ. We are complete in Him!

Healing isn't "out there" somewhere. God's healing virtue is already inside of you. Jesus doesn't have to come and place His mighty hand on you to heal you because by His stripes you were already healed. (1 Peter 2:24.) You just have to believe it, speak it in faith, act upon your confession of faith, and expect it to manifest in your physical body.

Ask the Lord today for a revelation of what is really yours in Christ Jesus. Quit trying to get what you already have and enjoy your inheritance.

Compel Them to Come
Luke 14:16-24

Then said he unto him, A certain man made a great supper, and bade many…
And the lord said unto the servant, Go out into the highways and hedges,
and compel them to come in, that my house may be filled.
Luke 14:16,23

The man who made the supper represents God who has invited "whosoever will" to come to dine (have a close relationship) with Him. The parable teaches that it is not God who fails to offer salvation to people, but rather it is the invited guests who reject His offer.

The people in Jesus' parable had feeble excuses, and they were no different from the excuses of people today. All of the excuses had to do with their material wealth or family obligations being more important than a relationship with God. As a result, the master told his servant to go out and ask the poor, the homeless, and the downtrodden to come–and they did.

The Lord's marriage supper of the Lamb will be full of "undesirables" from the world's point of view, but not because God rejected the upper classes; it will be because they rejected Him. Those who have an abundance of this world's possessions don't tend to recognize their need for God as much as those who are without. God also offered salvation to the Jews first, but as a whole they refused Him; so He sent His servants to the Gentiles to fill His kingdom.

This parable proves the Lord does not advocate using force to convert people to Christianity. He respects the free will of all people to either accept or reject Him. However, He admonishes us to compel them to come by persuasion and love. The word *compel* denotes aggressiveness, so we are not supposed to simply hang out our "shingle" and wait for the world to come to us. We are supposed to aggressively pursue them with the Good News.

You are urgently commanded to be a witness of the love and redemption of Jesus Christ because the time before His return is short. Do not waste any opportunity today to share the Good News with someone!

The Cost of Discipleship
Luke 14:25-35

For which of you, intending to build a tower, sitteth not down first,
and counteth the cost, whether he have sufficient to finish it?
Luke 14:28

The parable of the man building a tower is a continuation of Jesus' teaching about what it takes to be His disciple. This parable stresses commitment. Jailhouse religion, where a person is only sorry they got caught and are just trying to get out of a bad situation, will not produce true discipleship. They must forsake all to be Jesus' disciple, and He is simply saying, "Count the cost."

Jesus' teaching on discipleship emphasizes steadfast loyalty and faithfulness to Him before anyone or anything else. Just as a king wouldn't engage in war without thoroughly considering all the possible outcomes, no one should attempt to become a disciple of Jesus without counting the cost. It would be better not to follow Him at all than to begin, experience some unexpected hardship, and then turn back.

When a person first comes to Jesus, it is impossible to know everything that following Him might entail. No one, however, should be afraid of making a total commitment to Him because of all the *what ifs* that may never happen. All they have to do is take one look at the Cross to know that Jesus can get them through anything!

Have you begun following Jesus and then turned back a few times? Perhaps today is the day you should sit down, count the cost, and make that solid commitment that no matter what life throws at you, you will continue to trust Him and follow Him. I promise that once you make that decision, He will live through you (Gal. 2:20) in an amazing way. You will experience a strength that is not your own but equal to whatever test you encounter.

Hard Knocks or God's Word?
Luke 15:11-17

And when he came to himself, he said, How many hired servants of my father's have bread enough and to spare, and I perish with hunger!
Luke 15:17

God's Word makes it clear that the wages of sin is death. (Rom. 6:23.) Romans 1:18-20 reveals that even those who don't know God's Word have an intuitive knowledge of right and wrong and God's judgment against sin. Therefore, for anyone to live in sin, as depicted by this prodigal son, they have to be deceived. This is exactly what the Bible says is the case in 2 Corinthians 4:4. When Jesus said, "He came to himself," He was referring to the deception being removed and the son's spiritual eyes being opened.

Like this story of the prodigal, tragedy often brings people out of deception and back to their senses. It's not that God sends the tragedy. God spoke through the prophet Jeremiah, "Thy way and thy doings have procured these things unto thee" (Jer. 4:18). However, tragic situations do clearly illustrate that "it is not in man that walketh to direct his steps" (Jer. 10:23), and they can cause us to look somewhere else for help. Although turning to God is always beneficial, hard knocks are not the best teacher.

Paul said in 2 Timothy 3:16-17, "All scripture is given by inspiration of God, and is profitable for doctrine, for reproof, for correction, for instruction in righteousness: That the man of God may be perfect, thoroughly furnished unto all good works." God's Word was given for reproof and correction, and if we will submit to it, we can "be perfect, thoroughly furnished," without having to experience tragedy first.

Today you can be taught, corrected, and instructed by God's Word. In this way you can make good decisions that will avoid failure and calamity and not only give you success and joy but bless those around you.

Life-Changing Repentance
Luke 15:18-19

I will arise and go to my father, and will say unto him, Father,
I have sinned against heaven, and before thee.
Luke 15:18

This is a good example of true repentance. This son did not claim any goodness of his own or try to justify his actions. Instead, he humbled himself and appealed to the mercy of his father. Likewise, we cannot approach God in self-righteousness; we have to humble ourselves, put all of our faith in the Savior, and turn from our wicked ways. (2 Chr. 7:14.) That is true repentance—changing our mind and heart inwardly that then changes our attitude and actions outwardly.

Repentance is a necessary part of salvation. In another devotion (April 30) I talk in more detail about the difference between godly sorrow and ungodly sorrow. This young man had godly sorrow about his actions, and his godly sorrow led to repentance. Ungodly sorrow, or the sorrow of this world, is self-centered and just brings self-pity and a victim mentality that blames everyone else for their problems. With that mindset, of course, there will be no repentance; and without repentance, there can be no restoration to the Father.

This young man felt bad about his sins and recognized that he had sinned against both his natural father and his heavenly Father. That was the beginning of his full restoration to both of them. Today, as you seek the Lord, don't let anything stand between you and Him. If you have godly sorrow about anything, take it to Him and be forgiven and cleansed of it forever. It will change your day–and the rest of your life!

The Father's Love
Luke 15:20

And he arose, and came to his father. But when he was yet a great way off, his father
saw him, and had compassion, and ran, and fell on his neck, and kissed him.
Luke 15:20

For this boy's father to have seen him "a great way off," would imply that the father had been eagerly awaiting his son's return. Certainly, in the spiritual application of this parable, our heavenly Father longs to cleanse and receive any sinner. All they have to do is just repent and come to Him for forgiveness.

Jesus used this parable to rebuke the Pharisees for their harsh, self-righteous, unforgiving attitude toward sinners. The older brother in this parable was symbolic of the Pharisees and all religious people who believe their good works earn their salvation and acceptance with God. Like this older brother, the Pharisees had not lived an outward life of rebellion, and they thought that others who didn't measure up to their standards were surely hated by God.

But the Word says, "God so loved the world," and "Christ Jesus came into the world to save sinners." These and other scriptures reveal the heart of the Father toward sinners. He just wants them to come home! He wants relationship with them restored so that He can be involved in their lives and bless them. He loves sinners.

The repentant prodigal son had learned the vanity of materialism and immorality, and he had come home to a relationship with his father that neither he nor his older brother had known before. What is the condition of your relationship with the Father today? If you need to be restored to Him in any way, His arms are open wide, and He longs for you to run to Him right now.

Do the Right Thing
for the Right Reason
Luke 15:25-28

And he was angry, and would not go in: therefore came his father out,
and intreated him.
Luke 15:28

If relationship with his father had been the greatest desire of the older brother, he would have rejoiced to see his father restored to his other son. The joy that gave his father would have brought tears of joy to his own eyes. Furthermore, if this elder son had had any compassion for his brother, he also would have rejoiced at his return just like his father did. Instead, he was totally self-centered (that's pride) and became angry. This illustrates Proverbs 13:10, which says, "Only by pride cometh contention."

This elder brother was proud because he thought he was better than his younger brother, and we can't love and respect someone we think is beneath us. Some people are better athletes than others. Some are better businessmen than others. Some are better speakers than others, and so forth. This is an ungodly comparison. (2 Cor. 10:12.) We need to recognize that our accomplishments don't make us better—or worse—than others. God doesn't value us or define us by what we do; He looks at our hearts and why we do what we do.

Better performance does not make a better person. A person's character can be severely wanting even though their performance is good. A classic example of this was this older brother. He did all the right things for all the wrong reasons. Inside he was corrupt and selfish. He performed righteously to get his father's favor and eventually his fortune.

Why do you do what you do? What is your real motivation for wanting to excel in some gift, talent, or skill? Today ask the Lord to show you any area of endeavor where you are doing the right thing for the wrong reason. If there is something, don't get under condemnation for it! Just repent (change your mind and attitude), and move forward to do the right thing for the right reason.

Blessed to Be a Blessing
Luke 16:1-18

And he said also unto his disciples, There was a certain rich man, which had a steward; and the same was accused unto him that he had wasted his goods.
Luke 16:1

The unjust steward was covetous. He had not been faithful to his master or to his master's debtors. He had wasted his master's goods on himself. When found out, his self-serving nature considered the options and decided there had to be a change. He decided to use his lord's money to make friends so that when he was fired, he would have someone to help him.

His master was apparently wealthy enough that he didn't take offense at the steward's discounting of the debts owed to him, but rather he commended the steward. He didn't commend his dishonest ways, but he was commending the fact that he had finally used his lord's money to plan for the future instead of wasting it on himself. Although the steward was motivated by what he would ultimately gain, there was prudence in his actions. This was lacking before.

In this sense, Jesus said the children of this world (lost people) are wiser than the children of light (born-again people) because they plan for the future. Jesus told us to use money (the unrighteous mammon) to make friends that would receive us into "everlasting" habitations. The use of the word *everlasting* denotes that Jesus is now talking about our eternal future. The people who have been saved and blessed by our investments in the kingdom of God will literally receive us into our everlasting home when we pass on to be with the Lord.

God gave you your material possessions, so you are actually a steward of His resources. He gave you this wealth to establish His covenant on the earth—not so you could consume it upon your own lusts. Today, use your money and possessions with this in mind: You have been blessed to be a blessing.

The Right Righteousness
Luke 16:14-15

And he said unto them, Ye are they which justify yourselves before men; but God knoweth your hearts: for that which is highly esteemed among men is abomination in the sight of God.
Luke 16:15

Justification is not something to be earned but a gift to be received. Seeking to earn salvation is the only sin that will prevent a person from being saved. You cannot submit yourself to the righteousness of God, which comes as a gift through faith, as long as you are seeking to establish your own righteousness.

Most people are unaware that there are two kinds of righteousness. Only one type of righteousness is acceptable to God. There is our righteousness, which is our compliance with the Law; and there is God's righteousness, which is a gift through our faith. Our righteousness is imperfect because our fallen nature is incapable of fulfilling the Law; but God's righteousness is perfect because Jesus fulfilled all the Law.

God calls our righteousness "filthy rags." (Isa. 64:6.) A person who believes they must earn God's acceptance by their actions does not believe in God's righteousness, which is a gift. We must choose whether we will surrender our lives in faith to God and receive and walk in His righteousness or try to fulfill the Law in our own strength. God's righteousness is not what Jesus did for us plus any works on our part. It's either all His righteousness or all ours. We cannot mix them!

You probably already know that you cannot achieve right standing with a holy God by keeping the Law. You can only be saved through humble trust in the person and work of Jesus Christ. Today you cannot trust in your own righteousness in any way and still enjoy the benefit of Christ's righteousness. They don't mix. But when you place all your faith and trust in Him, He makes you as righteous as He is—and that is the right righteousness.

Freed From the Law
Luke 16:16-17

The law and the prophets were until John: since that time the kingdom of God is preached, and every man presseth into it.
Luke 16:16

The Bible teaches that there are different dispensations or divinely ordered ways of God dealing with mankind throughout the ages. A dispensation is simply a period of time in which God deals with mankind in a certain way.

The Old Testament law was only a temporary dispensation and ruled from the giving of the Law (Ex. 20) until the ministry of John the Baptist. When Christ came, He put an end to obtaining righteousness by the Law and sacrifices. (Rom. 10:4.) Anyone who advocates the keeping of the Law for the purpose of right standing with God is going back to an Old Testament system that was abolished by the work of Jesus Christ through the Cross and His resurrection.

The New Testament believer is under the dispensation of God's grace, but that doesn't mean the Law has passed away. Jesus didn't do away with the Law; He fulfilled the Law. (Matt. 5:17.) He fulfilled every jot and tittle of the Law for us, and when we accept Him as our Lord and Savior, His righteousness is imputed to us. We are right with God not based on our performance but on our faith in Him.

The purpose of the Law was to reveal that you were a sinner in need of the Savior. It still serves a purpose for those who are not born again. In this present age, Jesus said He didn't come to condemn you but to save you by His grace and through your faith and trust in Him. Thank God for His grace today.

Your Debt Was Paid
Luke 16:17

And it is easier for heaven and earth to pass, than one tittle of the law to fail.
Luke 16:17

The jot was not only one of the smallest letters of the Greek alphabet but also one of the most insignificant. It was sometimes deleted at the writer's pleasure. The tittle was only a mark or a point on a line that helped distinguish one letter from another and corresponds to our period or apostrophe. The point Jesus made here was that even the tiniest detail of the Law would not pass away.

Jesus Christ fulfilled every jot and tittle of the Law, which is a good thing because no one else could. He did what no sinful person had ever done or will ever do. He kept the Law, and the prize for keeping it was the eternal life of God. This granted Him eternal life, which qualified Him to pay our debt for not being able to keep the Law. Before He could give us eternal life, He had to pay for our sins.

This is similar to someone receiving the death penalty for a hideous crime, and some billionaire leaves his whole estate to him. It would do the condemned man no good unless that blameless billionaire took that criminal's place and died for him. Then the criminal would go free and enjoy the billionaire's wealth. That's what Jesus did for us. He took our sins and gave us His righteousness.

Jesus did much more than just obtain eternal life for us; He also paid all the wages of our sins. (Rom. 6:23.) God literally placed the condemnation and judgment that was against us upon His own Son. Jesus' perfect flesh was condemned so our defiled flesh could go free. What a trade! Jesus bore your sentence of condemnation, guilt, and shame so that you would no longer have to bear it. Today, be at peace inside knowing that your debt for all your sins has been paid in full.

Comfort in Eternity
Luke 16:19-31

And it came to pass, that the beggar died, and was carried by the angels into Abraham's bosom: the rich man also died, and was buried.
Luke 16:22

This story clearly teaches that there is life after death. It shows there is no "soul sleep" where our souls are awaiting the resurrection of our bodies, but we go into a conscious eternity immediately. It also shows that there are only two possible destinations after death. Either we go to a place of torment for the wicked or we go to a place of blessing for the righteous. There is no "limbo" or "purgatory," and there is no second chance. This story illustrates the finality of our eternal destiny once we die.

Abraham's bosom is a symbolic term for an actual place where those who believed under the Old Covenant but had not yet been born again went after they died physically. It was located in the heart of the earth, in the same region as hell, which is where those who never gave their lives to God go. The rich man's body was in the grave, and yet this Scripture speaks of him lifting up his eyes and seeing Lazarus in Abraham's bosom. This demonstrates that our spirit mirrors our physical shape so closely that we are recognizable after we die.

Part of this man's torment was from the flames of hell. However, he was also tormented by the thought of his loved ones' on earth having the same eternal destiny he was experiencing. Surely his desperation to warn them would make his misery worse. Also, the fact that he could see Lazarus and Abraham in a place of God's blessing and comfort would keep him from ever adjusting to his situation.

In the light of Jesus' words, we can see that hell will be much more than just a place of physical torment. Those who are consigned to that place will also be tormented with the thoughts of what could have been if they had trusted Jesus, and how they influenced others to follow them to hell. Knowing this, your heart can go out to anyone who does not know the Lord today. Don't ignore any opportunity to share the Gospel with them!

Abraham Believed in Hope
Romans 4:16-22

Who against hope believed in hope, that he might become the father of many nations, according to that which was spoken, So shall thy seed be.
Romans 4:18

Hope seems to be lacking today. Many people intentionally resist hope because they don't want to face the pain and disappointment that comes if their hopes are dashed. Their philosophy is: "Don't get your hopes up, and you'll never be disappointed." They obviously don't know Jesus who is our blessed hope (Titus 2:13) in all situations and for all time.

People who break away from the pack and accomplish great things are those who believe in hope. That's why most of the major inventions have been discovered by Jews or Christians who trust in God. Abraham was one of these people. This verse says he believed in hope. He knew the power of hope and wouldn't let it go. When Abraham was nearly a hundred years old and his wife was over ninety, he still held on to the hope of God's promise to give him a child. Although his faith gave him the victory, his hope kept his faith alive.

Where does hope come from? This verse says that Abraham's hope that he would become a father was according to the words God had spoken to him. The Holy Spirit constantly ministers hope to us as we meditate on the words God has spoken to us. God's Word releases His hope into our hearts. If we have no Word from God, then we have no hope. Certainly the world doesn't give out hope; it actually destroys it by rampant pessimism, skepticism, and fear. Our only source for true hope is in what God has promised us.

Make a special effort to spend time listening to God's Word today, and let hope begin to work in your life. Let God paint a picture on the canvas of your heart of what you can be and do through His ability!

Spiritual Eyes of Hope
Romans 8:20-25

*For we are saved by hope: but hope that is seen is not hope: for what a man seeth,
why doth he yet hope for?*
Romans 8:24

Did you know that you receive more input from your eyes than any other sense? Just think how drastically your life would change if you couldn't see. Therefore, it is easy to understand why you are so dependent on your physical sight. However, there are things you can't see.

In the kingdom of God, hope believes in things that have no physical evidence. Hope is a confident trust and reliance on God for results that can't be seen in the natural. Those who cannot break free from their senses, especially their sight, will never be able to operate in God's kind of hope.

How do we overcome what our physical eyes tell us? If our circumstances are contrary to what we know God wants us to have, how do we conquer the negative input? The answer is God's Word. Through meditating and acting on God's Word, we gain spiritual sight and can see more clearly with our spiritual eyes. We do have spiritual senses. This is what Jesus meant when he said, "He that hath ears to hear, let him hear" (Matt. 11:15). We have spiritual ears and eyes that enable us to perceive things that are hidden to our natural senses.

If you haven't begun to use your spiritual senses, start today. Here's a tip: you can't see with your physical eyes if they are closed; likewise, you can't see with your spiritual eyes if they are not open to the Spirit and the Word. If you don't see your world through the Holy Spirit's impartation of God's Word, you are spiritually blind—and you don't want to be blind in your spirit! Open up your spiritual eyes by opening up your heart to God's Word, and then hope will manifest.

Sure Hope = Strong Patience
Romans 8:20-25

But if we hope for that we see not, then do we with patience wait for it.
Romans 8:25

Have you ever noticed the patience that athletes possess? They only compete in the Olympics every four years, but they train and participate in other games and competitions incessantly. Some work their whole lives for one brief moment of glory. How can they do that? What motivates them to persevere? They have a strong hope.

Athletes who want to win must deny themselves things that other people take for granted. There are special foods they eat and others they avoid. Practices and workouts require a huge commitment, most of their time, and all of their effort. They work while others play. There are no summer vacations for those who "go for the gold." What is it that enables them to bind themselves to such a disciplined course of action? Their hope of winning the prize!

Likewise, in the Christian race those who have a strong hope are able to endure to the end. Believers without hope are like athletes who don't expect to win so they don't try very hard. Patience, which is a component of calm endurance, only operates in those who believe there is an obtainable reward for their efforts.

Moses was able to refuse the riches of Egypt and commit himself to the Israelites "because he was looking ahead to his reward" (Heb. 11:26 NIV). Those who succeed in the Christian life are those who have a sure hope in what awaits them. They know they will spend eternity in heaven with the Lord. This enables them to stay on track all the way to the finish line.

Your life in Jesus Christ isn't a fifty-yard dash; it is a full marathon. The Bible says the prize doesn't go to those who start well but to those who finish well. So maintain your sure hope in Him, and you will be able to finish strong.

God's Word Gives You Hope
Romans 15:1-4

For whatsoever things were written aforetime were written for our learning,
that we through patience and comfort of the scriptures might have hope.
Romans 15:4

People look for hope in many different places. Some consult horoscopes or fortunetellers, while others look to spouses, friends, or government agencies. This verse makes it clear that the Scriptures are where our hope comes from. Of course, God is the God of all hope (Rom. 15:13), but He uses His Word to impart His hope to us.

Many people choose to learn everything the hard way. They don't want to believe God's Word until they have personally experienced victory, but if they don't believe His Word they won't experience victory! By biblical standards this is what we would call foolishness. So what's the solution?

Any problem we face—and even worse problems—have already been encountered by someone in the Bible. The Scriptures graphically record the struggle and victory of those who trusted God. That gives us hope. If God is truly not a respecter of persons (Rom. 2:11), then He will do for us what He has done for others. We can live vicariously through the lives of Bible characters and have hope for situations we encounter.

You don't have to wait until you are in a crisis and under pressure before you gain hope. Through the pages of Scripture, you have "been there, done that," and received the hope and faith necessary to overcome. You don't have to prove God anew every time trouble comes. He has already been tried and proven countless times by saints through the centuries in the Bible. Today, draw on their experiences. It's much better to learn at someone else's expense.

Hope Causes Rejoicing
Romans 12:9-15

Rejoicing in hope; patient in tribulation; continuing instant in prayer.
Romans 12:12

Hope is what causes us to rejoice, yet 1 Peter 1:8 says, "Yet believing, ye rejoice with joy unspeakable and full of glory." Which is it that causes us to rejoice—faith or hope? The answer is both. Hope is just future-tense faith. Hope is believing God for something that's not presently manifest. Faith is believing God to bring something into manifestation now (Heb. 11:1), but hope is faith that sees a future fulfillment. If we really believe God will supply what we hope for, we will rejoice.

If I were to promise you that one year from today I would deposit one million dollars in your bank account, and you believed it, you would rejoice in that hope. Likewise, if you really believe the promises God gives you, you will rejoice in that hope. Those who don't rejoice, don't believe in what they are hoping for.

Expectant joy is a sure sign of hope. Just as you can distinguish real gold from other look-alike metals by its characteristics, you can distinguish real hope by its rejoicing. If rejoicing is not present, then real hope isn't there either.

Our emotions are like the tail of a dog. The tail isn't the dog itself, but you can sure tell what's going on inside a dog by watching its tail. You can learn a lot about yourself by checking your emotions. Are you rejoicing? If you have true biblical hope today, you will be!

God Is a God of Hope
Romans 15:8-13

*Now the God of hope fill you with all joy and peace in believing,
that ye may abound in hope, through the power of the Holy Ghost.
Romans 15:13*

God is a God of hope. With God nothing is impossible. This is foreign to our finite thinking, but there is no situation in which God doesn't have an answer. Just picture the children of Israel at the Red Sea. It looks impossible, but only to those who fail to consider that God can do the unthinkable. Envision Daniel in the lions' den. His accusers thought there was no way out for him, but they didn't know God. Remember the Hebrew children in the fiery furnace? How much more impossible can you get than that? Yet God made a way for each one of them.

Look at the resurrection of Lazarus, Jesus walking on the water, and thousands of other examples in Scripture with God doing the impossible. He is a miracle-working God! Therefore, there is always hope for those who trust in Him. Regardless of where you are now or what situation you find yourself in, God can chart a course for you back into the center of His perfect will. No one is too far gone, and no situation is too desperate for His miraculous intervention.

The first step out of a desperate situation is to hope. Before you can totally believe, you must hope. Faith only produces what you hope for. (Heb. 11:1.) Hope comes from the promises of God. Embrace the hope that God can turn your situation around, and be encouraged in your heart today. Find the miracle you need in the Word and recognize if He did that for them, He will do it for you!

Hope Produces Purity
1 John 3:1-3

Every man that hath this hope in him purifieth himself, even as he is pure.
1 John 3:3

Every time the apostle Paul preached grace, the question arose, "Are you saying that I can sin because I'm under grace?" Paul dealt with that question three times in his writings (Rom. 3:8; 6:1-2,15; Gal. 2:17) with the resounding answer, "God forbid!" Certainly that is not what Paul was communicating, and reading the Gospels will show you that although Jesus was compassionate and merciful to sinners, He always said, "Go, and sin no more" (John 8:11).

The Bible is clear that every born-again person who has the hope of the resurrection is seeking to purify themselves and be pure like Jesus. That doesn't necessarily mean they are accomplishing that goal. There are many things that can make the grace of God have no effect in their lives and keep them in bondage to sin. But it is also an irrefutable fact of Scripture that those who are God's children and are looking forward to that moment when Jesus comes to get them at the resurrection desire to live a life He will look upon with pleasure. This is one of the distinguishing characteristics of true Christians.

This is the same reasoning Jesus used when He said, "For ye know not what hour your Lord doth come" (Matt. 24:42). Keeping the coming of the Lord in view affects our actions. Those Christians who aren't living a pure life have forgotten the promise in God's Word that the day is coming when they will stand before Jesus to give an account for their lives and receive His rewards. Today, remember that this world and everything that affects you is temporary and will fade into obscurity at the appearance of your Lord. You will be able to prioritize much easier.

Hope Overcomes Sorrow
1 Thessalonians 4:13-18

But I would not have you to be ignorant, brethren, concerning them
which are asleep, that ye sorrow not, even as others which have no hope.
1 Thessalonians 4:13

The hope of being reunited with loved ones who have died puts the believer in a different situation than those who don't have that hope. Death is final to the unbeliever. There's no way to bridge the gap between the living and the dead, and those who die are lost forever. Forever is a long, long time…

For the believer, death is just a temporary separation from other loved ones who are believers also. We have the hope of seeing each other again in heaven and dwelling together in the glory of God forever. This hope disarms the ungodly sorrow of the unbeliever. A Christian may still miss someone who has died, but it's not the same hopeless sorrow the unbeliever experiences. That type of sorrow produces death (2 Cor. 7:10), which is why the death of loved ones can tear the living apart.

Anyone can handle separation as long as they know it is not permanent. We see our children off to school, we go to work, and our friends leave for vacation. It would be illogical to grieve as if they had died because they are going to be gone for just a little while. Likewise, those who believe in the resurrection and are assured of eternal life with God in heaven know they will see their loved ones again.

Make sure you view all your situations through hope today. Just as the sorrow of losing someone you love is diminished through the hope that you'll see them again, so the pressures of everyday life are lessened through the hope that God's promises are true. Every negative situation in your life is only temporary!

Vengeance Is God's
Luke 17:2

It were better for him that a millstone were hanged about his neck, and
he cast into the sea, than that he should offend one of these little ones.
Luke 17:2

God takes the persecution of His children personally. In Acts 9:4 when Jesus appeared to Saul on the road to Damascus and spoke to him about his persecution of the saints, Jesus said, "Saul, Saul, why persecutest thou me?" Saul was not directly persecuting Jesus, but he was persecuting His saints. Yet Jesus said, "Why are you persecuting Me?" Judgment against those who persecute God's children will not always come in time to prevent their harm, but as this warning makes very clear, God will avenge His own. (Rom. 12:19.)

Letting God be the one who defends us is a matter of faith. If there is no God who will hold people accountable for their actions, then turning the other cheek would be the worst thing we could do. But if there is a God who promises that vengeance is His and He will repay, then taking matters into our own hands shows a lack of faith in Him and His Word.

We are not to take matters into our own hands and defend ourselves. "Vengeance is mine; I will repay, saith the Lord" (Deut. 32:35,36; Rom. 12:19; Heb. 10:30). Striving to vindicate self actually shows a lack of faith that God keeps His promises. It also indicates spiritual nearsightedness, which is only looking at the present moment instead of seeing things in view of eternity.

Jesus did not come to condemn the world, and He is not holding people's sins against them. We should do the same. If someone has taken advantage of you, betrayed you, or slandered you, remember what Jesus told Saul: "Whatever you say and do to My followers you say and do to Me!" Your heavenly Father knows all, and He will defend you.

The Faith to Forgive
Luke 17:5

And the apostles said unto the Lord, Increase our faith.
Luke 17:5

It is very interesting to note that the apostles asked Jesus to increase their faith after He spoke of forgiveness. They observed all of the wonderful miracles He performed, and yet that never inspired them to ask for greater faith. Truly, walking in love and forgiveness toward others takes as much faith as any miracle we will ever believe for.

The basis of forgiveness is the love and mercy of God. It is only because God first loved and forgave us that we can love and forgive others. If we aren't walking in the love and forgiveness of God for ourselves, we won't minister them to others. He loved us when we were (and sometimes are still) unloveable, and He forgave us before we repented or asked for forgiveness.

The Scriptures admonish us to forgive as Christ has forgiven us. God offered His forgiveness toward us while we were yet sinners, so forgiveness was offered to us unconditionally. Likewise, we are to forgive others their trespasses, just as God has forgiven us our trespasses. We forgive whether the other person repents or wants our forgiveness.

Only God can bring a person to repentance, save them, and restore them. In the meantime, our part is to love them and forgive them the way He loves and forgives us. This takes great faith! At the same time, while we must always love and forgive, the Holy Spirit and the Word may not have us continue the relationship. For example, if our business partner steals from us, not once but several times, after we have forgiven them, we need to sever our partnerships with them. Forgiveness is unconditional, but restoration of a relationship has godly conditions like true repentance and regained trust.

Be wise in your relationships today. You can walk in love and forgiveness and at the same time make decisions about your relationships that will keep you from harm and emotional distress.

Correction or Condemnation?

John 11:5

Now Jesus loved Martha, and her sister, and Lazarus.
John 11:5

It is interesting to note that special mention is made of Jesus loving Martha. This is after the incident recorded in Luke 10:38-42, where Martha was caught up with serving instead of worshipping Jesus. He did not rebuke her but rather exhorted her that her priorities were not in order. When the Lord deals with problem areas in our lives, it is always for our profit—not punishment—and we should not take it as rejection. This is one way to discern God's correction from the devil's accusation: Is it condemning?

God convicts us of sin, but He doesn't condemn us. Conviction is solely for our good, while condemnation includes punishment. Satan condemns Christians, but he does it illegally because Romans 8:1 says, "There is therefore now no condemnation to them which are in Christ Jesus." If we feel condemned, we have received condemnation and shame from the devil. Those things are not from God.

The way the Lord convicts us is through the inner ministry of the Holy Spirit. This is always done in a positive manner that encourages us to turn from sin. The enemy's negative way condemns us for sinning, which makes us feel trapped in it; but the Holy Spirit gently and firmly leads us away from sin and gives us hope and faith to overcome it completely.

Are you under condemnation in some area or maybe several areas of your life? If so, you have allowed yourself to be manipulated and put down by the devil. Today you can be free of all condemnation by simply telling the enemy to go in Jesus' name and declaring you are righteous through the blood of Jesus Christ. Then continue to walk in the power of the Holy Spirit. If you are about to sin or have sinned, He will let you know about it! Just stick with Him, and He will correct you and keep you out from under the devil's condemnation.

Walk in the Light
John 11:9-10

*Jesus answered, Are there not twelve hours in the day? If any man walk
in the day, he stumbleth not, because he seeth the light of this world.*
John 11:9

Jesus compares His decision to return to Judaea to a man traveling during the
day. Daytime travel doesn't guarantee a hazard-free trip, but the light allows
him to see the hazards. It is inevitable that we will stumble in the dark at night.
Likewise, walking in the light of God's direction doesn't mean that there won't
be problems, but the alternative of doing our own thing (walking in darkness) is
guaranteed to get us into trouble.

Jesus was obeying the leading of the Holy Spirit to return to Judaea. He could
see exactly what was going to take place, and He was going to walk in the light
that His Father had given Him. Our decisions should not be based on whether we
will be hurt in some way as a result of our actions, but we must discern God's will
and do it regardless of the cost.

The misconception that, "If God is in it, there will be no problems," is not only
wrong but dangerous. This kind of thinking has caused many people to back off
from what God has told them to do because things didn't go the way they expected.
The Bible tells us we should not be shocked when trials come (1 Peter 4:12), and we
should continue to walk in the light that we have from the Lord, which is His will.

Today you can walk in the light and see clearly as long as you are in God's will.
If you are doing what He has called you to do, even when problems arise, you will
see clearly how to deal with them in a godly way.

Your Resurrected Body
John 11:11-14

Howbeit Jesus spake of his death: but they thought that he had spoken of taking of rest in sleep.
John 11:13

Jesus' friend Lazarus had died. There are many Scriptures where death is referred to as sleep; however, here the disciples thought Jesus was saying Lazarus was only resting. He eventually corrected their misunderstanding by using the word *death*, but that was not His first choice because God's perspective on the death of the human body is different than ours. Physical death is final to people but not to God. There will be a resurrection.

In the same way that a seed is different than the plant that it produces, our resurrected bodies will be different from our physical bodies here on earth. Our glorified bodies will be similar to our physical bodies in appearance. We know this because of what the Scriptures reveal about Jesus' glorified body. He still looked human. He ate food. He retained the scars of the crucifixion nails in His hands, side, and feet. He said He had flesh and bones. Yet He could appear and disappear. Our resurrected bodies will be immortal (not subject to death) and will be like Jesus' resurrected body.

In the same way that your physical body is a miraculous creation, your glorified resurrected body will be even more amazing. It will no longer be subject to disease or death, and it will easily move from heaven to earth and from place to place just like Jesus. You can rest assured that God never serves dessert first! If your physical body is wonderful—or even if you have had chronic problems that you have not been able to fully overcome—you have this great blessing to look forward to. Your resurrected body will be perfect in every way.

Confess God's Truth
John 11:14

Then said Jesus unto them plainly, Lazarus is dead.
John 11:14

At first Jesus spoke of Lazarus being asleep, but now He speaks plainly that Lazarus is dead. He did this because to their carnal minds death was final, but sleep was not. When He said, "Lazarus is dead," it looked like a contrary statement to what He was going to do (raise Lazarus from the dead), but He went on to say in verse fifteen, "I am glad for your sakes that I was not there, to the intent ye may believe." He was referring to raising Lazarus from the dead, which turned His statement of a negative fact (his death) into a positive confession of faith (being raised from the dead).

Many people have been confused over this issue. They will refuse to speak of or acknowledge any situation that is contrary to a promise God has given them. It is certainly desirable to avoid talking about our problems, and there is scriptural precedent for this. (2 Kings 4:20,26.) In this instance, Jesus avoided using a word to describe Lazarus' situation that would have instilled fear into His disciples' hearts, but when they didn't understand, He stated the natural facts.

A true, positive confession doesn't deny natural circumstances. We just refuse to let the natural realm have the last word! We speak the greater spiritual truth, which is what Jesus did, and we should follow His example. Therefore, it is not wrong to acknowledge a physical problem such as sickness, just as long as we acknowledge to an equal or greater degree the spiritual truth, "by whose stripes ye were healed" (1 Peter 2:24).

Don't deny any problems that exist in your life today, but deny those problems the right to continue to exist in your life by confessing your faith in God and His Word.

Live Forever in Him
John 11:26

And whosoever liveth and believeth in me shall never die. Believest thou this?
John 11:26

Some people have interpreted this to mean it is possible to never die physically. Therefore, there are people today who believe they will live until the Second Coming of Jesus, even if that is thousands of years away. Although it is understandable how someone could interpret this verse in that manner, it is doubtful that is what Jesus meant.

First, a doctrine as profound as this would certainly be well documented in other Scriptures. There are some Scriptures that might support this claim, but they do not state it outright themselves. To interpret them to mean that a believer might live until the Second Coming of Christ would be prejudicial, and that is not a sound method of Bible interpretation. Secondly, there is not a single scriptural example of anyone who obtained this. That should make anyone suspect of this teaching. Enoch or Elijah might be cited as examples, but they were translated and taken to heaven. They are not still in their physical bodies on this earth.

Finally, some truths have been lost and then revived throughout church history, but living until Jesus returns is not one of them. No believer has ever done this. Therefore, this Scripture about never dying is generally accepted as referring to our spirits. When we are born again, we receive God's eternal life, and we will never die spiritually again. This promise is made many times in Scripture to every believer.

Because you believe Jesus was raised from the dead and have confessed Him as your Lord, you are saved (Rom. 10:9,10); and that also means your spirit will never die or be eternally separated from God. Your spirit will be communing with His Spirit now and forever! As you face the difficulties of your day, remind yourself that this, too, shall pass; and your future is eternal life, love, and blessing.

Groaning in the Spirit
John 11:33

When Jesus therefore saw her weeping, and the Jews also weeping
which came with her, he groaned in the spirit, and was troubled.
John 11:33

The Greek word translated *groaned* expresses that Jesus was deeply moved, but not necessarily with sorrow. It was more a groan of anger at Satan who had caused all the grief He was seeing around Him. Jesus came to "destroy him that had the power of death, that is, the devil" (Heb. 2:14), and He was grieved to see the pain His enemy had inflicted on those He loved.

This is the type of groaning the Holy Spirit does for us. (Rom. 8:26.) It is not just the Holy Spirit sympathizing with us, but it is the Holy Spirit doing battle for us when we don't know how to pray. In this case, the Holy Spirit used Jesus to do battle against death and the doubt of those present, which would keep Lazarus in the grave.

Everyone who has the Holy Spirit in them has or will have this experience. The groaning of the Holy Spirit is not just grief but righteous anger and resistance against Satan's devices in our lives. Many times Christians don't discern this because they think they are just grieved over their situation, but the Holy Spirit is moving them to get into intercession with Him against their enemy.

Although the groaning of the Holy Spirit inside you is not uttered, you can react to it with audible groans or physical movement of some kind, like someone who is grieving. There is nothing wrong with this as long as you don't confuse your reaction with the Holy Spirit's action. Romans 8:26 says, "The Spirit itself maketh intercession for us with groanings which cannot be uttered." The Holy Spirit is not uttering anything; you are responding to His silent groanings inside you.

The genuine groaning in the Spirit is priceless and always produces good fruit in your life, so when it happens, just flow with the Holy Spirit. Today you can be grateful that you have Him as your Comforter and Teacher in all situations.

Be Loosed!
John 11:44

And he that was dead came forth, bound hand and foot with graveclothes: and his face was bound about with a napkin. Jesus saith unto them, Loose him, and let him go.
John 11:44

Symbolically Lazarus is like many Christians. The Bible speaks of us passing from death unto new life when we get born again, but we bring our grave clothes (bad habits, negative attitudes, and wrong ideas) from our old life and need to be "loosed" from them in order to fully enjoy our new life in Christ. We do this by changing what we think about.

Our emotions, attitudes, and actions follow what we think. When we focus our attention on our problems, they are magnified; when we think on God's provision for our problems, our answer is magnified. Whatever we think upon is going to dominate us. We will either be bound by negative thoughts or loosed by godly thoughts. If we think on depressing things, we will be depressed. If we think on uplifting things, we will be uplifted. If we think on sickness, we will be sick. If we think, *By His stripes I am healed,* we will be healed.

Godly contentment is not dependent upon circumstances, but that is what the world believes. They think contentment will come when their situation is right. That's why so many are depressed. They don't believe they can maintain positive emotions of peace and joy in the midst of any negative circumstances. But the Bible tells us that emotions follow the way we think, and we can be loosed from our old grave clothes by choosing to think on things that are lovely, true, of good report, and so forth. (Phil 4:8.) We respond emotionally to what we think.

You can turn your day around by simply focusing your attention on the blessings and truths of God that are eternal, instead of the circumstances of your physical world that will pass away.

Like Lightning
Luke 17:24-31

For as the lightning, that lighteneth out of the one part under heaven, shineth unto the other part under heaven; so shall also the Son of man be in his day.
Luke 17:24

This verse and the parallel verse in Matthew 24:27 make it very clear that the second return of Jesus will be no secret to anyone. In Matthew's account it is especially clear that Jesus uses the example of lightning so that we would not be deceived by false Christs. Just as lightning is visible to everyone, so the second return of Jesus will be witnessed by the whole world.

We do not have to be afraid of missing His return, anxiously following every report that He has come, and these verses completely destroy claims like that of the Bahài religion that Jesus has secretly come back already. We know this is false because Jesus told us His second coming would be visible to everyone.

Jesus also explained that until the very day of His coming, the world would continue on its present course. People would not discern the signs of His coming just as the people during Noah's day did not realize their impending judgment. (Luke 17:27.) This corresponds to the New Testament prophecies about His coming as a thief in the night. (1 Thess. 5:2; 2 Peter 3:10.) The world will see the "lightning" when He strikes the earth, but by then it will be too late. Jesus stressed that His coming will take unbelievers by surprise.

Jesus pointed out the urgent need to be ready for His return. In the same way a thief comes when people are the least prepared, He will return in a time when people are not looking for Him. There will be a condition of apathy in the latter days that will tend to lull even the faithful to sleep if they don't take heed to His words.

Don't fall asleep! Keep yourself stirred up with the things of God and sensitive to what the Holy Spirit is saying and doing today. Jesus urged you to be spiritually alert so you will be prepared for Him when He comes.

God Answers Prayer
Luke 18:1-8

Saying, There was in a city a judge, which feared not God, neither regarded man.
Luke 18:2

In Jesus' story about the widow and the unjust judge, He did not say that our Father is unjust, nor did He tell us to badger God until we wear Him out and He grants our requests just to get rid of us! Jesus was simply contrasting God's willingness to answer our prayers with the unjust judge's unwillingness to grant this woman's request.

Not only do we have a God who is a just Judge and who will avenge His elect speedily, but also we have Jesus as our Advocate or Attorney. He is always making intercession for us. Our adversary (the devil) is constantly accusing us and misrepresenting God (the Judge) to us. This can cause us to give up and not even plead our case with God because we doubt He will answer us.

To teach that we must pester God until He does what we want Him to do is not good theology. Jesus declared that our Father is not an unjust judge that we have to pressure into doing what is right. Satan has deceived us into thinking God is not willing to answer our prayers, and Jesus countered that deception with this parable. He encouraged us to pray and petition God in the knowledge that He loves us and desires to bless us and grant our requests.

This widow's actions were commendable. She knew what was rightfully hers, and she refused to take *no* for an answer. If you can be that confident and determined when dealing with unjust people, you can be much more confident when dealing with your faithful Father. You can trust Him to always come through for you today.

Righteousness Is a Gift

Luke 18:9-14

And he spake this parable unto certain which trusted in themselves
that they were righteous, and despised other.
Luke 18:9

P eople who are self-righteous often despise others. They cannot compare themselves to Jesus and feel good about themselves, so in order to trust in themselves, they have to constantly compare themselves to other fallible people. This breeds a critical attitude that exalts themselves by debasing others.

No one can ever be righteous in the sight of God through their own righteousness. Our actions benefit us in relationships with people and prevent Satan from having an opportunity against us, but they cannot make us right with God. We must receive His gift of righteousness completely on the basis of faith in what Jesus did for us. This is the truth that this parable is presenting.

Most people are unaware that there are two kinds of righteousness, and only one type of righteousness is acceptable to God. There is our own righteousness, which is based on our own performance; and there is God's righteousness, which is based on Jesus' performance.

God's righteousness is not something that you do but something you received as a gift when you put your faith in Jesus Christ. The moment you believed God raised Him from the dead and said, "Jesus, You are my Lord," the Holy Spirit transformed your spirit and made you righteous—as righteous as Jesus! Celebrate your right standing with God this entire day.

Divorce Is Not God's Best
Mark 10:2-6

And the Pharisees came to him, and asked him, Is it lawful for a man to put away his wife? tempting him.
Mark 10:2

The Pharisees didn't really want to know what Jesus thought about divorce. They didn't value His opinion. They were tempting Him to get entangled in the big dispute of their day, which was between liberal and conservative views on divorce. This was a very emotional issue then, just as it is today, and they thought they had Jesus in a no-win situation. However, as always, Jesus proved to be more than their match and gave them much more than what they asked for.

The Pharisees didn't question whether or not divorce was right; they took the right to divorce for granted. Instead of expounding on acceptable grounds for divorce, Jesus went to the root of the problem and showed that God never intended there to be divorce at all. If they really understood the extent of the one flesh covenant between a husband and wife, they would not be looking for an excuse to get out of marriage. This approach amazed the Pharisees and brought forth the question, "Why did Moses, in the law, make provision for divorce?"

Jesus answered that divorce was permitted but never intended. God allowed something He hated because of the hardness of people's hearts. This was also true of polygamy and slavery. Once a person begins to ask, "How can I get a divorce?" instead of, "How can I keep this marriage together?" their hearts have been hardened, and there is already a serious breach in the marriage.

Jesus came to remove your hard heart and give you a heart of compassion, so don't allow your heart to be hard in any way! Whether or not you are married, decide today that divorce is your enemy, and God's love and compassion will rule your heart and mind. Then you will walk in God's best in all your relationships.

One Flesh
Matthew 19:3-5

And said, For this cause shall a man leave father and mother,
and shall cleave to his wife: and they twain shall be one flesh?
Matthew 19:5

What does it mean for a man and a woman to become "one flesh"? The act of sexual intercourse between a man and a woman produces this one-flesh relationship. Whether or not the man and woman ever cleave to each other in marriage, the physical act still binds them together as one flesh.

This is the reason sexual relationships outside of marriage (whether extramarital or premarital) are so damaging. Whether or not individuals get caught, pregnant, or ever hurt anyone else with their sin, they are doing a lot of damage to themselves. God created us to become one through the sexual act. There is no biblical one-night stand, and that's all there is to it.

It is interesting that Jesus said the only scriptural reason for divorce was fornication. He did not say alcoholism, child abuse, hatred, or so many other things that are certainly wrong in a marriage. That shows us that there is something very powerful that takes place in the physical act of intercourse, and it explains why Satan has exploited what God gave as a blessing. The devil perverts and distorts the sexual relationship to use that power against us.

Becoming one flesh with someone (sexual intercourse) is not marriage. Marriage goes beyond becoming one flesh. This can be seen clearly in John 4:17-18. The woman at the well had five prior husbands, and the man she was currently living with was not her husband. It is certain she was having sexual relations with him, but Jesus didn't call him her husband.

Marriage involves more than sexual relations. It is a covenant or life-long commitment between a man and a woman. They are to be completely devoted to one another in every way—just as you are to Jesus. Meditate on the beauty of marriage as God designed it today, and then enter the reality of your eternal covenant with the Father. It will bring joy to your day!

It's Not What You Do— It's What He Did
Matthew 19:12-20

And behold, one came and said unto him, Good Master, what good thing shall I do, that I may have eternal life?
Matthew 19:16

The rich, young ruler seemed to approach Jesus to seek salvation. He ran, kneeled down to Him, and openly professed Him as a Good Master. What could be wrong with that? First, he acknowledged Jesus as good but not as God. Every major religion of the world acknowledges Jesus existed and that He was a good man, but they won't recognize Him as God. If Jesus was only a good man, He couldn't save anybody.

Jesus didn't come just to show us the way to God; He was the way—the only way—to the Father. (John 14:6.) Jesus had made this point publicly many times, and so He responded to the rich, young ruler accordingly. He said, "God is the only one who is good. You must accept me as God or not at all." Jesus was either who He claimed to be or He was the biggest fraud that ever lived. He has to be one or the other. He cannot be both.

Second, the young man asked what he could do to produce his salvation. He trusted in himself and believed he could accomplish whatever good work Jesus might request. This is completely opposite God's plan of salvation. Jesus obtained salvation for us by substituting for us on the Cross, and He offers salvation to us as a free gift. All we must do is believe and receive.

This rich, young ruler wasn't looking for the Savior; he was trying to be his own savior. Sometimes we get saved by grace through faith in Jesus, and then we try to live our Christian lives saving ourselves. It doesn't work that way! His is the salvation that just keeps on giving. Are you trying to save yourself today? All you have to do is look to Him for everything you need.

God or Money?
Mark 10:21-27

Then Jesus beholding him loved him, and said unto him, One thing thou lackest:
go thy way, sell whatsoever thou hast, and give to the poor, and thou shalt
have treasure in heaven: and come, take up the cross, and follow me.
Mark 10:21

The Bible makes special mention that Jesus loved this rich, young ruler, even after he said he had kept all of God's commands, which was not the truth. Jesus was showing him that he had broken the first commandment, "Thou shalt have no other gods before me" (Ex. 20:3), and the tenth commandment, "Thou shalt not covet" (Ex. 20:17). His tough answer, "Sell whatsoever thou hast, and give to the poor," was not intended to hurt this young man. It was said from a heart of love and intended for his good. This man's money had become his god, and it had to be dethroned before Jesus could become his Lord.

The one thing this young man lacked was faith in Jesus over anything else. Jesus had taught that you cannot serve both God and mammon; if you love one, you will hate the other (Matt. 6:24), and this young ruler loved his wealth. He "was sad...and went away grieved" (v. 22) after Jesus told him to sell all his possessions. As He left, Jesus shook His head and said how hard it was for the rich to be saved. Now, it is the disciples' reaction that is even more interesting! They were astonished and in verse twenty-six asked Him, "Who then can be saved?"

Jesus said, "With men it is impossible, but not with God: for with God all things are possible" (v. 27). We always quote this verse when we need healing or a financial breakthrough, but Jesus was saying that wealthy people need the supernatural intervention of God to get past their trust in money and put all their faith in God.

What are you putting all your trust in today? If you are looking to your paycheck or the stock market as your security, then you can lose your peace and joy at any moment. Put all your trust in Jesus, and not only will you have confidence of eternal salvation, but also nothing will shake you. You will know you are in the loving, capable hands of the Lord.

It's Not What You Do
Matthew 20:1-16

So when even was come, the lord of the vineyard saith unto his steward, Call the labourers, and give them their hire, beginning from the last unto the first.
Matthew 20:8

This parable begins with Jesus' statement that the kingdom of heaven is likened to a man who is a householder (owner of an estate). He goes out early in the morning to hire workers to work in his vineyard for the day. An agreed-upon price was set at a penny, the normal daily wage of a laborer. Later, around 9:00 A.M., the landowner encouraged those standing idle in the marketplace to work in the vineyard, not for a set wage but for "whatsoever is right."

The landowner employed more laborers at noon, at 3:00 P.M., and even some at 5:00 P.M., with just one hour left to work. According to Jewish law, wages must be paid each evening before the sun set. When it came time for the steward to pay the laborers, he paid each man a penny. Those working the entire day murmured, for they supposed they would have received more. They had agreed, however, to work for a penny.

This is a lesson on God's grace. This parable says that it is impossible to earn the generosity of the Master, and neither performing better or longer than someone else makes a difference with Him. The landowner gave the same reward to all who came to work in his vineyard, and God gives the same reward (eternal life) to all who come to Him by faith. Jesus was saying that the benefits of the kingdom are the same for all who have become subject to its King, regardless of what they have done or how long they have been saved.

It makes no difference how long you have known the Lord or the amount of work you have performed in His kingdom, you are going to heaven with the rest of us, and you have the same love, forgiveness, and favor of the Lord that every believer has. Be happy today that you are who you are and are able to do your part, and God is pleased with you.

Share in His Sufferings
Matthew 20:17-25

But Jesus answered and said, Ye know not what ye ask. Are ye able to drink of the
cup that I shall drink of, and to be baptized with the baptism that I am
baptized with? They say unto him, We are able.
Matthew 20:22

The Greek word for *baptize* is *baptizo*. Josephus used the word to describe the city of Jerusalem as being "overwhelmed" or "plunged" into destruction by the Romans, and Plutarch (also first century AD) used this word to refer to a person being "immersed" in the sea. In the Septuagint (the Greek version of the Old Testament), baptizo is used to describe Naaman dipping himself in the Jordan River. (2 Kings 5:14.) From classical Greek to New Testament Greek, the same basic meaning has been retained: "To immerse, submerge, dip, or plunge." Jesus was asking the disciples if they could be plunged and immersed into the same sufferings He would experience.

At this point the disciples had no idea what Jesus would suffer for them. It was inconceivable to them that He would ever be taken and executed by those He had alluded for three years, and He performed miracles on a daily basis. This is a picture of our Christian life as well. We have the Miracle Worker living inside us, and yet we suffer for His name's sake. We lead people to salvation, heal the sick, cast out demons, feed the hungry, clothe the poor—and still we suffer at times.

People talk about us and embarrass us. Sometimes they betray us and steal from us. But our suffering is not like "normal" people suffer because we share His sufferings. Our lives are not our own (1 Cor. 6:19), and like Jesus, we suffer for the joy set before us. (Heb. 12:2.) We know our future is eternity with Him in heaven, and we know that while we are here, we walk in the victory He has already obtained for us in every situation we face.

If you are partaking in the sufferings of the Lord, if people are making your life difficult because you love Him and serve Him, you will share in His rewards. With this in mind, today you can actually shout and take joy in times of suffering for His sake.

Jesus Ransomed You
Mark 10:45

For even the Son of man came not to be ministered unto, but to minister,
and to give his life a ransom for many.
Mark 10:45

Jesus told His disciples many times of His death, but this is the first time He indicated the reason for His death. Now it is clear that His death would be a "ransom," defined in the Greek as a means of purchasing the freedom of someone who had been taken captive. The words *ransom* and *redeem* are used interchangeably in Scripture.

Not only would Jesus pay the price for sin, but also His death would be substitutionary. In 1 Timothy 2:6, the word *ransom* is taken from the Greek word *antilutron*, which means, "a redemption-price." The Greek word *anti* means "in place of." In other words, Jesus would die in our place. He would put His life in the hands of the enemy in order for us to go free.

The price paid for our redemption was the life of Jesus, which was contained in His sinless blood. (Col. 1:14.) According to Hebrews 9:12, this redemption is eternal, is intended to purify us from all iniquity (Titus 2:14), and will inspire us to serve the living God. (Heb. 9:14.) Jesus ransomed us because He loved us, but also because we were created for a purpose.

There was a time when your worst enemy held you captive, an enemy that required a price to be paid before it would set you free. Your enemy was your sin nature, and it would take a miracle to change that! Thank God, Jesus became that miracle for you. He took all the chains and bondage of sin upon Himself so that you could go free. He ransomed you from sin, from death, and from all the power of the devil. That is something you can praise God for today.

Dealing With Unbelievers
Luke 19:1-8

And Zaccheus stood, and said unto the Lord; Behold, Lord, the half of my goods
I give to the poor; and if I have taken any thing from any man by
false accusation, I restore him fourfold.
Luke 19:8

Zaccheus was rich, but Jesus made no demands for him to give away all his goods to the poor as He had with the rich, young ruler. It was obvious Zaccheus had repented and money was no longer his god. Furthermore, he went beyond the requirement of restitution in Mosaic Law by offering to give half of his goods to the poor and to repay fourfold any theft he may have committed.

Zaccheus was a publican, and publicans were hated by their fellow Jews, especially the religious Jews. They were considered the epitome of sinners, and Jewish religious laws prevented devout Jews from keeping company with any publican. To eat with a publican was unthinkable, as that was considered to be partaking of the publican's sins. This is why the people reacted so adversely to Jesus eating with Zaccheus.

Jesus did not eat at Zaccheus' house to participate in his sin but to extend mercy and forgiveness to him. This is always the criterion whereby we can judge whether we should be involved in a certain situation. We must not participate in other people's sins, but the Lord doesn't want us to retreat from the world either. We are the salt of the earth (Matt. 5:13), and to do any good we have to get out of the "salt shaker."

If you can stay right with God in your heart and minister His love to someone, then you are right to associate with sinners. On the other hand, if you find you are being drawn into ungodliness, you need to repent and get back in the Spirit or withdraw. Today be prayerful about all your dealings with those who don't believe.

Be Faithful With a Little
Luke 19:12-13

*He said therefore, A certain nobleman went into a far country to receive
for himself a kingdom, and to return. And he called his ten servants,
and delivered them ten pounds, and said unto them, Occupy till I come.*
Luke 19:12-13

In this parable Jesus told the disciples He was going away, and it would be a long time before He came back to physically rule on the earth. In the meantime, we are His body, and He has given us the authority of His name to occupy until He returns.

The nobleman's servants were called to give an account for what they had done with their lord's money while he was away. These servants represent the followers of Jesus, and we can see that is more than simply not rejecting Him; it is an active commitment to serve Him.

One of the ten servants had served himself and not His master. He did nothing with what his lord had given him. This wicked servant was stripped of what he had, and it was given to the servant who had used his lord's money wisely. This illustrates that the Lord expects us to grow. In fact, in nearly every parable God expects growth or increase.

What was it that this wicked servant didn't have that caused his master to take back the money he had given him? It was faithfulness. Those who are faithful with what God has given them will be given more, and those who are wasteful, will have what God has given them taken away and given to another.

You are here on earth to occupy, and by "occupy" Jesus meant to use wisely everything God has given to you. Live today in the knowledge that one day Jesus will return, and you will have to give an account of what you did with all the gifts and resources He gave you.

Relieving Burdens
Luke 19:23

Wherefore then gavest not thou my money into the bank, that at
my coming I might have required mine own with usury?
Luke 19:23

The Law of Moses attempted to protect both borrower and lender. In Israel, borrowing and lending was not for big, commercial enterprises but rather to help the poor and needy that lacked everyday necessities. It was an act of love in which the lender actually lifted a burden by helping his fellow Israelite through a crisis. However, they were forbidden to charge usury. The Greek word for *usury* means primarily "a bringing forth, birth, or an offspring." It is used metaphorically for the profit received by a lender. Today, we would call it charging interest on a loan.

Although Jesus never condemned interest directly, in general He was hard on the improper attitude toward riches and the oppression of the poor. Making money from someone else's hardship has never been a godly way of doing business, and Deuteronomy 23:19-20 makes it clear that interest was never to be charged to a fellow Israelite. Today, that would be equivalent to never loaning money with interest to a fellow Christian. Borrowing money is not condemned in Scripture unless you interpret Romans 13:8 as speaking of borrowing: "Owe no man any thing, but to love one another."

The Scriptures make it clear that borrowing is not God's best. Deuteronomy 28:12 lists never having to borrow as a blessing, while Deuteronomy 28:44 lists borrowing as a part of the curse of the law. You can know what to do by simply being led by the Spirit. If He impresses you to relieve another person's burden, then do it. If He leads you to borrow and pay off the loan over time, you can do so in confidence knowing He is your Source of all happiness and provision.

What Is Jesus Worth to You?
Mark 14:3-6

*And being in Bethany in the house of Simon the leper, as he sat at meat, there came
a woman having an alabaster box of ointment of spikenard very precious;
and she brake the box, and poured it on his head.*
Mark 14:3

Spikenard was a fragrant plant, and its roots were used in Jesus' day to make an aromatic, costly perfume and ointment. The plant grows in the Himalaya mountains at an elevation of 11,000 to 17,000 feet. For centuries it was used by Hindus as a medicine and perfume and was an actively traded commodity. Because it had to be transported over six thousand miles to reach Palestine, it sold for as much as four hundred denarii per pound (750 dollars per ounce today). That made it more valuable than gold.

This ointment was worth at least two and one-half times more than the thirty pieces of silver Judas received for betraying the Lord, which is why he was so upset. He didn't care about the poor. He the treasurer for Jesus, and he wanted the money the perfume would sell for in his bag so he could steal it.

This story also reveals how each person valued Jesus. Judas valued Jesus at thirty pieces of silver, but to Mary, Jesus was worth everything she had to give. She had seen Jesus raise her brother from the dead, and her heart was overflowing with love and worship.

Judas' reaction to this act of pure worship is typical of the reaction toward worship of many people today. Those who cannot see beyond the monetary or physical realm will be offended by other believers' displays of worship. True worship comes from the heart and involves total surrender of all we have to our Lord and Savior.

What is Jesus worth to you today? When you answer that question, you will know what is most important on your "to do" list!

How Big Are You?
1 Samuel 17:1-11

And there went out a champion out of the camp of the Philistines, named Goliath,
of Gath, whose height was six cubits and a span.
1 Samuel 17:4

When I was a teenager, I went to a Golden Gloves boxing match where there were thousands of people. I noticed a bald-headed man close to the ring who looked like he was standing through the entire match. Then he stood up. This man was a giant! I found out he was called the Corn King Giant and was nine feet, six inches tall. I ran down to see if I could get up next to him. My eyes were level with his belt buckle. It was quite an experience.

Goliath was about that size, twice as tall as David. David probably weighed no more than the coat of mail Goliath wore, but he was bigger on the inside than Goliath was on the outside. We, too, often evaluate things only in physical terms. Physically, Goliath was a giant; but in trusting God, he was a dwarf. David was the giant in faith, and that was what won the battle. Anyone who is strong in believing God is a giant in the spiritual realm and able to do great exploits.

We overestimate and over-emphasize the problems that confront us because we forget who we are in Jesus Christ. David was God's anointed king, but Jesus is the King because He slew the greatest giant mankind has ever faced: sin. Everyone born of God is a spiritual giant with power and authority far greater than anything we encounter from the enemy, the world, or our flesh.

Ask God to open your eyes to who you are in the spirit. You will find that you are a giant who has been intimidated by dwarfs! The truth is that you are as anointed and powerful as David and even more today because you have the Holy Spirit living inside you.

You Have the Covenant
1 Samuel 17:12-30

And David spake to the men that stood by him, saying, What shall be done to the man that killeth this Philistine, and taketh away the reproach from Israel? for who is this uncircumcised Philistine, that he should defy the armies of the living God?
1 Samuel 17:26

There were a number of keys to David's ability to kill Goliath. One of those keys was His knowledge of and faith in God's covenant with the nation of Israel. The Lord had said that no one would be able to stand before His people. (Deut. 11:25.) Goliath was just a man—and an uncircumcised man at that! This meant he didn't have a covenant with God. David placed his faith completely in the promises God had given him through the covenant He had made with Israel.

Every one of the Israelite soldiers had that same covenant, but the covenant is of no effect until it's believed. Hebrews 4:2 says, "For unto us was the gospel preached, as well as unto them: but the word preached did not profit them, not being mixed with faith in them that heard it." David believed God's Word and activated His covenant power in his life.

King Saul tried to give David his armor to wear, but he wouldn't take it. (vv. 38,39.) His trust was in the God of the covenant, not what he wore. And after all, Saul's armor wasn't doing him any good. He was hiding along with the rest of the soldiers. David's faith rested in God alone.

God's covenant with you is a better covenant based on better promises. (Heb. 8:6.) Through the blood of Jesus you are walking in the victory He has already purchased for you. There's simply no reason for you to cower before your enemies. You have God's covenant promises. Activate them by faith today, and watch your giants fall.

The Convicting Power of a Pure Heart

1 Samuel 17:28-30

Eliab his eldest brother heard when he spake unto the men; and Eliab's anger
was kindled against David, and he said, Why camest thou down hither?
and with whom hast thou left those few sheep in the wilderness?
I know thy pride, and the naughtiness of thine heart; for thou
art come down that thou mightest see the battle.
1 Samuel 17:28

There was more to Eliab's anger than believing David had abandoned their father's sheep to see the battle. Eliab was the oldest son, and he was there when Samuel passed him by and anointed David. (1 Sam. 16:13.) God had chosen his younger brother to be king, so he was jealous of David.

"Only by pride cometh contention" (Prov. 13:10). Eliab's love for himself caused him to lash out at his younger brother. He was afraid because if David was right, then Eliab was a coward. He had to condemn David's words, or they would condemn him! This is exactly why the self-righteous religious people were always attacking Jesus. His pure heart of wisdom and compassion put them under conviction all the time.

Purity of heart toward God causes religious persecution. If you throw a rock into a pack of dogs, the one that yelps the loudest is the one that got hit. So it is with persecution. Those who protest the loudest are the ones feeling the pressure of the Holy Spirit's conviction when they hear a believer speak the truth.

Before you can defeat the giants in your life, you must withstand the critical remarks of others—especially your own family. If David hadn't overcome his older brother's criticism, he never would have overcome Goliath. If Jesus had compromised to please the religious Jews, He never would have gone to the Cross and defeated sin and death for us.

Understanding that persecution is actually a defensive act of a person under conviction will help you keep your focus and fight the real battles today.

When No One Is Looking
1 Samuel 17:31-47

Thy servant slew both the lion and the bear: and this uncircumcised Philistine shall be as one of them, seeing he hath defied the armies of the living God.
1 Samuel 17:36

In Matthew 6:18, Jesus said that what we do in secret God will reward publicly. This was the secret to David's success with Goliath. David had faith that God would enable him to kill Goliath and win the war because prior to this both a lion and a bear had attacked his father's sheep, and he had killed them both. No one was around. He wasn't showing off or trying to act brave. In fact, he could have run and no one would have known! But he chose to stand in faith and believe God.

It was David's victories over the lion and the bear that gave him the assurance and faith that God would also be with him to conquer Goliath. After all, the nation of Israel was His people—much more precious to God than a few sheep. David learned to trust God when no one was looking so that when they were looking, his faith was strong and established, and he was doing the right thing for the right reasons.

Many people dream of slaying some giant of a problem or doing some great exploit, but they aren't faithful in life's everyday trials because they aren't doing things for God. They are only doing things that will promote themselves. They are waiting for the grandstands to be full before they give it all they have. But those who don't win the local trials never make it to the Olympics.

David's faithfulness in the relatively small things was what enabled him to be ruler over much. (Luke 16:10.) Be faithful in the trials you face today, and your faith will be strong and your heart in the right place for when the big tests come your way.

Make Sure They're Dead
1 Samuel 17:48-58

*Therefore David ran, and stood upon the Philistine, and took his sword, and
drew it out of the sheath thereof, and slew him, and cut off his head therewith.
And when the Philistines saw their champion was dead, they fled.*
1 Samuel 17:51

We fight giants every day, but we often make the mistake of quitting before the battle is complete. Instead of destroying our enemies, we just chase them out of sight and leave them to return and fight another day. David declared, "I have pursued mine enemies, and overtaken them: neither did I turn again till they were consumed" (Ps. 18:37). Never was that illustrated in David's life more than when he fought Goliath.

David had a holy hatred for his enemy. He wasn't just trying to scare him off; he was out to kill him. David wasn't tentative; he ran toward Goliath! He boldly slung the stone, and God made sure it hit its mark. Goliath, the giant of Gath, fell on his face before both armies. But David wasn't through yet.

The Scriptures don't say, so Goliath may or may not have been dead. The Philistines, who were on the mountains watching, couldn't tell for sure; so David left no doubt. He climbed up on top of the giant, drew Goliath's sword, and cut off his head. Once David held the giant's head in his hand, there was no doubt in anyone's mind who was dead and who had won.

The Bible says that Jesus did the same thing to the devil. "And having spoiled principalities and powers, he made a shew of them openly, triumphing over them in it" (Col. 2:15). Today you walk in the victory He already obtained for you. If you have been battling something and have obtained some relief, don't quit until you are experiencing everything Jesus died to give you.

All One in Christ
John 12:20-23

And Jesus answered them, saying, The hour is come, that the Son of man should be glorified.
John 12:23

Philip and Andrew had just brought word to Jesus that certain Greeks or Gentiles were seeking Him at the feast. He had ministered to other Gentiles, but this is the first time that the Gentiles came specifically to seek Him instead of what He could do. Apparently, this was an added signal to Jesus that His time had come and He could no longer confine His ministry to the Jews. Therefore, He made statements about His death and glorification that would break down the middle wall of partition between the Jew and the Gentile.

There was a physical wall of partition that symbolized this division in the Jerusalem Temple. The Gentiles could come into a designated area of the Temple known as the Court of the Gentiles, but a stone wall, about five-feet high, stopped them from going farther. A sign standing before the wall stated, "No man of another nation is to enter, and whosoever is caught will have himself to blame for his death!"

Many regulations and rules separated Jews and Gentiles for centuries, but Christ's work on the Cross abolished that barrier by removing the Law. "For he himself is our peace, who has made the two one and has destroyed the barrier, the dividing wall of hostility, by abolishing in his flesh the law with its commandments and regulations. His purpose was to create in himself one new man out of the two, thus making peace" (Eph. 2:14,15 NIV).

In the New Testament church, "Ye are all one in Christ Jesus" (Gal. 3:28). The world tries to bring people together in all kinds of ways, but only Jesus destroyed that barrier and made people one through the indwelling of the Holy Spirit. Today you can celebrate the fact that you are a part of the body of Christ, the "one new man," made up of all kinds of people through centuries of time.

Choose to Believe
John 12:37-40

Therefore they could not believe, because that Esaias said again, He hath blinded
their eyes, and hardened their heart; that they should not see with their eyes,
nor understand with their heart, and be converted, and I should heal them.
John 12:39-40

No one has ever been denied the opportunity to accept salvation. (Titus 2:11.) The Word of God declares, "Whosoever shall call upon the name of the Lord shall be saved" (Rom. 10:13); "Behold, I stand at the door, and knock: if any man hear my voice, and open the door, I will come in to him, and will sup with him, and he with me" (Rev. 3:20); and "Whosoever will, let him take the water of life freely" (Rev. 22:17).

Mark 6:5 says, "He could there do no mighty work, save that he laid his hands upon a few sick folk, and healed them." In that instance, it is evident that the reason Jesus couldn't do any miracles was not because He didn't possess the power but because He chose not to use that power against a person's will. He couldn't perform the mighty works because of His decision to uphold our freedom of choice.

Furthermore, these Jews could not believe because they rejected Jesus. They could not believe because they chose not to believe. "They stumbled at the stumblingstone" (Rom. 9:32), which was Jesus.

Isaiah did not predestine people to not be saved; he just saw that very few would receive the report (Isa. 53:1) about the Messiah. They would be kept from the knowledge of salvation because they rejected Him in whom all the treasures of wisdom and knowledge are found. (Col. 2:3.)

Today, be careful what you choose to receive and reject. Reject any thought or word that opposes God's Word, but gladly receive everything spoken in the name and power of Jesus. Then you will see, understand with your heart, be changed, and be whole.

The Fig Tree
Mark 11:13-24

And Jesus answered and said unto it, No man eat fruit of thee hereafter for ever.
And his disciples heard it.
Mark 11:14

Jesus was hungry and saw a fig tree that already had leaves, which led Him to believe it had figs. But that wasn't the case. There were no figs. In response, Jesus cursed the fig tree with His words, saying, "No man eat fruit of thee hereafter for ever."

Jesus talked to the fig tree. This verse says, "Jesus answered and said unto it." That means the fig tree had been talking to Him. Some people think this is weird, but things talk to us all the time. Your checkbook tells you that you don't have enough money to make it. Your body tells you that you're sick. Situations speak negative things to us without saying a word. Most of us pick up on these negative comments and speak them right out of our mouths, thereby giving them power over our lives.

Jesus did the right thing. He used His words to silence the hypocrisy of this fig tree. It professed fruit by having leaves, but it didn't possess it. It had spoken something to Him that it couldn't deliver. Jesus said that it would never yield fruit to anyone ever again—and it didn't! It immediately died at its roots, and its death was visible the next day. (Mark 11:20.)

Jesus' disciples were overwhelmed with this miracle and questioned Him about it. He said that this was the power of words. Anyone who speaks in faith, without doubting in their heart, will have whatsoever they say. This works in the positive or negative.

Whenever a negative circumstance starts speaking to you today, talk back to it in faith, and watch the situation change.

Faith That Moves Mountains
Matthew 21:18-22

Jesus answered and said unto them, Verily I say unto you, If ye have faith, and doubt not, ye shall not only do this which is done to the fig tree, but also if ye shall say unto this mountain, Be thou removed, and be thou cast into the sea; it shall be done. And all things, whatsoever ye shall ask in prayer, believing, ye shall receive.
Matthew 21:21-22

What is different about mountain-moving faith? For one thing, God's kind of faith understands and uses authority. Notice that Jesus said we should speak to the mountain. Most people are praying to God about their mountain, but the Lord said we should speak directly to it. This reflects our God-given authority.

Once I had a toothache that bothered me for two weeks. I prayed and asked God to heal it many times. As I was traveling, I listened to a tape where the minister was talking about speaking to the mountain instead of speaking to God. It dawned on me that I hadn't done that. I hadn't used my authority in Jesus' name. I was asking God to do something that He told me to do!

When I got to my hotel, I looked in the mirror, stuck my finger into my mouth, pointed to my tooth, and said, "You are healed in the name of Jesus. Pain, leave right now!" In less than ten minutes all the pain was gone, and I never had another problem with that tooth.

Mountain-moving faith believes that God has already provided healing for us. In Jesus' name you can speak directly to the problem instead of speaking to God about the problem. Use your God-given authority, and speak to your mountain today. If you believe, it will move.

Forgiveness and Prayer
Matthew 21:20-22; Mark 11:20-26

And when ye stand praying, forgive, if ye have ought against any:
that your Father also which is in heaven may forgive you your trespasses.
Mark 11:25

There are qualifications for believing and receiving, and one of them is that we forgive those who hurt and offend us or someone else. Harboring unforgiveness in our hearts will keep our prayers from being answered.

We should forgive others as quickly as we make the decision to pray. When we stand praying, we must forgive anyone we are holding something against. Why is this so important? God dealt with all men's offenses by placing sin upon Jesus, who was judged in place of every sinner of all time. To demand that others must earn our forgiveness when we did not earn ours is not being like Jesus. He forgave us, and we should forgive others.

It is doubtful that a person who refuses to forgive has ever experienced forgiveness. This is comparable to the servant Jesus talked about in Matthew 18:23-35. He was forgiven a debt of over 3 million dollars and yet he refused to forgive his fellow servant who owed him 3,000 dollars. Jesus called him "wicked" (v. 32). Can you see why God cannot answer our prayers if we are acting like this wicked servant and refusing to forgive others the way we have been forgiven?

The forgiveness you have received from the Lord is infinitely greater than any forgiveness you will ever be asked to extend to others. Freely forgive as you have been forgiven, and then you can pray confidently in faith, and God will hear and answer your prayers.

Made Right With God
Matthew 21:23-30; Mark 11:27-33; 12:1-2; Luke 20:1-9

But what think you? A certain man had two sons; and he came to the first, and said,
Son, go work to day in my vineyard. He answered and said, I will not: but
afterward he repented, and went. And he came to the second, and said
likewise. And he answered and said, I go, sir: and went not.
Matthew 21:28-30

There were many ways Jesus showed the religious leaders that they were not really right with God. In this parable He revealed who truly did the will of God. It was not the son who talked about it; it was the son who may have begun in rebellion but then repented and did his Father's will.

These leaders had a form of godliness like this second son, but they were not doing the will of God. The publicans and harlots had no form of godliness, but when confronted with the preaching of John, many of them repented and began to do the will of God like the first son in the story.

These religious Jews, who sat in the seat of Moses, disqualified themselves from being God's representatives here on earth because of their hypocrisy and hard hearts. Even the publicans and harlots who repented were ahead of them. There is no sin more frequent among religious people than that of self-righteousness: they honor the Lord with the mouth when their hearts are far from Him. (Matt. 15:8.)

Terrible sinners were repenting and entering the kingdom of God ahead of the very religious Jews because they knew they were sinners and put their faith in Jesus. One of the deadliest things about religious self-righteousness is the deception that we will be saved because of our good deeds. We cannot save ourselves regardless of how good we act.

Remember how you were saved and who saved you. If you stay humble, knowing you are right with God because of Jesus, instead of being continually under pressure to prove yourself right with God, your heart will be filled with joy and praise for the One who has already made you right with God.

Your Life Belongs to God
Matthew 22:20-22

And he saith unto them, Whose is this image and superscription? They say unto him,
Caesar's. Then saith he unto them, Render therefore unto Caesar the things
which are Caesar's; and unto God the things that are God's.
Matthew 22:20-21

The image on the denarius, the only small silver coin acceptable for imperial tax payments, was probably that of Tiberius Caesar (reigned AD 14-37). The inscription on one side of the coin read, "Tiberius Caesar Augustus, Son of the Divine Augustus," and the reverse side read, "Chief Priest." This inscription was a claim to divinity and, as emperor, the right to be worshiped.

The religious Jews had tried many times to trap Jesus on issues of the Law and had always failed. Now they approached Him about paying taxes, hoping His answer would give them the opportunity to deliver Him to Pilate for prosecution. They reasoned any answer He gave would be wrong. If He approved of the Roman taxes, then He would lose popularity with the masses. If He spoke against the Roman taxes, then the Jews would hand Him over to the Roman government and Pilate would dispose of Him. It looked like they finally had Jesus in their power.

Jesus, however, answered with such simple wisdom that these Pharisees and Herodians were caught in their own trap and made to look like fools. He declared, "Render to Caesar the things that are Caesar's, and to God the things that are God's" (Mark 12:17). People are made in God's image, so they must render to God the things belonging to God (our lives) and to Caesar the things belonging to Caesar (his money and other benefits of his rule).

People today tend to grumble a lot about paying taxes and bills, but even Jesus saw the need for these things. When you know that God is your source and your life belongs to Him, then you want to give to and bless others like He does. The next time you pay your taxes and bills, honor God and do it joyfully, knowing you are contributing to the lives of others.

The Resurrection Power
Matthew 22:23

The same day came to him the Sadducees, which say that there is no resurrection,
and asked him.
Matthew 22:23

The resurrection is a major theme of New Testament teaching. Of the thirteen sermons in the book of Acts, eleven stress or imply the resurrection. To understand the power of the resurrection, we first have to understand how God made us. We consist of three parts—spirit, soul, and body. (1 Thess. 5:23.) A fallen human being is spiritually dead (separated from God), and their soul is darkened by sin. A born-again believer is spiritually alive (reunited with God), and their soul is being transformed by the light of God's Word. Spirit and soul are immortal, so the believer will die physically and their spirit/soul will go to heaven; while the unbeliever will die physically and go to hell.

The bodies of both the believer and the unbeliever are mortal. At death, every person's body goes through the decomposition process and returns to its original elements. At the resurrection, all departed spirit/souls will be called forth from either heaven or hell. God will supernaturally raise, reassemble, and unite the material elements of their bodies with their spirit/souls. Thus they will be completely reconstituted by God—spirit, soul, and body. Everyone will be resurrected, some to eternal life with God in heaven, and some to eternal damnation in the lake of fire.

The hope of the believer is the resurrection unto eternal life with God. Their natural, earthly, corrupt body will be raised and fashioned into a heavenly, glorious, immortal body. This is the completion of everything that has been purchased for us by the blood of Jesus. The transformation from this physical condition to our glorified bodies will be a huge difference, but the power of God can accomplish it easily.

If the Lord can work the miracle of resurrection, then surely He can heal your body and free you from other bondages. As you pray for your miracle today, let the hope of the resurrection build your faith.

Marriage Is for This Life
Luke 20:27-40

Therefore in the resurrection whose wife of them is she? for seven had her to wife.
And Jesus answering said unto them, The children of this world marry,
and are given in marriage.
Luke 20:33-34

I t is doubtful that the situation the Sadducees related ever took place. It is more probable they were stating a hypothetical case to discredit the resurrection, which they did not believe was scriptural. If you accept their basic supposition (marriage continues in heaven), then their reasoning was correct. It would not be possible to administer marriage in heaven after having multiple mates on earth. Their reasoning wasn't flawed, but the facts their reasoning was based on were not scriptural.

The Bible speaks of two becoming "one flesh" in marriage, and angels are not flesh. Paul said, "Flesh and blood cannot inherit the kingdom of God" (1 Cor. 15:50). Therefore, marriage is an earthly institution limited to flesh and blood mortals and will not exist in heaven. Marriage, as is death, is temporary for mortals while they are on earth. This is why a person whose mate has died is free to remarry. Marriage pertains only to this life.

That is not to say that a couple who have loved each other deeply here on earth will love each other less in heaven. They will love each other infinitely more, but it will be God's agape love, not human romantic love, and it will not be limited to just one person. We can be sure heaven will surpass any expectations we may have so that no one will be disappointed!

Today, many people use logical reasoning to try to discredit certain doctrines of God's Word, but Jesus said they are in error because they do not know the Scriptures. (Mark 12:24.) Only reasoning based on Scripture has any merit. When you decide what you believe concerning any doctrine of the church, make sure you know what the Bible really says about it. Then you will be standing on a firm foundation for your life.

The Two Greatest Commands
Matthew 22:34-46

Master, which is the great commandment in the law? Jesus said unto him, Thou shalt love the Lord thy God with all thy heart, and with all thy soul, and with all thy mind. This is the first and great commandment. And the second is like unto it, Thou shalt love thy neighbour as thyself.
Matthew 22:36-39

Jesus revealed that all of the Old Testament laws were designed to instruct us how to love God and love others. Therefore, the two commands that dealt directly with loving God and others (Lev. 19:18; Deut. 6:5) were the most important.

The religious leaders had become so obsessed with keeping every minor detail of the law that they had lost sight of its ultimate purpose. They neither loved God nor their fellow man, yet they thought they were keeping the Law. The same thing is happening today. Some of the cruelest acts have been done in the name of the Lord by those who thought they were defending God's commandments. However, if we violate one of the two greatest commandments in an effort to enforce some other commandment, we are misapplying God's Word just as these religious Jews were.

The Old Testament Law and the New Testament concept of grace compel us to love God and all people. However, the Old Testament Law motivated men to love God and other people through fear of punishment if they failed to comply, whereas the grace given to us in the New Testament is to love others unconditionally as God loves us.

It is possible to act holy but not love God or people, but it is impossible for God's love not to produce holiness in a person. Look at all your relationships through the eyes of God's unconditional love today. As you love, you will be holy.

You Have God's Wisdom
Matthew 23:1-39

Then spake Jesus to the multitude, and to his disciples.
Matthew 23:1

Matthew 23 contains the worst rebuke of the Jewish religious leaders Jesus gave to any group. He chastised them for their hypocrisy, hard hearts, and total lack of understanding of God, His Word, and His ways. Matthew tells us He did this publicly before the multitude, the very people the hypocrites wanted to impress and control.

Jesus had faced many prior battles with the scribes and Pharisees. On this particular day, the encounter started with the chief priests and elders challenging Jesus' authority. He stunned them by replying with a question that challenged their authority. He then used three parables to illustrate that the leaders of the Jews had rejected the rule of God in their lives, despite their pious religious acts.

The Pharisees countered by tempting Jesus with a question about paying taxes to the Roman government. Then the Sadducees tried to stop Jesus with a question about the resurrection. Finally, a lawyer tried to snare Him with a question about the greatest commandment. Jesus did so well in each test that "no man after that durst ask him any question" (Matt. 22:46).

As a believer you may have encountered unbelievers who tried to trap you as these religious people tried to trap Jesus. The devil will use these people to try to get you to doubt what you believe. But the Bible says that Jesus is "made unto us wisdom" (1 Cor. 1:30), and the same Spirit that raised Jesus from the dead dwells in you. (Rom. 8:11.) That means you can answer any question anybody throws at you! Be confident today that you can remain strong in your faith no matter what question comes up.

God Recognizes Our Sacrifices
Mark 12:41-44

*And Jesus sat over against the treasury, and beheld how the people cast money
into the treasury: and many that were rich cast in much. And there came
a certain poor widow, and she threw in two mites, which make a farthing.*
Mark 12:41–42

The treasury that is spoken of here is a place located in the Women's Court
that was in the Temple complex but was not part of the Temple itself.
Women were not allowed in the Temple.

Jesus used this incident to teach His disciples a very important lesson. God's
promises concerning giving are an assurance that the widow's offering pleased God
and that He blessed her for it, but the widow did not hear Jesus' commendation.
There is no indication that she ever knew anyone had known the extent of her
sacrifice.

Likewise, there are times when you may feel that no one knows or appreciates
your financial sacrifices. This might not just be your sacrificial giving to the church
or to a ministry but to the people in your life. However, just as surely as Jesus saw
this woman's gift and knew the sacrifice involved, your heavenly Father takes note
of your smallest gift and one day will reward you.

Do not compare what you give with what someone else gives whether it is
money or time or service. Remember that God looks at your heart. Take joy when
you have the opportunity to give because in that way you are being like your Father.
Today, be a giver just like He is a giver.

Guard Against Deception
Matthew 24:3-5

And Jesus answered and said unto them, Take heed that no man deceive you.
Matthew 24:4

Deception can be avoided or Jesus would not have said, "Take heed that no man deceive you." Satan can only deceive those who allow him to do it. Ephesians 6:11 tells us, "Put on the whole armor of God, that ye may be able to stand against the wiles of the devil." God said the "whole armor." Many Christians have been running around with only the helmet of salvation on. There is more to overcoming the devil than just being saved. We have to understand our righteous position in the Lord. We also must possess faith, know the Word, and understand the gospel of peace.

The Christian life is a constant struggle against Satan who is trying to corrupt us. Most of us are aware of the warfare but don't know where the warfare is occurring. The battle is in our minds. Just as the serpent didn't come against Eve with brute force but used words to deceive her, Satan tries to corrupt us through thoughts contrary to the Word of God. His original tactic was deception, and that is still his method of operation today.

One of the characteristics of children is that they are easily deceived. They are gullible. In order for a believer to move from childhood to sonship, they must develop spiritual discernment. This comes from being grounded in the Word of God. The way to recognize deception is not to analyze all the false claims but to become so familiar with what is genuine that a counterfeit will be easily recognizable.

Today if you abide in God's Word and continue to walk according to God's Word, you will not be deceived. You will easily spot any thought or idea that is contrary to what you know of the truth.

Base Your Relationships on God
Matthew 24:12

And because iniquity shall abound, the love of many shall wax cold.
Matthew 24:12

The only reason an abundance of iniquity would make anyone's love for the Lord wax cold would be if they were not separated from that iniquity. Lot was a righteous man whose soul was vexed from day to day by hearing and seeing the unlawful deeds of the ungodly. (2 Peter 2:8.)

We have to deal with the world's system and those in it, but we need to be careful and maintain proper distance. We should shun relationships with those who influence us negatively more than we influence them positively. Marriage is one area where this principle is especially true. There is no closer union in life than the marriage relationship. A believer who marries an unbeliever is directly violating Scripture and is toying with disaster. (2 Cor. 6:14.) The Lord should be the most important person in our lives. How could we possibly become one with a person who doesn't love our Lord?

It is folly to think that after marriage an unbelieving spouse will accept the Lord. Although it does happen, it cannot be guaranteed. In fact, statistics are overwhelmingly against this happening. However, if you are in this situation and are believing God for your spouse to be saved, you must have the support of other believers in your church so you can stand strong and continue growing in the Lord yourself. You cannot allow your unbelieving spouse to keep you from growing spiritually. No one will benefit from you backsliding just to please your mate!

Being unequally yoked with unbelievers just doesn't work. Believers and unbelievers are as different as righteousness and unrighteousness, light and dark, and Jesus and the devil. One has faith and the other has none. I hope you have avoided this if you are already married. If you are not married, decide today that you will not fall for this deception.

Your Nature in Christ
Matthew 24:13

But he that shall endure unto the end, the same shall be saved.
Matthew 24:13

Here Jesus teaches that the believer must persevere in faith to receive complete salvation. Salvation is a gift that cannot be earned or maintained by our own works. It has to be received by faith, and there is effort on our part to maintain that faith.

Holiness will not produce relationship with God, nor will a lack of holiness make God turn away from us. He deals with us according to our faith in Jesus, not our performance. Holiness will keep Satan from stealing our faith, while a lack of holiness is an open invitation for the devil to do his worst. A person who wants to endure to the end cannot live a lifestyle that permits Satan free access to them.

Although God is not imputing our sins unto us, we cannot afford the luxury of sin because it allows Satan to have access to us. When a Christian does sin and allows the devil an opportunity to produce death in their life, the way to stop this is to confess the sin. God is faithful and just to take the forgiveness that is already present in our born-again spirits and release it in our flesh (1 John 1:9) thereby removing Satan and his strongholds.

Holiness is a by-product of an intimate relationship with God; it does not produce relationship with God. It is the nature of a Christian to want to do right. If I were to ask you, "Do you really want to sin?" You would say no because you are living from your new nature of God's righteousness within. Remember this truth today whenever the devil comes to tempt you, and keep the faith!

Resist the Temptation of Sin
Luke 22:3

Then entered Satan into Judas surnamed Iscariot, being of the number of the twelve.
Luke 22:3

Some people have speculated that Judas betrayed Jesus in an effort to force Jesus into a confrontation with the Roman government. Then He would have had to use His supernatural power in self-defense and overthrow the Romans thereby giving independence back to the nation of Israel. This idea is based mainly on Judas' response when he saw that Jesus was condemned. He "repented himself" (Matt. 27:3), implying that the condemnation of Jesus was never his intent. However, the Bible does not say Judas possessed noble virtues. He was simply a thief.

This verse makes it very clear that Satan entered into Judas and was responsible for putting the betrayal of Jesus into Judas' heart. We can be assured that Satan's only purpose in motivating Judas to betray Jesus was to steal, kill, and destroy. (John 10:10.) Moreover, that Satan possessed Judas does not acquit Judas of the responsibility for his actions. The devil goes about seeking whom he may devour. (1 Peter 5:8.) He cannot devour just anyone. They have to give place to him. By being a thief, Judas gave Satan access to him. He may have never intended to betray Jesus when he began to steal from Him, but once he submitted to Satan in thievery, it was hard to stop.

Sin cannot be controlled. You cannot sin "just a little." Sin is sin in God's eyes, and the more you give in to it, the more it captures you. In order to resist the devil and overcome his temptations to sin, you must first submit yourself to God. (James 4:7.) Once you have submitted to Him, the Holy Spirit will supernaturally empower you to say no to whatever the enemy is trying to do in your life.

Communion Is Sacred
Luke 22:19

*And he took bread, and gave thanks, and brake it, and gave unto them, saying,
This is my body which is given for you: this do in remembrance of me.*
Luke 22:19

The bread of communion symbolizes the body of Jesus, which was broken for us through His sufferings. He not only died for us on the Cross, but also He bore thirty-nine stripes on His back by which we are healed. (1 Peter 2:24.) Partaking of communion should remind us of the emotional and physical salvation Jesus provided for us.

The Lord's Supper comes from a part of the Passover meal that was celebrated only once a year. However, the early Christian church took communion weekly and sometimes daily. There is no specific frequency of the Lord's Supper prescribed in Scripture.

As we take communion, we are solemnly remembering the Lord's death, as well as our union with Him in that death. We died with Him and then rose with Him to the eternal life we now enjoy. (Col. 1:12.) Partaking of the bread is partaking of healing and wholeness because His body was broken so ours could be whole. Partaking of the wine is partaking of His righteousness, which His shed blood imparted to us.

Communion is one of the most powerful professions of your faith in the redemptive work of Jesus, and 1 Corinthians 11:27 tells us that you should not take it lightly. Today, remember the miraculous way Jesus saved you and transformed your life. And whenever you have the opportunity or feel the unction to take communion, make it the special time with the Lord He intended it to be.

Let God Minister to You
John 13:5-8

Peter saith unto him, Thou shalt never wash my feet. Jesus answered him,
If I wash thee not, thou hast no part with me.
John 13:8

Peter's refusal to let Jesus wash his feet came from the knowledge that he was totally unworthy to have the sinless Son of God serve him like a common servant. Peter was correct in his assessment of his relative worth, but what he missed was that God doesn't minister to us because of our worth but because of His love.

Even though Peter's attitude looked holy and humble, he was actually resisting God's will and being proud. Pride is being self-centered and self-willed instead of God-centered and submitted to God's will. Peter should have been humble enough to know that Jesus knew what He was doing! Instead, he thought he knew better.

This same pride causes many Christians to refuse to let God bless them, thinking they are unworthy of His favor. While it is true that their actions don't warrant His goodness, they will receive more of the Lord's blessings when they receive them as an expression of His love and grace toward them.

Misguided humility is every bit as damaging as exaggerated pride. Peter wanted to serve Jesus, but he was too proud to be served by Jesus. Jesus was telling Peter that unless he received His ministry to him, Peter would be unfit to serve Him. Symbolically He was saying, "Peter, you cannot cleanse yourself. You must allow Me to do it."

You cannot cleanse yourself or others. Be totally dependent on the work of God's grace in your life, and He will cleanse you and equip you to minister to others. Before you can be the blessing you desire to be to God or to the people around you, you have to let God be the blessing to you that He desires to be.

Love Comes First
John 13:35

By this shall all men know that ye are my disciples, if ye have love one to another.
John 13:35

Jesus didn't say that all men would know we are His disciples by our doctrine, our rituals, our hatred for sin, or even by the way we express our love for God. He said very clearly that the one characteristic that would cause the world to identify us as His followers was our love for one another.

This same night, the Lord prayed to His Father using this same thought saying, "That they all may be one; as thou, Father, art in me, and I in thee, that they also may be one in us: that the world may believe that thou hast sent me" (John 17:21). The only way that the body of Christ will be one as the Father and Jesus are one is through God's kind of love.

According to Jesus, unity of believers through a genuine God-kind of love is the greatest tool for evangelism that the church has or ever will have. The early church didn't have the massive organizational structures that we see today or the ability to travel anywhere in the world in just a matter of hours. They certainly did not come close to spending as much money, in proportion to us, to spread the Gospel. Yet, the pagans of Thessalonica said of Paul and his companions, "These that have turned the world upside down are come hither also" (Acts 17:6). They had evangelized the known world in less than thirty years.

Before we can ever fulfill the great commission of Matthew 28:19-20, there must be a revival of love in the church, where doctrine and ritual take a back seat to love for one another. Today, ask the Lord to show you how you can express your love to your brothers and sisters.

Peter's Faith Did Not Fail
Luke 22:31-61

But I have prayed for thee, that thy faith fail not: and when thou art converted, strengthen thy brethren.
Luke 22:32

Jesus informed Peter that Satan desired to sift him as wheat. (v. 31.) We know through Scripture that later that night Peter denied knowing Jesus three times. (Luke 22:54-62.) It looked like the devil succeeded even after Jesus prayed for him. Did Jesus pray a prayer that wasn't answered? Certainly not!

In this verse, Jesus also spoke of what Peter should do when he was converted. Therefore, He foresaw Peter's denial, prayed that his faith wouldn't fail, and it didn't. It is possible to fail in our actions but not fail in our hearts.

That night Peter said he would follow Jesus to the death. (v. 33.) He proved it by trying to defend the Lord against the Roman soldiers who came to arrest Him. (Luke 22:50,51.) This was a suicide mission. If Jesus had not intervened, Peter would have been killed. There is no doubt Peter's heart was committed to Jesus.

Just like many of us, after his great show of courage Peter was unprepared for the spiritual battle he encountered later. If the war had been in the physical realm, with fists and swords, he would have fought to the death. But he didn't know how to stand spiritually. Peter denied the Lord with his mouth but not in his heart. He proved this by the remorse he experienced after seeing Jesus turn and look at him. (Luke 22:61.)

Maybe you have failed the Lord some way in your actions. Jesus has prayed for you that your faith would not fail. Knowing this, you can get up again, just like Peter, and serve the Lord with all your heart in whatever you do. Remember, God used Peter to preach the first Gospel message on the Day of Pentecost.

The Comfort of Eternity
John 14:2

In my Father's house are many mansions: if it were not so, I would have told you.
I go to prepare a place for you.
John 14:2

This is Jesus' last teaching to His disciples before His crucifixion. They were about to go through the greatest test of their faith, and He was preparing them for what was to come. Why speak of preparing them a mansion in heaven? He wanted to comfort them and help them put things in perspective. In 1 Thessalonians 4:18, Paul tells us to comfort one another with words about being gathered unto the Lord in the air. Paul said again, "I reckon that the sufferings of this present time are not worthy to be compared with the glory which shall be revealed in us" (Rom. 8:18). Someday, all of our trials will seem like nothing, and this can be a great comfort to us now.

When we think about being with the Lord throughout eternity, it helps us to put our present problems in proper perspective. It is easy to get fearful about our troubles and think all is lost. However, for those of us who are born again, if worse comes to worse, we still have the promise of Jesus wiping all the tears from our eyes and preparing a habitation for us where all our former sorrows will have passed away. This keeps us from despairing and inspires us to keep going in faith.

In heaven there are many dwelling places, and Jesus is preparing a special one for you. The thing that is going to make heaven "heaven" is that you will be with Him. No doubt, there will be things to see and do that will be wonderful, but nothing will compare to being with the One who loves you and died for you.

One Way
John 14:5-6

Thomas saith unto him, Lord, we know not whither thou goest; and how can we know the way?
John 14:5

Thomas knew Jesus; he just didn't know Jesus was "the way." When he asked Jesus this question, Jesus didn't say: "I am a way, a truth, and a life that will lead you to the Father in heaven." Rather, He claimed to be the only way, the only truth, and the only life. He said, "No man cometh unto the Father, but by Me" (v. 6). This means that anyone who claims to honor Jesus while advocating other ways to get to God, to know the truth, or to have eternal life apart from Jesus alone is deceived and deceiving others.

Jesus' claims about Himself leave no room for any other means of salvation. He is either who He says He is or He is the greatest deceiver of all time. His statements about Himself leave no other alternative. Therefore, other religions that recognize Jesus and His teachings as wonderful examples but don't believe He is the only way to achieve salvation are false.

Jesus said He is the Truth, and John revealed He is the Living Word. (John 1:1,14.) People today may know portions of the Bible, but they don't realize that the words written in the Book are the way to victory in every area of their lives. They will cry out to God to speak to them while their Bible lays unopened on their nightstand. If they would only open it, read it, and receive the Word into their hearts, they would know Jesus is the way, the truth, and the life.

The Word of God is a spiritual book written by men under the direction of the Holy Spirit. It was not written to our heads but to the innermost part of our hearts. This is why some people find the Bible so hard to understand. They are trying to comprehend it in their minds. The Word of God has to inspire our hearts before it can enlighten our minds.

Today, open your Bible and read it as though the Lord was speaking to the deepest part of you—because He is.

God Is in the Simple Things
John 14:7

If ye had known me, ye should have known my Father also: and from henceforth ye know him, and have seen him.
John 14:7

To know Jesus is to know the Father. This is not only because Jesus did exactly what He saw His Father do, but also because Jesus was God in the flesh. He wasn't made in God's image and likeness as Adam and we are (Gen. 1:26); He was "the express image of his person" (Heb. 1:3), which means He was exactly like God in every way.

The disciples didn't realize that seeing Jesus was seeing God. They were expecting something more. Many times we miss God in our lives and circumstances because we are looking for something spectacular. Although God is totally awesome, He doesn't always choose to manifest Himself that way. He spoke to Elijah, not in the fire, wind, or earthquake, but in a still, small voice. (1 Kings 19:12.) Jesus didn't come to this earth in a grand way but was born to poor parents in a stable. Isaiah 53:2 says that Jesus had no form nor beauty that would make us think He was anything more than a mere man.

Paul reveals in 1 Corinthians 1:27-29 that God chooses to do things this way so that no flesh will glory in His presence. He wants us to focus on Him through faith and not concentrate on the physical things He uses. In the Old Testament when He did use visible instruments to release His power, the Israelites made idols out of those things.

Just as the disciples saw Jesus but didn't realize that what they saw was God, you may be missing Him because your focus is on what is going on around you instead of what His Spirit is communicating within you. You may be looking for Him to do something stupendous, like raise the dead, when He just wants you to speak a kind word to someone who is having thoughts of suicide. He wants to use you in great ways, but He also wants to use you in the little things. Keep that in mind as you follow Him today.

God Is Your Comfort
John 14:16-17

And I will pray the Father, and he shall give you another Comforter,
that he may abide with you for ever.
John 14:16

Again, Jesus said these things to His disciples so they would not be offended or cast down when He was crucified and buried. Now He is telling them about the Holy Spirit who is the Comforter. The ministry of the Holy Spirit in the life of the believer is the front line of defense against the devil and his devices of defeat. The phrase, "the God of all comfort" (2 Cor. 1:3), carries the idea of a divine comforter who encourages, refreshes, strengthens, aids, assists, and is an ever-present help in the time of need.

The ways God chooses to comfort are not always the same. In a tough situation He may deliver you, remove the cause of the affliction, or comfort and strengthen you to endure it, giving you hope for the future. He may send other believers to share their faith by prophesying, fellow laborers who will serve and strengthen you. He uses the body of Christ as a means to comfort you with exhortation and prayer. The point is that the source of all comfort is God, no matter what channel He chooses to use.

In 2 Corinthians 12:9 God revealed to Paul that His strength is made perfect in our weakness. Paul, who had experienced God's comfort in a way that perhaps no other believer has, revealed how the Lord accomplished this. It was through the power of the Holy Spirit. True Christianity is not the absence of trials, but the strength and comfort that Jesus through the Holy Spirit will bring us through them.

You cannot withstand the pressures of everyday life apart from the comfort of the Holy Spirit. He is there to give you wisdom, courage, and compassion when you encounter all the difficulties of this life. He is also there to keep you humble when the victories come! For everything you need today, just look within you.

Jesus in the Flesh
John 14:28

Ye have heard how I said unto you, I go away, and come again unto you.
If ye loved me, ye would rejoice, because I said, I go unto the Father:
for my Father is greater than I.
John 14:28

Jesus declared His divinity and His union with the Father so clearly that He was accused of blasphemy more than once. In this verse, He said the Father was greater than He. How does this statement not contradict His other claims?

A key to understand this statement is given in Philippians 2:6-8, where Paul says that Jesus didn't think it robbery to be equal with God but humbled Himself, taking on the form of a servant, which refers to His humanity. Jesus was equal to God in His divine nature, but He made Himself inferior to the Father in regard to His humanity. Jesus didn't lose any of His deity when He became a man, but He was clothed in flesh and had to submit to its limitations. In this sense, the Father was greater than Jesus.

Jesus was the pre-existent God who chose to become a man so he could redeem us by His own blood sacrifice. When He became a man, He was still 100 percent God in His spirit, but His physical body was 100 percent human. His body was sinless, but it was still flesh and subject to the natural things we all experience. The physical Jesus had to grow in wisdom and in stature just like we do in the natural sense.

When Jesus was born, His physical mind did not know all things. He had to be taught how to talk, walk, eat, and so forth. He had to learn that He was God in the flesh and accept that by faith. His physical mind grew in awareness of who He was by faith—the same way we do when we believe who we are in Him.

Jesus' mental comprehension of His deity was something He learned and accepted by faith. He had to become aware of His true identity through revelation and knowledge. Today, you must do the same. Isn't it nice to know that you serve a Lord who has gone through everything you are going through?

Let God Prune You His Way
John 15:2

Every branch in me that beareth not fruit he taketh away: and every branch that beareth fruit, he purgeth it, that it may bring forth more fruit.
John 15:2

*P*urging has been interpreted in many ways. The illustration Jesus used was pruning, and some have said purging is a very painful process. The Lord cuts away our flesh and carnal habits with things like sickness, death, poverty, and other forms of tragedy. Then we will bear more fruit. This teaching not only promotes problems as being good and from God but makes them necessary to bear more fruit.

That thinking is not consistent with the rest of God's Word or even the context of this verse. The text makes it very clear that the purging Jesus spoke of is done through the Word that He has spoken unto us. Paul said in 2 Timothy 3:16-17, that God's Word was given to us "for doctrine, for reproof, for correction, and for instruction in righteousness: That the man of God may be perfect, thoroughly furnished unto all good works." That is God's method of pruning us, and He doesn't need the devil's help! His Word will make us "perfect, thoroughly furnished unto all good works."

If you mistakenly think God is bringing tragedy into your life to make you more fruitful, then you will not resist the enemy, the one who is really bringing them. You can learn from God through trials and tragedy because He is always with you, but that is not His schoolroom. Today, He will teach you through His Word by His Spirit, gently leading you and guiding you through whatever you face.

Your Life Is in Him
John 15:4

Abide in me, and I in you. As the branch cannot bear fruit of itself,
except it abide in the vine; no more can ye, except ye abide in me.
John 15:4

This is a profound truth that is the key to bearing fruit, but it is so easy to forget. Because the fruit is borne on the branch, it is easy to credit the branch with the fruit. However, it is the vine that drew the life from the earth and channeled it through the branch. Likewise, since we are the branch through which the life of God flows, we sometimes think it is our own holiness that produces the fruit. The moment we think that way, we are no longer abiding in (trusting in; clinging to) the vine. We will become fruitless if we persist in this mindset.

This truth is a great relief to believers who understand and apply it properly. It puts all the responsibility on Jesus. Our only responsibility is to respond to His ability. In the same way that we have never seen a branch travailing to bring forth fruit, so all we have to do is labor to enter into His rest. (Heb. 4:11.) We simply depend upon and completely trust Jesus as our source for everything. If we abide and live in Him, fruit will come naturally.

Like the life of a plant is found in the soil, a branch in a vine, or a fish in the sea, your life is found in your union with Jesus Christ. Your faith in what He did for you saved you, and your faith and trust in Him is what will allow you to enjoy the full benefits of salvation today. Just rest in Him, commune with Him, and follow Him. You will find all kinds of fruit start manifesting in your life!

Embrace the Holy Spirit
John 16:7

Nevertheless I tell you the truth; It is expedient for you that I go away: for if I go not away, the Comforter will not come unto you; but if I depart, I will send him unto you.
John 16:7

The Greek word translated *expedient* means "to be an advantage; profitable." How could any situation be more advantageous or profitable than having Jesus physically with you? However, when Jesus walked on this earth in His physical body, He was subject to many physical limitations. For instance, He could not always be with every one of His disciples all the time. Through the ministry of the Holy Spirit He could.

The list of advantages of having the Holy Spirit in us compared to having Jesus with us in His physical body goes on and on. Instead of dealing with one Jesus, Satan saw 120 "little Christ's" (that is literally what the word *Christian* means) come out of the upper room on the Day of Pentecost, and three thousand more were born again after Peter preached that day.

Jesus taught His disciples as no teacher ever had, yet they had very little understanding because they were not born again. After the Holy Spirit came, He led them into all truth and even showed them things to come. The advantages can all be summed up in that Jesus' power is now complete (Matt. 28:18) and no longer confined to one physical body.

You cannot live a victorious and satisfying Christian life without a moment-by-moment, hour-by-hour, day-by-day dependence upon the Spirit of God inside you. He is there to teach you, guide you, comfort you, and strengthen you. Draw upon His ability today in everything you do.

Be a Witness, Not a Judge
John 16:8

And when he is come, he will reprove the world of sin, and of righteousness, and of judgment.
John 16:8

The ministry of the Holy Spirit is to reprove sin. It is not our ministry. We are simply witnesses. A witness is not the judge or the jury. A witness simply relates what they have experienced, thereby providing evidence to the truth of something. We are to witness in word and deed to the truth of Jesus being alive in us. Then we step aside and let the Holy Spirit be the one to convict.

In their zeal, some believers have gone beyond the witness stage and have tried to bring people under conviction. Assuming the job of the Holy Spirit not only frustrates their witness, but also it drives many people away from God. We make a very poor Holy Spirit! We should stick to our job of being witnesses and stay out of the Holy Ghost's business.

Just before Jesus ascended to heaven, He declared that the Holy Spirit was given to empower us to be His witnesses, and He specified where we should witness. (Acts 1:8.) We start in Jerusalem (where we are), then Judea (those nearby), then Samaria (other religious and racial groups), and finally the uttermost parts of the earth (other countries). There are some practical reasons for this. Jesus said that a prophet is honored everywhere except in his hometown. (Matt. 13:57.) Typically, the hardest place to witness is to family and friends. Starting with those who know us best will cause us to humble ourselves and give God all the glory. Any rejection tempers us and our witness, so that we will be more effective and more resilient when we go to the other peoples of the earth.

Today, be mindful that you have a responsibility to share the Gospel as the Holy Spirit leads you, but then it is all up to Him. Knowing this takes all the pressure off you, and if you are rejected, you know they are rejecting Jesus, not you. You can continue to have a great day knowing you have done the Lord's will.

Experience Eternal Life
John 17:3

And this is life eternal, that they might know thee the only true God,
and Jesus Christ, whom thou hast sent.
John 17:3

In order to fully understand what eternal life is, it is helpful to understand what it is not. Eternal life is not living forever. Everyone lives forever in either heaven or hell. Also, eternal life is not living forever in the blessings of heaven after physical death. John 3:36 and 5:24 show that eternal life is a present tense possession of the believer.

In John 17:3, Jesus defines eternal life as knowing God the Father and Jesus Christ. The word *know* is speaking of intimacy and revelation instead of mere intellectual knowledge. Therefore, eternal life is having an intimate, personal relationship with God the Father and Jesus the Son.

According to John 3:16, this intimacy with God is what salvation is all about. Forgiveness of our sins is not the point of salvation; forgiveness of our sins is the means of obtaining our salvation, which is intimacy with the Father. We cannot be intimate with a holy God if we are unholy sinners. Sin was the obstacle that stood between us and God. It had to be dealt with, and Jesus did; but if our salvation stops at being forgiven, we miss out on eternal life—an intimate relationship with God.

It is wonderful to be forgiven and cleansed of all sin and unrighteousness through the blood of Jesus Christ. It is a tremendous hope to look forward to eternity in heaven. However, you can enjoy the greatest blessing of your salvation today: the intimate, face-to-face relationship with God the Father and Jesus the Son.

Seek the Will of God

Luke 22:41-42

Saying, Father, if thou be willing, remove this cup from me: nevertheless not my will, but thine, be done.

Luke 22:42

Jesus knew it was the Father's will for Him to be made an offering for the sins of the world. He had prophesied His own death and resurrection many times. But because of His unique relationship with God, Jesus asked Him to accomplish His will some other way. At the same time, He affirmed His commitment to do His Father's will and not His own.

Jesus knew God's will and left this time of prayer trusting that whatever the Father deemed best for Him would happen. He knew when He began praying what the Father's will was, and He knew at the close of His prayer that God's will could not be accomplished any other way.

For us to pray, "Lord, if it be thy will" in response to a promise God has given us is nothing but unbelief and is not even remotely related to what Jesus did in the Garden of Gethsemane. One of the foundational principles of answered prayer is that we must believe that we receive when we pray. (Mark 11:24.) There is no way we can fulfill that condition if we don't know God's will in that situation. Praying, "if it be thy will" takes us out of the active position of believing and puts us in the passive position of waiting and letting circumstances rule our lives.

If you are seeking direction in an area where God's will is not already expressed in His Word, then you should pray James 1:5 and ask for wisdom. You should not be ignorant but understand what the will of the Lord is. (Eph. 5:17.) The only appropriate time to pray, "if it be thy will," is when you are dedicating yourself to the service of God.

Always Willing
Matthew 26:36-45

Watch and pray, that ye enter not into temptation: the spirit indeed is willing,
but the flesh is weak.
Matthew 26:41

If you are born again, your spirit is not your problem. The Holy Spirit made your spirit new when He came to live in you. Now your spirit is just like Jesus (1 John 4:17) and is always willing to do God's will. It is your flesh that is your problem.

The flesh, as Jesus describes it here, not only includes your physical body but also your soul. God has given you everything it takes to walk in victory, but you also have the treasure of your born-again spirit housed in an earthen vessel. (2 Cor. 4:7.) That is saying that your spirit, where God has deposited all of His power and glory, resides inside your flesh.

Jesus had asked His disciples to watch and pray with Him in what was His most distressing time. He said to them, "My soul is exceeding sorrowful, even unto death," and asked that they pray for Him. None of them were able to do it. They all fell asleep! We think this is outrageous until we are physically exhausted and the Holy Spirit gives us an unction to pray. Our spirits (and sometimes our souls at first) are so willing, but our flesh is still tired. Eventually we will decide to either persevere in the Spirit or give in to our flesh.

What you need to remember is that you can tap into the power of the Holy Spirit inside your spirit by renewing your mind with God's Word. The more your mind is renewed, the more the power of God will flow through your soul and physical body. You must exercise your soul, mind, and body unto godliness. (1 Tim. 4:7,8.) Then, when the Holy Spirit asks you to intercede and stand in the gap for someone at three o'clock in the morning, your spirit—that is always willing—will easily dominate your flesh.

The Importance of Teaching
Matthew 26:55

*In that same hour said Jesus to the multitudes, Are ye come out as against a thief
with swords and staves for to take me? I sat daily with you teaching in the temple,
and ye laid no hold on me.*
Matthew 26:55

In this verse, Jesus is being arrested by the Temple guards, and He reminds them that He is the same person who preached and taught among them for the last three years. Even when He is being treated like a common thief, He tells them to remember what He has said to them. The four gospels refer to Him teaching 43 times, preaching 19 times, and preaching and teaching 6 times. This indicates that Jesus spent twice as much time teaching as He did preaching. Preaching brings people to Jesus, but teaching makes disciples out of them. Jesus was making disciples, not just converts.

The Greek word for disciple means "a learner," and indicates "learning by endeavor" or what we would call "on-the-job training." Jesus said in John 8:31, "If ye continue in my word, then are ye my disciples indeed." Anyone who continues to read, study, meditate on, and hear the teaching of God's Word is Jesus' disciple.

"Jailhouse religion," where a person is only sorry they got caught and just wants to get out of a bad situation, will not produce true discipleship. These people give their lives to Jesus, and the moment they leave the jail, they go back to their worldly ways. They are not a disciple of the Lord until they get in church and submit to the teaching of the Word.

Today you can examine your lifestyle and see whether or not you are acting like you have "jailhouse religion" or are a true disciple of the Lord. Every believer can get fired up and inspired by a preacher, but it is your pastor and other teachers that will bring the Word of God to you in ways that your heart will receive it with gladness and be transformed. The teaching of the Word is what will bring real stability and joy to your life in Christ.

Jesus Wants You Healed
Luke 22:51

And Jesus answered and said, Suffer ye thus far. And he touched his ear,
and healed him.
Luke 22:51

This verse describes Jesus' response to Peter's rash act of cutting off one of the Temple guard's ears when he was trying to take Jesus into custody. This guard was just doing his job. He may have actually been a follower of Jesus, or he may have hated Jesus like the other religious Jews did. The Bible doesn't tell us. But regardless of the feelings and beliefs this guard had about Him, Jesus immediately healed him. This demonstrates His great desire for all people to be well and whole, and it also shows one of the many ways He healed people.

Jesus often healed people by touching them, and others received their healing as they touched Jesus. You can transmit the power or the anointing of God through the laying on of hands. (Mark 16:18; Heb. 6:2.) The virtue of God can even be transmitted to objects and then brought to the person who needs healing or deliverance. (Acts 19:12.)

Healing has been purchased for us as part of the atonement of Christ. The Lord would no more refuse to heal us than He would refuse to forgive us. That does not mean we deserve healing—we don't—but we don't deserve to be forgiven either! They are both gifts from God. (Rom. 6:23; Eph. 2:8.)

Today you know you are saved by the redemptive work of Jesus, not your good deeds. You are also healed by the blood of Jesus, not your works. You cannot earn salvation or healing, but you can receive both by faith. When you doubt you are worthy of being healed, remember how Jesus healed the guard's ear. If Jesus healed him without even thinking about it, He fervently desires that you receive your healing as well.

The Rhema Word
Matthew 26:69-75

And Peter remembered the word of Jesus, which said unto him, Before the cock crow, thou shalt deny me thrice. And he went out, and wept bitterly.
Matthew 26:75

"Peter remembered the word of Jesus" says it all!

There are several Greek words used for *word*. The Greek word used here is *rhema*, and it literally means, "a spoken word; an utterance, a saying, but specifically a spoken word appropriate for the situation." It's not the Bible lying on your coffee table that makes the enemy flee. It is the Word of God hidden in your heart, activated by the power of the Holy Spirit, and spoken in the appropriate situation that destroys all deception and makes you free.

The word *rhema* brings to mind what Jesus said in John 6:63, that "the words that I speak unto you, they are spirit and they are life." The words that we speak from the written Word of God are empowered by the Holy Spirit. The Word by itself doesn't make us free. It is the Word we know and speak in faith that will deliver us. (John 8:32.) The Word is effective and powerful because it is God's Word. His Word supersedes all authority of the church, of reason, of intellect, and of the enemy. When we connect His Word with our heart, and our heart connects His Word to our situation—then we have a rhema word.

This is exactly what Peter was doing just after he denied Jesus the third time. Sometimes a rhema word will come after your worst failures, and that is because the Holy Spirit is reminding you of the only Word that can restore and get you moving again. You can rise above any failure today by listening to the Holy Spirit who will always put you in remembrance of the Word of God—and then that rhema word will set you free.

All About Miracles
Luke 23:8

And when Herod saw Jesus, he was exceeding glad: for he was desirous to see him
of a long season, because he had heard many things of him; and he hoped to have
seen some miracle done by him.
Luke 23:8

When Pilate could find no fault in Jesus, He sent Him back to the Jewish king, Herod. Herod was glad because for a long time he had wanted see Jesus perform a miracle. The questions he asked Jesus made this desire obvious, but Jesus did not say or do anything in response. Miracles are one way God meets the needs of those who seek Him in faith. Sometimes He will demonstrate His supernatural ability to inspire faith in people (Mark 2:10,11), but He will not perform a miracle for skeptics who are tempting Him and have no desire for Him. (Luke 4:9-12.)

A miracle is a supernatural intervention of God's power over natural law. Healings occur within the boundaries of natural law while miracles are not limited to natural law. A person with a high fever who receives prayer and then begins to recover is experiencing a healing. The Lord intervened, but in natural ways. The virus, infection, or whatever was rebuked, left the body (Luke 4:39), and then the natural healing process that the Lord built into people took over. When something totally supernatural happens, like reattaching the guard's ear and it being instantly whole (Luke 22:51), that is a miracle. It was also a healing, but it was a miraculous healing.

Feeding the five thousand (Matt. 14:19,20), walking on the water (Matt. 14:25), translating a ship and all aboard to the other side of the sea (John 6:21)—all these are miracles—and you, being in Christ, can do them too! Today you have the full authority of the name of Jesus, which means that anything He did, you can do also. As long as your heart is in the right place and you desire a miracle to reveal Jesus to someone, you should have no hesitancy in believing God for one.

Jesus—the Name Above All Names
Luke 23:9

Then he questioned with him in many words; but he answered him nothing.
Luke 23:9

When Herod questioned Jesus, he revealed how humble He was. He refused to defend Himself, and He refrained from venting His wrath against the man who had senselessly killed John the Baptist, who was His cousin and probably one of His closest friends. Because of His humility and obedience to the Father, God gave Him a name that is above every name in heaven, earth, and under the earth. (Phil. 2:9-11.) There is no exemption for anyone or anything from coming under the Lordship of Jesus. He is Lord of ALL.

Jesus has not only been exalted above every "being" that has a name, but He is also highly exalted above any "thing" that has a name. If you can put a name on it, Jesus is above it. Sickness, poverty, depression, anger, your car, your job, your family—everything has to bow its knee to the name of Jesus.

The day is coming when every knee of men, women, children, angels, and demons will bow and confess that Jesus is Lord. Every being from all ages will ultimately bow and acknowledge the lordship of Jesus Christ. This is the extent of the power and authority of the name of Jesus.

If you have already bowed your knee to Him today, you will not only look forward to eternity with Him in heaven, but you can enjoy a wonderful life here on earth because you can walk in the power of His name. Whatever you are facing, it must bow to the name of Jesus!

Pilate Violates the Truth
Matthew 27:11-17

Therefore when they were gathered together, Pilate said unto them, Whom will
ye that I release unto you? Barabbas, or Jesus which is called Christ?
Matthew 27:17

Although Pilate knew Jesus was innocent, he looked for some diplomatic way to release Jesus that would not cause him to lose favor with the Jewish leaders. This is why he sent Jesus to Herod. He hoped that Herod would pass judgment on Jesus and save him the trouble. When that scheme failed, Pilate drew on an old custom of releasing a prisoner to the people during a feast. It was time for Passover, and he gave them a choice between Jesus and Barabbas, who was a murderer. Pilate thought the crowd would certainly choose Jesus. However, through the insistence of the chief priests and scribes, the people chose Barabbas to be released.

Pilate was now out of ideas as to how to let Jesus go and still save face with the Jews, so he condemned Jesus to death. Pilate violated what he knew to be true in his heart because of the fear of men (Prov. 29:25) and what he thought they might do to him. Without the chief priests' cooperation, he ran the risk of unrest among the Jews, which could bring punishment by Caesar for failing to govern well.

As it turned out, Pilate was deposed a few years later anyway by Tiberius Caesar, and he died in exile in Gaul in AD 41. At the most, sentencing Jesus to death gave Pilate a five-year extension of his troubled rule and damned his soul in the process. What a person compromises to keep, they will always lose. Going against the truth is never worth the price.

As you make decisions and evaluate situations today, set your heart to stand with the truth of God's Word and to be led of His Holy Spirit. You have no reason to fear what people will do when you follow after the Lord's will.

Jesus Set You Free
Luke 23:18

And they cried out all at once, saying, Away with this man,
and release unto us Barabbas.
Luke 23:18

What happened to Barabbas is a picture of what happens when we are born again. Barabbas was guilty; Jesus was innocent. Jesus suffered the death that Barabbas deserved, and Barabbas went free. Likewise, we were guilty (Rom. 3:23) and condemned to death (Rom. 6:23), yet Jesus suffered our punishment so that we could go free. (2 Cor. 5:21.) Just as Barabbas didn't ask for this substitution, so "God commended his love toward us, in that, while we were yet sinners, Christ died for us" (Rom. 5:8).

Jesus' death set Barabbas free, but he had to choose whether to accept this new freedom or to continue in his old selfish ways and come under the judgment of Rome again. In the same way, we have all been freed through the substitutionary death of Jesus, but we have to choose whether to accept our freedom by putting our faith in Him and surrendering our lives to Him.

As Christians, we need to develop a continual awareness that our lives are not our own. We do not have the liberty to do as we please; we have the liberty to love, serve, and worship God through Jesus Christ our Lord. We should present our bodies as living sacrifices unto God, recognizing that this is just our reasonable duty to the one who gave His life for us. (Rom. 12:1.)

The lordship of Jesus should be the determining factor in every action of your life today. (Rom. 14:7-10.) Every thought, word, and deed should pass the test, "Is this what Jesus wants?" This is the key to having a great day!

Is It the Truth?
Matthew 27:4

Saying, I have sinned in that I have betrayed the innocent blood. And they said,
What is that to us? see thou to that.
Matthew 27:4

The religious Jews who had courted Judas' favor to obtain his cooperation in arresting Jesus cared nothing for him. They simply used him. The devil's crowd will flatter you and see that you prosper as long as they can use you, but when there is no longer anything in it for them, they will forsake you just as the chief priests did Judas.

The serpent didn't come to Eve in the Garden threatening to bite her if she didn't eat of the forbidden fruit. Instead, he came with deception, presenting himself as being concerned for her welfare. Satan's greatest weapon is deceit, which is bending the truth, using half-truths, and outright lying. He will take the Word of God and twist it just a little, add to it, and eventually he will say the exact opposite of what God originally said.

Just as an athlete or military person's success depends partly on how well they know their opponent, believers must not be ignorant of Satan's devices. (2 Cor. 2:11.) Jesus stripped Satan of all his authority (Matt. 28:18), and the only influence Satan has over us now is deception. If he can get us to believe a lie, something that does not line up with God's Word, he can get us to use our own power and authority against us. The thing that makes deception so deadly is that those who are deceived don't know it. Once they realize they are deceived, they aren't deceived any more.

The best defense against the devil's deception is to be so Word-centered that you give no place to him. Whenever you sense the presence of evil or discern an idea or thought that might be evil, run to the Word of God to check it out. Ask the Holy Spirit to show you what is the truth.

God's Forgiveness Is for All Sins

Luke 23:34

Then said Jesus, Father, forgive them; for they know not what they do.
And they parted his raiment, and cast lots.
Luke 23:34

Forgiveness of sins is one of the great themes of the Bible, which says so much about it that it would take volumes to adequately deal with the subject. It will suffice to say that the blood of Jesus is what provided us with forgiveness of sins. His sacrifice was so great that it outweighed all our sins for all time. It covered all the sins of the world—past, present, and future.

Most Christians have the concept that the sins they committed before they professed faith in Christ are forgiven at salvation, but any sins they commit after salvation are not forgiven until they repent and ask for forgiveness. This is not the case. All our sins—past, present, and future—were forgiven through the one offering of Jesus. If God can't forgive future sins, then none of us can be saved because Jesus only died once, nearly two thousand years ago, before we had committed any sins. All our sins have been forgiven.

Being forgiven for all time is one of God's greatest gifts to His children. We can proceed with our lives in confidence that even if we do miss it or fall to temptation, He still loves us and forgives us. All we have to do is turn to Him, be washed by His Word, and begin to walk in the Spirit again. A lot of people hear this and say, "Well, you're just telling Christians it's all right to sin." On the contrary, when believers understand the full extent of God's forgiveness, it gives them an even greater desire not to sin.

It is through the riches of God's grace that you received forgiveness for your sins and continue to receive that forgiveness when you need it. That is one of the great blessings and the strong confidence you can walk in today.

Paradise
Luke 23:39-43

*And Jesus said unto him, Verily I say unto thee, Today shalt thou be
with me in paradise.*
Luke 23:43

Paradise was also called "Abraham's bosom," which He mentioned in the story of the rich man and Lazarus. (Luke 16:22.) After His death, Jesus descended into the lower parts of the earth (Eph. 4:9), and John 20:17 shows that it was some time after His resurrection before Jesus ascended to His Father. Therefore, Paradise was "Abraham's bosom," located in sheol in the lower parts of the earth.

The phrase "led captivity captive" from Ephesians 4:8, refers to Jesus liberating the Old Testament saints from a part of hell called *sheol* in Hebrew. It is this Hebrew word that is translated *hell* in Psalm 16:10, which prophesies Jesus saying, "For thou wilt not leave my soul in hell; neither wilt thou suffer thine Holy One to see corruption" (Acts 2:27-30).

The ungodly dead also went to sheol, or hell, but Jesus taught in Luke 16:19-31 that there was a great gulf fixed between the godly and the ungodly. Those in the torment of hell envied those who were enjoying the blessings of the Lord in Abraham's bosom or Paradise.

Even though these Old Testament saints were blessed, they were not able to enter into the presence of the Lord because the atonement of Jesus Christ had not been completed. In that sense, they were captives. When Jesus died, He descended into sheol and took the captives captive. He took them to heaven, into the very presence of God, and vacated Paradise. After that, all that remained was the torment of hell.

The thief next to Jesus, when they were being crucified, asked Jesus to remember him, and Jesus assured him they would meet shortly in Paradise. Today, whether you are raptured to meet Jesus in the air or simply pass from your body in old age, you have nothing but heaven to look forward to also.

The Veil Is Torn
Luke 23:45

And the sun was darkened, and the veil of the temple was rent in the midst.
Luke 23:45

T he veil reached from the ceiling to the floor, from wall to wall, and separated the Holy of Holies from the Holy Place in the Temple. Solomon's Temple was thirty cubits high (1 Kings 6:2), but Herod increased the height to forty cubits according to the writings of Josephus, a first-century historian. Therefore, depending on what standard you use to convert cubits to feet (there is uncertainty as to exactly what a cubit equaled in feet and inches), this veil was somewhere between sixty and ninety feet high.

It is significant that this veil was rent from top to bottom. (Matt. 27:51; Mark 15:38.) No man could have torn the veil in this fashion. It was definitely God who rent the veil. It is also significant that the time this veil tore down the middle corresponds exactly to the moment Jesus died on the Cross.

Hebrews 9:1-9 tells us that the veil separated the Holy of Holies, where God dwelt, from the rest of the Temple, where people dwelt. This signified that mankind was separated from God by sin. (Isa. 59:1,2.) Only the high priest was permitted to pass beyond this veil and only once each year. (Ex. 30:10; Heb. 9:7.) This symbolized the Messiah, who would enter into God's presence for us and make an atonement for our sin.

The moment Jesus Christ died, the veil was torn in two, revealing that the sacrifice had been made and there was no longer a separation between God and you. Jesus tore the veil, that is to say His flesh (Heb. 10:20), in two and opened up the way to the Father through Himself—the way you are walking in today. Rejoice and be glad in it!

Honor Your Parents
John 19:26

When Jesus therefore saw his mother, and the disciple standing by,
whom he loved, he saith unto his mother, Woman, behold thy son!
John 19:26

John is the only gospel writer to give this account of Jesus' last ministry to His mother, perhaps because Jesus gave Mary to John. Even during His extreme suffering, Jesus thought of His mother and honored her by giving her into John's care. In this way, Jesus was fulfilling the second commandment of the Law, which said to honor His parents.

Christians are to honor their parents even after they are adults. However, the command to obey is temporary. (Gal. 4:1,2.) Honor naturally leads to obedience if nothing is asked contrary to God's laws, but honor and obedience are not synonymous. The Scriptures teach that when a man marries, he is to leave his father and mother and cleave unto his wife. (Gen. 2:24.) This is why parental interference in their son's or daughter's marriage is the source of many divorces and much marital strife. Yet, a believer is to honor their parents.

The definition of the word *honor* means "to esteem, respect," and the Greek word from which *honor* is translated means "to prize, i.e., to fix a valuation upon." When we are young, it is good to esteem and prize the opinions of our parents over our peers. The attitude that parents are out-of-date and out of touch dishonors them and deprives us of their wisdom and comfort. When we are older, we may disagree with our parents, especially if they are unbelievers, but we should never dishonor or show disrespect to them. If they have been abusive or ungodly, honoring them does not mean believing or acting like them. Honor is simply an attitude of respect for the position they hold as those who gave us life.

It says in Exodus 20:12, Deuteronomy 5:16, and Ephesians 6:1-3 that honoring your father and mother is the first commandment with a promise. This command is the first one of the Ten Commandments that gives a promise of blessing to those who obey it. Honor your parents as Jesus honored His, and you will live a long, prosperous life.

The Meaning of the Sabbath
John 19:31-37

The Jews therefore, because it was the preparation, that the bodies should not remain upon the cross on the sabbath day, (for that sabbath day was an high day,) besought Pilate that their legs might be broken, and that they might be taken away.
John 19:31

Prophecies about the Messiah continued to be fulfilled after Jesus died on the Cross, and one of these happened because of the Sabbath. No work could be done on the Sabbath, which meant Jesus had to die and be buried before it began. That is why the Jews asked Pilate to break His legs. Breaking the legs of those being crucified hastened death. Verse thirty-three says that Jesus was already dead, so the Scripture was fulfilled: "He keepeth all his bones: not one of them is broken" (Ps. 34:20)—all because of the Sabbath.

The Sabbath was first mentioned in Scripture in Exodus 16, then shortly after, the Lord commanded the observance of the Sabbath day in the Ten Commandments. (Ex. 20:8-11.) God connected the Sabbath with the rest He took on the seventh day of creation. According to Exodus 23:12, one of the purposes of the Sabbath was to give God's people and their animals one day of physical rest each week. Today's medical science has proven that our bodies need at least one day of rest each week to function at our peak.

In Colossians 2:16-17 Paul revealed that the Sabbath was only a shadow of things to come and had been fulfilled in Christ. Hebrews 4:1-11 talks about a Sabbath rest that is available to all New Testament believers, but is not necessarily functional in all of them. This New Testament Sabbath rest is simply our relationship with God in which we cease from doing things by our own efforts and allow God to work through us.

As you ponder the importance of the Sabbath in Jesus' death, think about the fact that He died to give you rest. If you are in turmoil or confused in any way today, cast your care upon Him and be restored to His continual Sabbath rest.

Death Lost Its Power
Matthew 27:51-53

And the graves were opened; and many bodies of the saints which slept arose.
Matthew 27:52

Only Matthew records this amazing event. The earthquake had apparently rolled the stones away from many of the graves in the vicinity of Jerusalem, and some of the saints buried there arose from the dead. Even at the death of Jesus, such power was released that death lost its grip on its captives.

After the resurrection of Jesus, these saints came out of their graves, went into Jerusalem, and appeared to many people. (v. 53.) We can only guess what effect this must have had on the people! The resurrection of Jesus puts Christianity in a class all by itself. Many people have come and gone professing some revelation from God or new way of approaching God, but only Jesus conquered death. This makes Him unique and elevates Him above any other man who has ever walked on the earth.

Because Jesus conquered death, the fear and sting of death have been removed for us. First Corinthians 15:55 cries out, "O death, where is thy sting? O grave, where is thy victory?" We all have to say good-bye to loved ones who pass from this life into heaven, and we can grieve for a season; but death has lost its power over us, and our grief passes quickly.

Unbelievers have no hope to see their loved ones again, so they grieve deeply and sometimes never stop grieving. You are different because you have a great hope: the certainty of seeing your loved ones again and being with them and with your Lord for eternity. Whenever you begin to lose hope over a temporary situation, just remember those "dead" saints walking through Jerusalem. It will put your life in perspective and give you a fresh outlook for today.

Your Expectation Dictates Your Experience
John 20:11-17

And when she had thus said, she turned herself back, and saw Jesus standing, and knew not that it was Jesus.
John 20:14

Mary didn't recognize Jesus. She was one of the women who followed Him and ministered to Him throughout His earthly ministry. (Luke 8:2,3.) She knew Him well and had heard His voice thousands of times. Jesus honored Mary by choosing her to be the first person He appeared to after His resurrection, yet she supposed He was the gardener.

Certainly, one of the principle reasons Mary didn't recognize Jesus was that she wasn't expecting to see Him alive! The thought that Jesus could be alive hadn't yet entered her mind. This illustrates how her expectations dictated her experience, and all believers are no different. What we expect from God is usually what we get from Him.

God is who He is regardless of what we think about Him. As far as our experience goes, we will only experience Him the way we think He is. For instance, those who believe God doesn't heal today won't be healed until they begin to believe differently. Those who don't believe in the baptism of the Holy Spirit won't receive it. Those who don't believe Jesus rose from the dead will not recognize the risen Christ, even if He stood before them.

Mary recognized Jesus when He called her name. It was the personal relationship between them that finally opened her eyes. What do you believe about Him today? If you think He's angry with you, you won't experience His pleasure, even though Scripture says you are accepted in the beloved (Eph. 1:6). If you believe He's forsaken you, you won't experience His presence, even though He never leaves nor forsakes you. (Heb. 13:5.) Believe everything the Bible says He is, and He will be all that to you and more.

Do You Remember God's Word?
Luke 24:1-9

And they remembered his words, And returned from the sepulchre.
Luke 24:8-9

The women who came to Jesus' tomb were greeted by two angels, who reminded them how Jesus had prophesied that He would rise from the dead on the third day. It wasn't until they remembered His words that they quit seeking a dead Jesus and started looking for the living Lord. Just think, two angels announcing the resurrection of Jesus didn't turn these women around, but the words of Jesus did.

Peter said that the written Word of God is a more sure word of prophecy than even an audible voice or a visible manifestation of the Lord. (2 Peter 1:16-20.) We often think that if something supernatural would just happen, then we would believe. The example of the women at the tomb and Peter's own testimony tell a different story.

The spectacular gets our attention, but faith only comes from God's Word. (Rom. 10:17.) God's Word is what we need. More specifically, we need faith in God's Word. The Lord has given us exceedingly great and precious promises (2 Peter 1:4), but our unbelief still causes some of us to mope around as if Jesus didn't come out of the tomb. Our unbelief negates the power of His resurrection in our lives.

Meditating on God's Word causes your faith to rise up and doubt and unbelief to run out the door. In the Word, you see a resurrected Lord and God who is alive and able to handle any problem you have. Until these women knew Jesus was alive, sorrow filled their hearts. If sorrow is filling your heart today, it is because you have forgotten the victory Jesus has given you. Remember He is alive and Lord over all your circumstances, and you will see the difference it makes.

Do You Recognize Jesus?
Luke 24:13-35

And it came to pass, that, while they communed together and reasoned,
Jesus himself drew near, and went with them.
Luke 24:15

Two of Jesus' disciples were walking to a city called Emmaus. They were sad because they were thinking about Jesus. They were even pondering the reports they had heard that He had been resurrected, but they were in unbelief. They wanted to believe, but reason wouldn't let them.

At that moment, Jesus joined them, but they didn't recognize Him. The very one whom they loved was with them, and they didn't know it. How could this be? If they could have perceived Jesus being with them, all their questions would have been answered and their sorrow turned to joy.

This same story is recorded in Mark 16:12-13. In this account, Mark said Jesus appeared to these two disciples "in another form," but that didn't mean He looked different. Later that day Jesus told His disciples to behold the nail prints in His hands and feet. (Luke 24:39,40.) He looked the same but was in a resurrected body. The natural mind cannot discern spiritual truth; spiritual reality must be spiritually discerned. (1 Cor. 2:14.)

Likewise, the Lord is always with us. He never leaves us, but we often miss Him. We fail to perceive His presence because we look through the eye of reason instead of the eye of faith. The disciples on the road to Emmaus recognized Jesus when He broke bread with them. (Luke 24:30,31.) It's when we have communion with Him by faith that our eyes are opened to His presence. Look through your eyes of faith today and see the one who's promised never to leave you nor forsake you at work in your midst. (Heb. 13:5.)

Let God's Peace Lead You
Luke 24:36

*And as they thus spake, Jesus himself stood in the midst
of them, and saith unto them, Peace be unto you.*
Luke 24:36

It is no accident that the first thing Jesus said to His disciples was, "Peace be unto you." His resurrection was the way they would all find complete and eternal peace with God. But His peace was not only a heaven or hell issue; it was also an everyday issue. Just as every sport has officials to settle any disputes, the peace of God is now our umpire that settles all disputes regarding His will for our lives. We must learn to listen to and heed the peace of God in our hearts.

God's peace is something that every born-again believer has. It's a fruit of the Spirit. That peace is always calling the shots; we just don't always pay attention. How many times have we acted contrary to the peace in our hearts and then experienced disaster? We then say, "I never did feel good about that." That was the peace of God trying to tell us not to go that way, but we chose to play by our own rules and reason.

There are some things you can do to facilitate the peace of God umpiring in your heart. First, consider all the options. Don't let fear rule out God's possibilities. Next, use your imagination to explore what will happen with each choice. You should be able to discern a greater peace as you consider the option the Lord would have you take. Just as an umpire has to make a call, be bold enough to follow the direction that gives you the most peace.

The rudder on a ship will not work until the ship is moving. The ship doesn't have to be going full-steam ahead for the rudder to work, but it does have to be moving. Likewise, we have to act before the peace of God will give us perfect direction. Even if you make a mistake, you will have made it in faith, trying to follow the peace of God in your heart. The Lord can bless a wrong decision made in faith from a pure heart, but He cannot bless indecision and lack of faith. (Rom. 14:23.) So act in faith and upon peace today; and if you make a wrong turn, you will know, and the Holy Spirit will get you back on track.

Power From on High
Luke 24:49

*And, behold, I send the promise of my Father upon you: but tarry ye in
the city of Jerusalem, until ye be endued with power from on high.*
Luke 24:49

In Luke 3:16, John the Baptist declared that Jesus would baptize people in the
Holy Ghost and fire. Then, after His resurrection and just before He ascended
to heaven, Jesus commanded all His followers to stay in Jerusalem and not go
anywhere or do anything until He sent "the promise of my Father" upon them. At
that time they would be "endued with power from on high."

On the Day of Pentecost, Jesus baptized the 120 in the Upper Room in the
Holy Ghost, and they all spoke in tongues, but this blessing was not only for these
few individuals. Peter said in Acts 2:39, "For the promise is unto you, and to your
children, and to all that are afar off, even as many as the Lord our God shall call."
This same power is available to all believers today.

Speaking in tongues is unique to the Church Age. This is because when a
person speaks in tongues, their new, born-again spirit is speaking (1 Cor. 14:14), not
their mind. First Corinthians 13:1 denotes two kinds of speaking in tongues: "the
tongues of men and of angels." The tongues of men are known languages people
speak. The tongues of angels, or heavenly languages, are the tongues that all Spirit-
filled believers can speak and are what Paul spoke about in 1 Corinthians 12-14.
He said that when a tongue is given publicly in a service, it must be interpreted
(the gifts of tongues and interpretation of tongues). But there is also a personal
prayer language every believer enjoys, in which they communicate Spirit to spirit.

Being "endued with power from on high" is not just about speaking in tongues.
In Acts 1:8 Jesus said this was to empower His disciples to be His witnesses. Today,
you can build your faith by praying in the Spirit (Jude 20) and be the powerful
witness God created you to be. That is what praying in tongues and the baptism
of the Holy Spirit are all about.

Water Baptism Is a Sign
Mark 16:15-16

*He that believeth and is baptized shall be saved; but he that believeth
not shall be damned.*
Mark 16:16

Water baptism is a command of Jesus and the initial action taken upon believing. Mark's statement could be rendered, "He who believes with saving faith (faith that produces action) will be saved." In this sense, water baptism is very important. It is an opportunity to act on your new profession of faith. Anyone who refuses to follow Jesus' command to be water baptized may be suspected of not really believing.

On the other hand, there are scriptural examples of people being born again before they were baptized in water. Cornelius and his friends were filled with the Holy Ghost and spoke in tongues before they were baptized in water. (Acts 10:44-48.) John 14:17 records Jesus saying that an unbeliever cannot receive the Holy Ghost, so Cornelius and his friends must have been born again before their water baptism.

Water baptism is the sign of the New Covenant in the same way that circumcision was the sign of the Old Covenant. The apostle Paul made it clear in Romans 4 that Abraham's circumcision was only a sign. Abraham was justified by faith before he was circumcised. Paul goes on to state in Galatians 5:1-6 that anyone who trusts in circumcision has fallen from grace; Christ will profit him nothing.

It is faith in the redemptive work of Jesus Christ that produces salvation—not our actions. However, James writes that faith without works is dead. (James 2:20.) Faith alone saves, but saving faith is never alone; it must be acted upon. This is what Jesus meant when He commanded all believers to be water baptized.

If you have not had the joy of being water baptized, today is your day. I'm sure your pastor would be delighted to baptize you in water. And remember, going under the water symbolizes that you have partaken of Jesus' death to sin, and coming out of the water symbolizes that you have been raised to new life with Him. Hallellujah!

One More Time
John 21:1-6

And he said unto them, Cast the net on the right side of the ship, and ye shall find.
They cast therefore, and now they were not able to draw it for the multitude of fishes.
John 21:6

This wasn't the first time Jesus performed this miracle. When He first called these disciples to follow Him, He did the same thing. They had been fishing all night and had no fish. There was no logical reason why casting the net one more time on either side of the boat would make any difference. But in obedience they did it anyway. On both occasions they caught a multitude of fish!

There are many parallels between the miraculous catch of fish and our lives. Most people basically do the same things. They try to be productive and raise good families, but there's a world of difference between doing it in our own strength and doing it in the Word of the Lord.

These disciples were in the same place, using the same net, but the difference was the interjection of God's Word mixed with their faith in it and obedience to it. The difference between acting on God's Word and doing our own thing isn't in the action itself but in our heart attitude.

You may have done everything you know to do without receiving the results you desire, but have you stepped out in obedience to God's Word? What does the Lord have to say to you about your situation? Find out. Then obey it and expect miraculous results.

The Most Important Question
John 21:15-17

When they had dined, Jesus saith to Simon Peter, Simon, son of Jonas, lovest thou me
more than these? He saith unto him, Yea, Lord; thou knowest that I love thee.
He saith unto him, Feed my lambs.
John 21:15

This was one of the very last times Jesus was with His disciples before He ascended to the Father. The whole plan of God was just hours away from being committed into the hands of these men. Everything Jesus had accomplished and was yet to accomplish would soon be committed into their trust. What a profound moment!

What would the Lord deem the most important thing to say to these disciples? What last-minute instructions would He give? Surprisingly, the Lord questioned Peter about his love. Three times Peter denied that he had known Him. Now, three times Jesus asked Peter if he loved Him.

The most important issue for all of us is our love for the Lord. Everything else revolves around this issue. It's easy to get so busy serving the Lord that we don't have any time to fellowship with Him. Ultimately, this leads to emptiness, frustration, and ineffectiveness.

Prior to his denial, Peter loved Jesus enough to be willing to fight to the death for Him. (Luke 22:33; John 18:10.) But it's easier to fight than it is to suffer. Peter didn't love the Lord more than himself. That's why He asked Peter if he loved Him more than these. Peter had denied Him because he valued the opinion of people more than he loved Jesus.

Do you love Jesus more than anything or anyone? Like Peter, Jesus is asking you that question today so that you can be sure you love Him more than anyone or anything else in your life. His love for you and your love for Him is what will see you through any situation.

Mind Your Own Business!
John 21:18-24

Jesus saith unto him, If I will that he tarry till I come, what is that to thee?
follow thou me.
John 21:22

In verse eighteen, Jesus told Peter that he would glorify Him in his death as a martyr. It's impossible to know the exact effect this had on Peter. No doubt, it was profound. But one thing is obvious—it caused Peter to wonder what would happen to John.

One of the critical mistakes we often make is to examine what God has called us to do in the light of what others are called to do. This isn't wise. Jesus wisely told Peter to mind his own business. What would happen to John shouldn't have affected Peter.

Early church tradition says that John was boiled in oil but miraculously didn't die. He was then banished to the isle of Patmos where he wrote the book of Revelation and eventually died a natural death. How would this knowledge have affected Peter? Would it have made him bitter? Would he have thought it unfair for him to die a martyr's death while John escaped the same? Who knows?

Comparing ourselves with others isn't smart. (2 Cor. 10:12.) Like water, we tend to seek the lowest level. Comparing ourselves with others often makes us compromise God's best for us or feel condemned because we haven't reached someone else's "stature." We don't need those comparisons. What we need to do is just keep our eyes on the Lord and fulfill His will for our lives.

Your life shouldn't be a race with others but a race to be more and more like Jesus every day. True happiness and a sense of fulfillment are found in focusing on what He has called you to do and doing it with all your heart.

God Is Good
John 21:25

*And there are also many other things which Jesus did, the which, if they should
be written every one, I suppose that even the world itself could not contain the
books that should be written. Amen.*
John 21:25

Every detail of every man's life who has ever walked on the earth has not
impacted the world as much as the few recorded details of Jesus' life. Jesus
was not just a man; He was God manifest in the flesh. (1 Tim. 3:16.)

In Acts 10:38, Peter gave a brief yet descriptive summary of the life and
ministry of Jesus. He was anointed with power and with the Holy Ghost. He used
this power to do good, not evil. This is one of the main characteristics of God and
is one of the easiest ways to discern what is from God and what is from the devil.
God is a good God and the devil is a bad devil. If it's bad, it's from the devil; if it's
good, it's from God.

Tragedy can come from three sources: God, Satan, and natural law. God's wrath
rests upon unbelievers only. (Rom. 1:18.) Believers will never experience His wrath.
(Rom. 5:9.) New Testament believers are exempt from the punitive judgment of
God since Jesus bore it for them.

As for natural law, as mankind violates the laws of God, in both a natural and
moral sense, they will reap what they sow. If a person drives recklessly and kills
themselves and others, it is not God or the devil that killed them. They violated
natural law and thus paid the price. Unfortunately, the devil often steps in to accuse
God of being behind all tragedy. But our God is a good God. James 1:17 says that
every good and perfect gift comes from Him.

It is incorrect to believe that God controls everything and has some redemptive
purpose in tragedies. This type of thinking will lead you to ignore the devil and
give him a free hand to destroy your life. It will also cause you not to use wisdom
concerning natural laws. You will think nothing can happen unless God wills it.
But today you will decide to either walk in the Spirit by the Word or to go your
own way. It will be a lot easier to go with God when you know how good He is.

How to Baptize
Matthew 28:19

*Go ye therefore, and teach all nations, baptizing them in the name of the Father,
and of the Son, and of the Holy Ghost.*
Matthew 28:19

Jesus commanded us to baptize in the name of the Father, the Son, and the Holy Ghost, yet there is no recorded instance where the believers did so. Instead, the instances of baptism that are recorded in the book of Acts show people being baptized in the name of Jesus only. Because of this noticeable difference, doctrines have arisen that teach there is no Trinity, and that unless water baptism is administered in the name of Jesus only, a person cannot be saved. This is a false teaching that has led many people astray.

Water baptism is an outward witness of the inner change that has already taken place in our spirits at the new birth. In Acts 10:44-48, Cornelius and his friends were filled with the Holy Ghost and spoke in tongues, proving that they were already born again before they were baptized in water.

The harmony between the commission of Jesus and the practice of the early church is simple. When we baptize people in the name of the Father, Son, and Holy Ghost, we are baptizing them in the name of Jesus because "in him dwelleth all the fullness of the Godhead bodily" (Col. 2:9). Therefore, baptizing in the name of either the Father, Son, and Holy Ghost, or in the name of Jesus, is correct as long as Colossians 2:9 is understood.

This is just one example where the Word of God will always agree with itself. Sometimes we just haven't studied it enough. Today, if you have any questions about something in the Word that seems to present a contradiction, just study it out. Get with your pastor—he will be thrilled you asked! The Word always explains itself.

Use Your Delegated Authority
Mark 16:18

They shall take up serpents; and if they drink any deadly thing, it shall not
hurt them; they shall lay hands on the sick, and they shall recover.
Mark 16:18

This either means we have supernatural protection if we pick up a snake, or it is symbolic of God's protection when we encounter the devil. Since the other four signs in this list are literal, it is most probable that this means physically picking up snakes. The apostle Paul experienced this supernatural protection from a viper when he was shipwrecked on the island of Melita. (Acts 28:3-5.) However, this is the only recorded example of this type of protection in the New Testament.

There is no record of the disciples picking up snakes just to prove they were believers. That would be tempting God. (Luke 4:9-12.) This, as well as drinking any deadly thing, is a promise that if we pick up snakes accidentally or are forced into that position because of our stand for Christ, we can believe for supernatural protection.

The power that is now working in believers is the same power that worked in Christ to raise Him from the dead. Everything we have as believers in Christ comes from our union with Him. Therefore, what is true of Him is true of us too. We have come to share in His throne (Eph. 2:6), which means we partake of the authority that His throne represents and exercise divine power and dominion on this earth.

There is no place in the New Testament that tells you to ask God to do something about the devil. Instead, you are told to do something about the devil. This is because you have been delegated His authority over the works of the enemy. Let the eyes of your understanding be enlightened to His exceeding power toward you. (Eph. 1:18,19.) Today, take authority over the devil, and walk in victory!

Speaking With Tongues Is for Today
Mark 16:17-20

And they went forth, and preached every where, the Lord working with them,
and confirming the word with signs following. Amen.
Mark 16:20

The Lord confirmed the preaching of His Word with miracles. If Jesus and the first century Christians needed the Word confirmed with the miraculous (Heb. 2:4), then we do too. There is no Scripture that says these miraculous signs have passed away.

Some people have interpreted "that which is perfect" in 1 Corinthians 13:10 to be the complete Bible. This has led them to believe that the gifts of the Spirit have ceased. Although God's Word is perfect (Ps. 19:7), it is not the perfect thing Paul is referring to here. 1 Corinthians 13:8 does say that tongues shall cease, but it will not happen until "that which is perfect is come."

In 1 Corinthians 13:12, Paul says, "when that which is perfect is come, we shall see face to face." This speaks of seeing the Lord face-to-face instead of vaguely, as through a dark glass, as it is now. Some might argue that this is speaking in a symbolic sense, instead of literally face-to-face. But the next comparison in this verse says that then, "when that which is perfect is come," we shall know all things even as we are also known. There is no other way to interpret this, except as a description of when we will stand before the Lord after this life. Then we will be face-to-face and know all things even as also we are known.

Verse eight says that at the time prophecies fail and tongues cease, knowledge will vanish away. This is talking about the next life, or the new heavens and earth because one of the signs of the end times is that knowledge shall increase. (Dan. 12:4.) So the "that which is perfect" Paul speaks of cannot be the Bible. It has to be either our glorified body or Jesus at His second coming. Either way, tongues and prophecy will remain until that time.

Jesus said that you would cast out demons, heal the sick, speak with new tongues, and signs and wonders would follow you. That means you have a very exciting life to lead today!

Experience Produces Hope
Romans 5:3-5

And patience, experience; and experience, hope.
Romans 5:4

T here was a time in my life when I believed God could miraculously supply my need because that's what His Word promised (Phil. 4:19)—even though I had never yet experienced such provision. However, the day came when I not only believed it, but my faith actually produced tangible results. I experienced what I believed.

That did something for me. I can't say it made me believe because I was already believing. If I hadn't believed, I wouldn't have received. (James 1:5-7.) However, it strengthened my faith by giving me new hope. Before, my hope was that it could happen. Afterwards, my hope became that it would happen again and again. After seeing His provision many times, I've come to expect that God will always provide. Experiencing God's supply has generated new hope in my heart.

In the heart of someone who has consistently experienced God faithfulness, there abides a strength and depth of hope that a novice can't understand or appreciate. A person who has already built a home has a confidence and security that a first-time builder can't understand. They may be able to duplicate the performance of the seasoned builder or even exceed it, but experience gives the veteran a definite edge.

There are no shortcuts to experience, but as the old saying goes: "Today is the first day of the rest of your life." Put God's Word to the test today, and begin enjoying the wonderful benefits of increased hope.

The Power of Memory
2 Peter 1:10-13

*Yea, I think it meet, as long as I am in this tabernacle, to stir you up
by putting you in remembrance.*
2 Peter 1:13

Peter's time on earth was limited. This was possibly his last exhortation to the people he loved so much. Yet, instead of imparting one more piece of information, he reminded them of what they already knew. He used the power of their memories to stir them up.

Memory is a powerful thing. One sight, sound, or smell can trigger emotions and actions we may not have experienced in years, all because it causes us to remember. Memory is a function of our minds. Peter said, "I stir up your pure minds by way of remembrance" (2 Peter 3:1). We must think to remember. It takes effort, but it's worth it.

One of the ways the Lord told us to remember is through setting aside special days to commemorate special events. This was one of the main purposes of the Sabbath (Deut. 5:15) and feast days of the Old Covenant. (Deut. 16:3.) They served as constant reminders of the Lord's blessings. This is also the purpose of the American holiday Thanksgiving. It was established specifically for reminding us of our meager beginnings and that without God's aid, the United States of America would not exist.

Regardless of your nationality, thanksgiving should be a regular activity in your life. You need to "forget not all his benefits" (Ps. 103:2). The reason the Lord told you not to forget is because remembering His benefits keeps your faith in Him strong and effective. Also, you will forget if you don't put forth some effort. Use this holiday to remember all the goodness of God toward you.

It's Good to Give Thanks
2 Corinthians 9:8-11

Being enriched in every thing to all bountifulness, which causeth
through us thanksgiving to God.
2 Corinthians 9:11

The American Thanksgiving holiday is rich in godly tradition. Of course, most people have heard of the original Thanksgiving, where the pilgrims gave thanks to God and the Indians for helping them survive their first winter in the New World. Many early presidents of the United States had celebrations commemorating this original event. However, it was in the midst of the U.S. Civil War, in 1863, that President Lincoln issued a proclamation making Thanksgiving an official holiday.

The original proclamation was actually written by William H. Seward, the Secretary of State. President Lincoln expressed similar sentiments when he called for a national day of prayer that same year. Here's an excerpt from that proclamation:

We have been the recipients of the choicest bounties of heaven; we have grown in numbers, wealth, and power as no other nation has ever grown. But we have forgotten God. We have forgotten the gracious Hand, which preserved us in peace and multiplied and enriched and strengthened us, and we have vainly imagined, in the deceitfulness of our hearts, that all these blessings were produced by some superior wisdom and virtue of our own. Intoxicated with unbroken success, we have become too self-sufficient to feel the necessity of redeeming and preserving grace, too proud to pray to the God that made us.

These are profound words that are even more true today than when they were first written. Use this holiday season to humble yourself and remember the God who's blessed you in so many ways.

Be Thankful Always
Romans 1:16-25

Because that, when they knew God, they glorified him not as God, neither were thankful; but became vain in their imaginations, and their foolish heart was darkened.
Romans 1:21

Once we know God, we must remain thankful. Why is this important?

A thankful person acknowledges what someone else has done for them. They realize the contribution of another. Therefore, a thankful person is a humble person. Humility is a must in the kingdom of God. One of the strongest ploys of the enemy is to try to get us to believe that we can make it on our own. Thankfulness constantly reminds us that God is our Source. We aren't self-made men and women; the Lord gave us life, health, talents, and opportunities. We should be thankful!

People who aren't thankful become vain in their imaginations. They lose the perspective of God as their Source and begin to imagine that it's some virtue of their own that promoted them. They move off the foundation of faith in the Lord, and as they continue to build, they're destined to fall.

Thankful people think of and appreciate others and what they do for them. In relation to God, a thankful person knows that "promotion cometh neither from the east, nor from the west, nor from the south. But God is the judge: he putteth down one, and setteth up another" (Ps. 75:6,7).

Who is your source? You can know this by who or what you are grateful for. Make it a habit to begin and end every day by thanking God for all He has done, all He is doing, and all He is going to do for you. Then you will never be deceived into thinking you are on your own in life.

God Has a Plan for You
Jeremiah 1:4-10

Before I formed thee in the belly I knew thee; and before thou camest forth out
of the womb I sanctified thee, and I ordained thee a prophet unto the nations.
Jeremiah 1:5

The Lord spoke to Jeremiah that he was called, sanctified, and ordained before he was born. But this wasn't unique to Jeremiah. John the Baptist (Luke 1:15,16), Jesus (Is. 49:1-5), and Paul (Gal. 1:15) were the same—and so are you!

Psalm 139:13-16 reveals how God knew you in your mother's womb. He knew exactly what you would look like before you were even born. Before you were formed, your life was written in His book. You didn't just happen. You didn't evolve from apes. You were created by a loving God, who has a specific purpose for you. He created you with special gifts to fulfill His purposes in this life. God has a plan for you.

Your greatest opportunity for happiness and success is in fulfilling God's purposes for your life. You may be able to use His talents to accomplish other things, but you won't experience His anointing and blessing on those other efforts as you would by devoting those abilities to Him and His work.

You may wonder, *How do I know what God wants me to do?* The answer comes in giving yourself completely to Him. When you make a total surrender to God, He begins working circumstances in a manner that leads you into His perfect plan. Your part is to surrender; His part is to reveal. If you do your part, He'll do His. Then you will experience a new fulfillment and joy that only those in the center of His will can know.

What's Your Excuse?

Jeremiah 1:4-10

Then said I, Ah, Lord God! behold, I cannot speak: for I am a child.
Jeremiah 1:6

God had just revealed to Jeremiah that He had created him for a specific purpose. He had sanctified and ordained him to be a prophet to the nation of Israel. What wonderful news! How awesome to know that God had a special purpose when He created him. He was not an accident. He was created to accomplish a work for the Lord.

However, Jeremiah wasn't blessed by this news—he was intimidated. He wanted out of God's plan for his life. He thought the call was too great for him, but the truth is, if what you feel called to do isn't greater than what you think you can do, then it's probably not God. God is a big God and He calls us to big things. We think small. God thinks big. Thank God, He is the one who empowers us and enables us to do what He calls us to do.

Jeremiah protested that he was only a child and couldn't speak. In truth, he was a grown man at this time. He was referring to his belief that he was inadequate for the task. Moses tried this same line on God. (Ex. 4:10.) We've all tried it. But the Lord commanded Jeremiah never again to say he was incompetent.

None of us are capable of accomplishing God's will on our own, but none of us are on our own when we are submitted to God's will. He gives us special anointings and gifts to accomplish His will. All we have to do is yield to Him, and He will do the rest.

Do you know what God's will is for your life? Are you lacking what it takes to get it done? You're in good company. Don't try to fulfill the task in your own strength, and never again refer to your weakness. Instead, just yield to Him and move forward.

None Are Insignificant
Acts 9:1-22

Then Ananias answered, Lord, I have heard by many of this man,
how much evil he hath done to thy saints at Jerusalem.
Acts 9:13

Everyone knows about Saul of Tarsus, who later became the apostle Paul. God used him to write much of the New Testament, but do you know the courageous person God used to heal Saul's blind eyes, minister the baptism of the Holy Spirit to him, and give him the prophecy he based his entire ministry on? We often forget the Anne Sullivans who reach the Helen Kellers of this world; but without these people who aren't as famous as their disciples, we wouldn't have people like the apostle Paul.

After this passage of Scripture, Ananias isn't mentioned again. As far as we know from the biblical account, he never did any other great exploits. Certainly, he never did anything as earthshaking as his ministry to Saul of Tarsus. Nevertheless, Ananias had to have great faith in the Lord to even go near a man who was persecuting and killing Christians, and he was a vital link in the chain of events that brought us one of God's greatest men.

In our modern day of distorted values, we have lost sight of the Ananiases of this world. We measure success by cold statistics that often overlook factors like loving parents who sacrificed so their children could succeed or teachers who took extra time and effort to make the difference in one pupil's life. Because of this we fail to realize the potential of our own small acts.

Anyone can count the seeds in an apple, but only God can count the apples in a seed. Likewise, the potential of your deeds of love and faith to others are beyond your comprehension. Don't pass up an opportunity to bless someone else today. You could be ministering to the next apostle Paul.

Where Are You?

Acts 9:10-22

And there was a certain disciple at Damascus, named Ananias; and to him said the Lord in a vision, Ananias. And he said, Behold, I am here, Lord.
Acts 9:10

God called Ananias' name, and he answered, "Behold, I am here Lord." What would have happened if Ananias had not been there? What if he had been doing something else and was not listening to God? The Lord might have found somebody else to do His will, but we don't know for sure. We can say this: Ananias would have missed the greatest opportunity of his life! How many people get to lead someone to the Lord who impacts the world like the apostle Paul did?

There is great significance in the fact that Ananias was there. He was in a place of communion with the Lord. He was listening and attentive to Him. This doesn't come overnight. Certainly Ananias had spent much time in God's presence. How many days, weeks, or years had Ananias spent seeking the Lord before this time? As far as we know, God hadn't done anything before in his life that was as spectacular as what He was leading him to do at this time. However, Ananias remained faithful. He was there when the big opportunity came.

We often fail to recognize that we aren't normally going to see angels or have visions during our times of fellowship with the Lord. We won't always have goose bumps running up and down our spines. There is just the gentle peace and assurance of faith that God is with us. The spectacular comes only on occasion, but we must constantly practice waiting on the Lord. We must always be on call.

Do you think God has ever called you and you weren't there? Don't let that happen today. Make sure your antenna is up and your faith is switched on so that when the Lord calls your name, you'll hear Him.

Kinds of Evangelism
Luke 24:45-48

And ye are witnesses of these things.
Luke 24:48

One of the great mistakes of the modern church is thinking that evangelism is something done within the four walls of the church building. Acts 8:1-4 makes it apparent that evangelism was not done by the pastor or clergy but by believers who went everywhere preaching the Word.

There are several methods of evangelism mentioned in the Scriptures:

1. House-to-house evangelism: "And in every house, they ceased not to teach and preach Jesus Christ" (Acts 5:42).

2. Personal, one-on-one evangelism: Philip ministered to the Ethiopian eunuch (Acts 8:26-38), Paul to Sergius Paulus (Acts 13:7), Jesus to Mary Magdalene, Nicodemus, the woman at the well, the thief on the cross, and others. There are about thirty-five such instances recorded in the Gospels alone.

3. Evangelism to large crowds: Peter ministered to the crowds in Jerusalem at Pentecost (Acts 2) and Paul at Lystra (Acts 14:8-18).

4. Evangelism to entire cities: "Then Philip went down to the city of Samaria, and preached Christ unto them" (Acts 8:5).

5. Public debate and preaching: Paul disputed in synagogues and market places (Acts 16:17); Peter and John preached in the temple (Acts 3:11-26); Paul declared, "And how I kept back nothing that was profitable unto you, but have shown you, and have taught you publicly, and from house to house, Testifying both to the Jews, and also to the Greeks, repentance toward God, and faith toward our Lord Jesus Christ" (Acts 20:20-21).

6. Tract evangelism: The first tract evangelism with ink and pen are the Gospels. In his Gospel, John stated, "These are written, that ye might believe that Jesus is the Christ, the Son of God; and that believing ye might have life through His name" (John 20:31).

Today, be wise in the way you speak and act with unbelievers. Make the most of every opportunity.

Proven Authority

Numbers 17:1-11

And it came to pass, that on the morrow Moses went into the tabernacle
of witness; and, behold, the rod of Aaron for the house of Levi was budded,
and brought forth buds, and bloomed blossoms, and yielded almonds.
Numbers 17:8

God will always prove those He has set in authority by their fruit. Throughout His time on earth, Jesus proved His authority came from God not only because of all the signs, wonders, and miracles He performed but by the multitudes who followed Him and whose lives were dramatically changed by His teaching.

The religious Jews never accepted and submitted to the authority Jesus carried, but lack of respect for authority has always been one of the most common problems in our world. Today we see it in the home, in the church, and in the attitudes people have toward government. In this story in Numbers, the people of Israel questioned Moses' and Aaron's authority to govern the nation of Israel.

In Numbers 16, Korah slandered Moses' character and authority, and the earth immediately swallowed him and all those associated with him. Then another fourteen thousand Israelites criticized Moses for the way he handled Korah and died by a plague of the Lord. Moses' authority was under attack, and God was supernaturally proving him, but the people were still not accepting him.

To resolve the issue, the Lord had Moses command the leaders of each tribe to take their rods, which symbolized authority, and write their names on them. Then all the rods were placed in the Holy Place overnight. The next morning Aaron's rod had budded, blossomed, and produced almonds. The other rods were still bare sticks. This forever settled the issue of whom God had chosen to rule the nation. The fruit made the difference!

You can always tell those who have God-given authority by the fruit they produce. (Matt. 7:20.) Although you must always honor and respect those in authority over you, some may not be producing fruit for the kingdom of God. Instead of judging them like Korah, pray for them. Be humble like Moses, and your own fruit will just naturally come forth.

Reconciled
2 Corinthians 5:17-21

And all things are of God, who hath reconciled us to himself by
Jesus Christ, and hath given to us the ministry of reconciliation.
2 Corinthians 5:18

Have you ever slaved over your checkbook trying to reconcile it with your bank statement? Sometimes it seems impossible. You think there must be a mistake. But through perseverance, the error is usually found and the two records agree. They are reconciled. *Reconciled* simply means "to bring into agreement, or to make the same." When Jesus reconciled us to God, He brought us into agreement with and made us just like God. Some people think this is blasphemy, but that's what this word means.

Our born-again spirits have been made completely new and are reconciled to God. Our spirits are just like His. The English word *reconciled* was translated from the Greek word *katallage*, which means "to change mutually." The word *mutually* means "possessed in common; as mutual interests." Since God never changes, it was our spirits that were changed to be just like His.

Some people can't accept this because they know themselves only from a carnal point of view. They look in the mirror, search their thoughts, and find obvious things that aren't like Jesus. But in your spirit—if you are born again—you have been reconciled to God. Whatever God's Spirit is like is what your born-again spirit is like. Praise the Lord!

God's Word functions like your bank statement, with one major difference: It's never wrong. It's a perfect account of what has taken place in your born-again spirit. Your spirit has been reconciled to God. Today you must reconcile your mind to what the Word says about you: You are just like Jesus on the inside, which means you can act like Him on the outside.

Are You in the Right Place?
2 Samuel 11:1-27

And it came to pass, after the year was expired, at the time when kings go forth to
battle, that David sent Joab, and his servants with him, and all Israel;
and they destroyed the children of Ammon, and besieged Rabbah.
But David tarried still at Jerusalem.
2 Samuel 11:1

The reason Jesus was always in the right place at the right time while He was here on earth was because He was the Living Word. He obeyed the Word of God and walked in the Spirit. In the Old Testament, there never was a better example of the opposite of this than this time in David's life. He had become the king of Israel, and it was the time when kings went to battle; but he decided to stay home. That one decision to disobey and subsequent decisions to disobey brought sorrow to his family and nearly cost him the throne.

Of course, David must have had deeper problems than just not being in the right place and doing what he was anointed to do. His relationship with the Lord must have been in decline for some time. Failure to be in touch with God causes restlessness, which often propels us into the wrong place at the wrong time.

Successful people often abandon the very things that brought them to the top. When Saul was little in his own eyes, the Lord promoted him (1 Sam. 15:17), but when he became a success he abandoned his dependency on God. Solomon did the same thing. He started out in great humility and sought only to be faithful to God, but his success corrupted him. This is also what happened to David.

David had reached a point of success where he no longer had to seek God. He no longer had to fight his own battles. He had others who would do it for him. This left him free to draw closer to God or wander away, and he chose to wander away.

Hard times aren't the true test of what's inside you. Everyone seeks the Lord when their backs are against the wall. Life's greatest test is success. Make fellowship with the Lord your first priority—in both good times and bad—and you will maintain the success He has given you.

You Give What You Have
2 Samuel 12:1-6

And David's anger was greatly kindled against the man; and he said to Nathan,
As the Lord liveth, the man that hath done this thing shall surely die.
2 Samuel 12:5

Have you ever noticed that the guilty are usually the most vocal opponents of the very things they are doing? As Shakespeare wrote, "Methinks thou dost protest too much." David was miserable inside, and his hatred for his own sin came out in his judgment of "that man"—who turned out to be him!

There have been many times that I've told a woman who was battered by her husband that this treatment wasn't personal. He can only give what he has. Because he's miserable inside, he can only mistreat her and make her miserable. This has caused wives to look at the situation differently and actually have compassion instead of judgment toward their husbands. That key often unlocks the door to their husband's heart and starts the healing process in him and between them.

Are you short-tempered with others? Do you constantly find fault with everything? It's possible that the problem really isn't with others, but with you. Are you upset with yourself? Are you never satisfied with your own performance? Have you not found true forgiveness in the grace of God?

We can't control what others around us do, but we can control ourselves. As we appropriate the love of God that's available to us personally, we'll be able to extend that love to others. If we are void of God's love, it'll show in our treatment of others.

The hatred you have for your own sin can manifests in judgmental or critical attitudes toward someone else. Don't make that mistake. Receive God's love and forgiveness today, and then you can pray for and help those who are caught in the same trap you were caught in.

You Get What You Give
2 Samuel 12:1-14

And Nathan said to David, Thou art the man.
2 Samuel 12:7

This parable isn't really about a rich man taking a poor man's sheep; it's about David taking another man's wife and then killing him. Why the pretense? It appears that the Lord was letting David dictate his own punishment. Matthew 7:2 says, "For with what judgment ye judge, ye shall be judged: and with what measure ye mete, it shall be measured to you again." This is what happened to David. He received what he gave.

David demanded the death penalty and much more. This man not only had to pay with his life but was made to make a fourfold restitution. This is what happened to David. His son had to die, and the sword of war would never stop pursuing him. More than that, evil arose in David's own family and greatly afflicted him. David's wives were taken from him, as he had taken Uriah's wife, by his own son! And although David committed his sin privately, God executed His judgment publicly.

Praise the Lord for our superior covenant. God will not judge us the way He judged David. Jesus bore that judgment for us. However, there is still the principle of reaping what we sow. People treat us the way we treat them. If we're harsh and unforgiving, then people will treat us that way. Those who show mercy receive mercy. (James 2:13.)

You don't have to learn everything the hard way; you can learn from other people's mistakes and especially from the Word of God. (2 Tim. 3:16.) In the meantime, it is always a good idea to show mercy and grace to those who fall short. Then, when you are the one who needs mercy and grace, someone will be there to give it to you.

It Ain't Over Yet!
Psalm 73:1-28

Until I went into the sanctuary of God; then understood I their end.
Psalm 73:17

This Psalm was confusing to me until I spent some time studying it and praying about it. Then I saw that it expresses the feelings every true child of God has felt at one time or another. In the first sixteen verses, Asaph lamented the prosperity of the wicked. He said that it looked like evil people were getting away with sin. They seemed to prosper and not have the worries that godly people like himself had. Sound familiar?

In our society today, the only people who can be discriminated against are Christians. Every value we hold dear is being assaulted, and if we speak out we are called bigots and labeled intolerant. Immorality isn't only practiced—it's flaunted! Television programs, movies, newspapers, magazines, and books are filled with pictures of immoral acts. The people who influence us the most are, as a whole, the most immoral people in the nation; yet they receive infinitely more money and attention than the people who are godly. It's been said that character is no longer an issue in politics. At times, as we read what our governmental leaders say and do, it appears that way.

This Psalm reveals that their seeming prosperity is only temporary. In the end their sin "will find them out" (Num. 32:23). Payday is coming. There is a reward for the godly and a punishment for the ungodly. Our responsibility as believers is not to hate and despise the ungodly; we are to pray for them and continue telling them the truth about salvation through Jesus Christ.

Take a lesson from Asaph today, and look at the ungodly through the eyes of your Savior. Then you will be able to love them, forgive them, and be a powerful witness of the truth to them.

The Law of Confession
Mark 11:22-26

For verily I say unto you, That whosoever shall say unto this mountain,
Be thou removed, and be thou cast into the sea; and shall not doubt in
his heart, but shall believe that those things which he saith
shall come to pass; he shall have whatsoever he saith.
Mark 11:23

The Lord used the word *say* (or *saith*) four times in this verse alone, stating that we will have what we say. This can work for or against us. We can either have what we say (which enables us to change our circumstances) or say what we have (which makes us victims of our circumstances). Think about it—words are important!

Eleven times in Genesis 1, it is recorded that God speaks things into existence. When the Lord created the heavens and the earth, He spoke them into being. "Through faith we understand that the worlds were framed by the word of God, so that things which are seen were not made of things which do appear" (Heb. 11:3). God created everything—including us—by words. The universe was made and is now held together by words. (Heb. 1:3.)

Words are keys that unlock the powers of God's universe. When the words we speak are in line with His Word, His power is released. If we agree with the devil and speak forth his thoughts of doubt, we unleash his power. "Death and life are in the power of the tongue: and they that love it shall eat the fruit thereof" (Prov. 18:21).

What words are coming out of your mouth? Are you saying what you have or what you want? If you learn the power of speaking God's Word in faith, you can begin to change your life. Today, pray the prayer David prayed, "Set a watch, O Lord, before my mouth; keep the door of my lips" (Ps. 141:3).

Faith Operates by Love
Galatians 5:1-13

For in Jesus Christ neither circumcision availeth any thing, nor uncircumcision;
but faith which worketh by love.
Galatians 5:6

The dictionary defines *work* as "to operate, or cause to operate, especially effectively." The driving force behind true biblical faith is God's kind of love. When we have a clear revelation of God's love for us, faith comes naturally. Faith is a byproduct of God's love.

Once a man argued with me that God doesn't heal all the time. His motivation for this belief was the fact that his twelve-year-old daughter was quadriplegic and mentally retarded. He believed God made her that way. I shared Scriptures, he shared Scriptures, and we arrived at a stalemate.

Finally I asked, "What kind of father are you that you don't love your daughter enough to see her healed?" He became really mad and assured me that he would do anything to see his daughter healed, even to the point of taking her place if that could happen. I responded, "Do you think God loves her less than you do?"

He could argue doctrine, but when it came down to love it was inconceivable that a God who not only has love but is love (1 John 4:8) would not use His power to see us whole. Those who don't believe that He will act on their behalf are people who don't understand His love for them. Faith works when we know the great love God has for us.

Ask the Lord for a revelation of how much He loves you today, and watch your faith come alive.

Faith Comes by Hearing
Romans 10:13-17

So then faith cometh by hearing, and hearing by the word of God.
Romans 10:17

This verse doesn't say that faith comes by having heard. The word *hearing* is a present-tense word and is continuous. Hearing is an action that is currently taking place.

Faith that comes from God's Word is like the energy we receive from food. We don't have to eat every moment of every day, but we can't live off the food we ate a year ago. The food we eat today fuels us for a relatively short period of time. Likewise, faith that comes from God's Word has to be appropriated on a regular basis. We can't cram when we are in the midst of a trying situation, expecting faith to work, any more than a student can study just once before an exam and expect to score 100 percent.

The food we ate as a child isn't just gone; it was used to increase and nourish bones, muscles, and body tissue. We still benefit from that food today but constantly need a fresh supply to continue in health and strength. In the same way, the time we have spent in the Word, which produced faith, is not lost. It has become a part of who we are and provides a structure for us to continue to build upon. However, faith for today must come from our current relationship with the Lord, which includes meditating on His Word.

There are many analogies that can be drawn between your body's need for food and your heart's need for faith. Certainly, one of the clearest comparisons is that you don't just eat once a week. Therefore, you need to be in God's Word every day. If this has never been your habit, start today. You will find that a daily meal of God's Word will give you a clearer head and even a more healthy body.

God Speaks to You Through Creation
Psalm 19:1-6

The heavens declare the glory of God; and the firmament sheweth his handywork.
Psalm 19:1

The physical creation all around us is awesome. Man has never fully appreciated the wonder in the simplest actions of God. Take for example the sunrises and sunsets. The sun rises and sets with such precision that almanacs can predict its exact arrival and departure down to the minute, years in advance. The rising and setting of the sun is also spectacular. It's like a trumpet calling attention to the glory and faithfulness of God. There are no words to adequately describe the beauty when the rays of the sun first appear through the clouds in the early morning or begin to leave in the evening.

These daily events often go unnoticed or unappreciated by the vast majority of us. There is no language that doesn't understand this form of communication, but our preoccupation with ourselves makes us deaf to it. The Lord speaks to us through His creation, but few of us listen.

Regardless of how dark your situation may be, a dawn is coming if you trust in God—just as surely as the sun will rise in the morning. Regardless of how hard your labor may be, a time of rest is coming—just as surely as the sun sets each day. Nothing people do will change the rising and the setting of the sun, and nothing people do will change the faithfulness of God to you. That is what He is saying to you today as you watch the sun rise and set.

Are You Available?
Luke 2:21-24

And to offer a sacrifice according to that which is said in the law of the Lord,
A pair of turtledoves, or two young pigeons.
Luke 2:24

The Old Testament passage being quoted above is from Leviticus 12:6-8. There the Lord commanded a lamb and either a young pigeon or turtledove as the prescribed sacrifices. If the woman was unable to offer a lamb, then two young pigeons or two turtledoves were acceptable. Mary would not have offered the lesser offering if it had been in her power to provide the lamb. This reveals that Joseph and Mary were not well off financially, yet the Lord chose them to be the earthly parents of His only begotten Son.

The Lord doesn't choose the way man chooses. Man looks on the outward appearance, but God looks on the heart. (1 Sam. 16:7.) Mary and Joseph were chosen when they were without: without fame, without position, without money. God entrusted the most precious gift He had to a couple who would surely have been overlooked if the Sanhedrin had appointed a committee to conduct the search.

God isn't looking for ability; He's looking for availability. When D. L. Moody heard a preacher say, "The world has never seen what God can do with one man who is totally yielded to Him," he thought, *By the grace of God, I'll be that man.* This uneducated man went on to shake three continents for God—and you can too. If God chose two good yet ordinary people to bring His Son into the world, then it is certain He has great plans for you. Today, just make yourself available to Him. (1 Cor. 1:26-28.)

Can You Believe It?
Luke 1:5-25

And Zacharias said unto the angel, Whereby shall I know this?
for I am an old man, and my wife well stricken in years.
Luke 1:18

Zacharias and Elisabeth were righteous people (v. 6) who prayed for a child for many years. They felt the same disappointments and frustrations that we would feel, but they kept believing God. The Lord finally answered their prayers and sent His angel to announce the good news.

What was Zacharias' reaction? He couldn't believe it! The very thing that he had been praying for was granted, and he doubted that it was true. In Zacharias' case, he received his miracle anyway. (Perhaps his wife Elisabeth's faith pulled him through!)

Likewise, you may be praying for the right things. You may even be sincere and earnest, but would you be shocked if those prayers were suddenly answered today? Have you made preparations for your prayers to be answered?

Before the children of Israel were actually delivered from Egypt, they ate the Passover meal by faith. Their bags were packed and ready to go. We need to anticipate our prayers being answered like they did.

Right now, imagine how you would feel or what you would do if the answer to your prayer manifested this very moment. Then, as much as possible, begin to think and act that way. You will find that your whole perspective on how your day is going will change.

The Sinless Sacrifice
Luke 1:26-38

To a virgin espoused to a man whose name was Joseph, of the house of David;
and the virgin's name was Mary.
Luke 1:27

The virgin birth of Jesus is so incomprehensible that it has always been one of Christianity's main targets of criticism. Skeptics cite the impossibility of such a thing as proof that the Bible can't be true. Nevertheless, the virgin birth of our Lord is one of the cornerstones of the Christian faith.

Mankind produces offspring in their own likeness and image. (Gen. 5:3.) Therefore, if Jesus had been the natural product of a man and woman, He would have had a sinful nature. (Rom. 5:12.) He would not have qualified to take our sin upon Himself on the Cross because He would have had to be the debt of His own sin. Isaiah prophesied that the Messiah would be born of a virgin (Is. 7:14), which denotes that God would be His Father. This had to happen to give Him sinless blood.

The Messiah also had to be born without sin for God to legally raise Him from the dead. Our faith rests on the resurrection (Rom. 10:9) because the only legal way God could raise Him from the dead was if He Himself was without sin. Once He died for our sins, God was legally bound to resurrect Jesus (Rom. 1:4) because He was sinless. There is no room for compromise on this issue! If Jesus was not born of a virgin and the sinless sacrifice for our sins, we are all lost and going to hell.

Even true believers try to find natural explanations to the miracles of the Bible to make it more palatable to unbelievers. They try to reconcile the Genesis account of creation with evolution and have the children of Israel crossing the "Reed" Sea instead of the "Red" Sea. However, there is simply no way to explain away the supernatural fact of the virgin birth. Without it, there is no Christian faith.

Aren't you glad that the Bible is true, and you don't have to make any apologies for it? Your new life in Christ is proof that your sins were paid in full by the spotless Lamb of God, who is your Lord and Savior today.

What Do You Expect?
Luke 1:26-38

And when she saw him, she was troubled at his saying, and
cast in her mind what manner of salutation this should be.
Luke 1:29

The angel Gabriel didn't say anything negative or derogatory to Mary. He just told her to rejoice because she was highly favored of God, the Lord was with her, and she was the most blessed woman who had ever lived. What was so disturbing about that?

The reality is that most of us aren't accustomed to praise, and we are too focused on our faults. We may consider it rude for others to mention our shortcomings, but we can relate when they do. Praise, on the other hand, is uncomfortable. It causes us to blush, and when it comes from God it can be frightening! Why is that?

We don't know how to handle praise because we have a wrong image of God. We tend to see Him as harsh, demanding, and condemning instead of the loving Father He is. We expect judgment, not mercy, from Him—and certainly not praise. The Bible says that God is love. (1 John 4:8.) That doesn't mean He overlooks sin, but as His children, He forgives us and inspires us not to sin.

Like Mary, we don't tend to see ourselves as God sees us. If Gabriel had rebuked her, she probably wouldn't have been as troubled. She would've said, "It must be God." But Gabriel did nothing but praise her, and in the end she received all God had for her. Recognize today that all believers are blessed and highly favored of the Lord—and that includes you!

It's a Heart Issue
Luke 1:26-38

Then said Mary unto the angel, How shall this be, seeing I know not a man?
Luke 1:34

Contrast Mary's encounter with the angel to Zacharias' encounter just six months earlier. Gabriel told Zacharias he would have a son by a miraculous birth, and Zacharias asked him how a thing like that could be, since both he and his wife were beyond childbearing age. Zacharias' unbelief angered Gabriel, and he struck him dumb until the birth of his son. (Luke 1:18-20.)

Mary asked a similar question, but Gabriel's response was much kinder. Since God is not a respecter of persons (Rom. 2:11), we can assume the heart motivations behind their questions were different. Zacharias asked his question in unbelief, a statement of scorn rather than a true inquiry. Mary asked her question to gain information not because she did not believe what the angel said.

When God tells us something in His Word, by His Spirit, or even by an angelic messenger, there is nothing wrong with asking questions. Questioning God is not wrong if you have the right heart attitude. After all, if Mary had not asked Gabriel how this child was going to be conceived, she might have assumed He would come through the natural union between Joseph and her.

All of us have trouble understanding the ways of the Lord from time to time. He told us, "My thoughts are not your thoughts, neither are your ways my ways, saith the Lord. For as the heavens are higher than the earth, so are my ways higher than your ways, and my thoughts than your thoughts" (Is. 55:8,9). Today, you need wisdom that only God can give. He doesn't mind you asking questions, as long as your heart is in the right place.

All Things Are Possible
Luke 1:26-38

For with God nothing shall be impossible.
Luke 1:37

The virgin birth is inexplicable except as a miracle. There's no possible way for a virgin to have a baby, but with God all things are possible. The Bible reveals, however, that there are some things that are impossible: Hebrews 6:18 says that it is impossible for God to lie; it was impossible for Satan to keep Jesus in the grave (Acts 2:24); it is impossible for anyone who was once born again, fully enlightened, and then rejects Jesus Christ to be "born again" again (Heb. 6:4); and it certainly is impossible to please God without faith. (Heb. 11:6.)

The Amplified Bible translates this verse as, "No word from God shall be without power or impossible of fulfillment." In other words, anything that God has promised in His Word is possible. His Word not only proclaims what He's willing and able to do, but it also carries His power to accomplish it.

God's Word becomes a self-fulfilling prophecy when mixed with faith. The one word, "Come," from the lips of Jesus had enough power in it to enable Peter to walk on water. (Matt. 14:29.) The word of the Lord Gabriel brought to Mary had the power to produce the virgin birth. When she believed it, her faith set God's Word into motion.

What has God spoken to you? It doesn't matter how impossible it may look. The only question is, "Lord, is this really from You?" If so, then the power it takes to accomplish the task is contained in the Word itself. Mix it with faith, and nothing that God has promised you is impossible!

The Word Became Flesh
Luke 1:26-38

And Mary said, Behold the handmaid of the Lord; be it unto me according to thy word. And the angel departed from her.
Luke 1:38

Everything about Jesus' birth was natural and normal except one thing: A man didn't provide the seed. The Holy Spirit of God placed the seed in Mary's womb. First Peter 1:23 calls God's Word the "incorruptible seed," and the Greek word translated *seed* is *spora*. This comes from the same root from which we get the word *sperm*. God's Word is His seed or sperm. (Mark 4:14.)

Gabriel took the Word of God that had been spoken through prophecy about the Messiah and brought it to Mary. Then the Holy Spirit moved upon her as He did over the waters of the earth in Genesis 1:2. He took God's seed and impregnated Mary with it. Therefore, John's description of this is very accurate. "And the Word was made flesh" (John 1:14).

A similar process is involved in every miracle we experience. In a very real sense, we must become pregnant with God's Word. The Word must be received into our hearts and nurtured over a period of time before there is actual manifestation of the miracle. A woman goes through stages of pregnancy. Likewise, when God's Word first takes root in our hearts, it's not always obvious—even to us. Eventually, it begins to show that His Word is working in us. Finally, there's the birth of what we have believed. This could be anything from growing in faith to becoming more responsible to prospering in our health and finances.

No one but Mary has ever had a virgin birth, but even that birth took a seed to make it happen. You must conceive (receive and believe) God's Word in your heart to give birth to your dreams in the natural realm. Put His Word in your heart today, and get ready to receive your miracle!

Choose to Rejoice
Luke 1:46-56

*And Mary said, My soul doth magnify the Lord, And my spirit hath
rejoiced in God my Saviour.*
Luke 1:46-47

Gabriel told Mary that her cousin Elisabeth was in the sixth month of
a miraculous pregnancy too. No doubt, Mary went to see her because
she hoped Elisabeth might understand that she was pregnant without
having had sexual relations with any man, including Joseph. Mary was bound to be
apprehensive. How could she expect anyone to believe she was pregnant without a
sexual relationship? These verses reflect the absolute joy Mary felt when her cousin
confirmed all that had happened before she told her anything.

Mary had already rejoiced in her spirit. She believed Gabriel and experienced
the Holy Spirit overshadowing her and conceiving Jesus. Now she rejoiced with
her soul too. This is very important. Sometimes people criticize believers for their
outward display of emotion toward the Lord. They say, "They aren't in the Spirit."
The truth is that rejoicing in the spirit and rejoicing in the soul are two different
things. Our born-again spirits always have the fruit of joy in them, but our souls
only rejoice at certain times. Rejoicing in our souls is our choice, and when you
think about it, it's actually hypocritical not to magnify the Lord with our souls
when our born-again spirits are already rejoicing.

The whole concept of being under the control of the Holy Spirit when we
dance, lift our hands, or speak in tongues has kept many people from doing these
things. Actually, our spirits are always rejoicing and praising God, and we can praise
Him with our souls and bodies whenever we choose to do so. Like Mary, we can
choose to rejoice and magnify Him with our whole being.

Follow the lead of your spirit today, and rejoice with your soul too!

Think About This

Luke 1:39-45

And it came to pass, that, when Elisabeth heard the salutation of Mary, the babe leaped in her womb; and Elisabeth was filled with the Holy Ghost.
Luke 1:41

This story has become so familiar to us that it's easy to miss the miracles! Mary and Elisabeth were cousins. (Luke 1:36.) They knew each other. Surely Elisabeth was aware that Mary was engaged but not yet married. She was just a teenager, yet Elisabeth prophesied about Mary being pregnant with the Messiah. That could not have come out of Elisabeth's mind. She never would have said those things because they were illogical.

Elisabeth also referred to Jesus as her Lord (v. 43). He had just been conceived. Today, He would have been called a fetus, yet she recognized Him as Her Lord and Savior. Many others proclaimed Him Lord at His birth (Luke 2:11) and after His birth, but Elisabeth proclaimed He was Lord from the moment of conception.

It is interesting to note that John the Baptist, who was just a six-month-old fetus at the time, leapt for joy in his mother's womb. This means that a six-month-old fetus has emotions. It is also when he was filled with the Holy Spirit. Before he was viable outside of the womb, God considered him a person and filled him with His Spirit!

Elisabeth spoke these words without reservation. She placed a blessing on Mary for believing what the Lord had told her and then reassured her that it would surely come to pass. (v. 45.) What an encouragement and confirmation this must have been to Mary. Meditate on these wonderful insights as you go about your day.

The Power to Serve
Luke 1:39-56

The babe leaped in her womb; and Elisabeth was filled with the Holy Ghost.
Luke 1:41

Upon hearing the greeting of Mary, John the Baptist leaped for joy inside his mother's womb. (v. 44.) A six-month-old fetus experienced unbridled emotion, voluntarily leaped for joy, and was actually filled with the Holy Spirit.

It is no coincidence that the man Jesus called the greatest of all Old Testament prophets was the only man in the Bible to be filled with the Holy Ghost in his mother's womb. (Luke 7:28.) The anointing of God that breaks every yoke is simply the manifest presence and working of the Holy Spirit. (Isa. 10:27.) The Holy Spirit is the part of the Godhead that empowers us for service.

God is not asking us to live for Him. He is asking us to let Him live through us. (Gal. 2:20.) The Christian life is not a changed life but an exchanged life. This can only be accomplished when the Holy Spirit is leading and empowering us.

Even Jesus didn't begin His ministry until he was anointed with the Holy Spirit, and He was the sinless Son of God. How much more do we need to depend on the power of the Holy Spirit in our daily lives?

Today, be conscious of the presence of the Holy Spirit in you and expect Him to supernaturally guide you and empower you. If you ask, you will receive. (Luke 11:9-13.)

Make God Bigger
Luke 1:46-56

And Mary said, My soul doth magnify the Lord.
Luke 1:46

Magnify means "to make greater in size, extent, or effect." How could Mary make God any greater in any of these ways? Furthermore, God is who He is regardless of what we think about Him. Our unbelief doesn't diminish who God is, but it can diminish how much of Him and His provision we receive. In that sense, we can limit (Ps. 78:41) or decrease His ability to move in our lives. Every time we think, *Can God?* we make Him smaller in our own minds. How can we change that?

"I...will magnify him with thanksgiving" (Ps. 69:30). That's what Mary was doing here. Thanksgiving magnifies God in our lives. Through thanksgiving, we exercise the power of our memory to recount all the times He has supernaturally saved us, healed us, delivered us—as well as all the prayers for others He has answered. Our memories stir us up (2 Pet. 1:13), and thinking about God's goodness and faithfulness builds our faith. (Col. 2:7.)

Whatever our minds focus on is what gets magnified. Too often we focus on the bad memories of the past or our fears about the future. Sometimes Satan puts no more than a toothpick in our path, but by the time we get through meditating on all the different ways it could hurt us, that toothpick has increased to the size of a log that completely blocks our path. We need to magnify the Lord by reminding ourselves that no log can stop Him if we just choose to believe.

Mary magnified the Lord and brought the greatest miracle into the world that's ever happened. You can see your miracle come to pass too. Start magnifying the Lord, and watch your perception of God's greatness increase today.

Joseph: Man of Great Faith
Matthew 1:18-25

*Then Joseph being raised from sleep did as the angel of the Lord had bidden him,
and took unto him his wife.*
Matthew 1:24

So many amazing things happened at the birth of our Lord Jesus Christ that the faith of Joseph is often overlooked. Think of how much faith he had to have operated in.

After the angel Gabriel appeared to Mary, there's no mention in Scripture of her telling Joseph anything. In fact, Mary went to see Elisabeth with haste. (Luke 1:39.) It's possible that in her excitement, she forgot to tell Joseph she was even leaving. When she returned three months later, "She was *found* with child" (Matt. 1:18, italics mine). This implies that Mary didn't tell Joseph what had happened, but when she returned, he observed she was pregnant.

How would a man today react if his fiancée turned up pregnant and told him it was a virgin birth? I'm sure Joseph had those same thoughts. His mercy toward her showed that he loved her, but he also planned to divorce her, which means he didn't believe her. Then the angel of the Lord appeared to Joseph in a dream and explained the situation to him. Even at that, it took a strong faith to believe what he was told!

This had never happened before and would never happen again. No one would believe him. To everyone else, it would appear that Joseph was marrying someone who had already been unfaithful. In the eyes of the world, this marriage would always be tainted. It is to his credit and a testimony to his great faith that Joseph obeyed the Lord by going ahead and marrying Mary.

If Joseph and Mary could believe God for the virgin birth of Jesus, surely you can believe what He has spoken to you today.

God Can Use Anyone or Any-thing
Luke 2:1-5

And Joseph also went up from Galilee, out of the city of Nazareth, into Judaea, unto the city of David, which is called Bethlehem; (because he was of the house and lineage of David).
Luke 2:4

The prophet Micah prophesied that the Messiah would be born in Bethlehem. Yet Joseph and Mary lived in the Galilean town of Nazareth. This was a problem. How would God work this out? He actually used Caesar Augustus to move Joseph and Mary into the proper place. This reveals some very important things to us.

First, we mistakenly think that the Lord only uses those who are totally devoted to Him. That certainly wasn't the case here! Augustus was one of the most corrupt Caesars of them all. He proclaimed himself to be god, yet he was the one God used to move the parents of our Lord to the proper place. Totally unknown to him, Caesar was used of God.

Secondly, it doesn't appear that Joseph and Mary were aware of Micah's prophecy. If they were, you would think they would have headed to Bethlehem on their own, in obedience to the Word of God. Instead, God used circumstances to get them to the exact spot Micah had prophesied the Messiah would be born. This tells us that we don't have to bring God's will to pass on our own; He's able to divinely structure our circumstances to direct our paths in His ways. All we must do is seek Him, and He will direct our paths. (Prov. 3:6.)

Have you been worrying about how the Lord is going to work things out? Be encouraged! God can use the most unlikely people and circumstances today to direct your path. Just trust in Him.

December 25

No-Frills Faith
Luke 2:6-7

And she brought forth her firstborn son, and wrapped him in swaddling clothes, and laid him in a manger; because there was no room for them in the inn.
Luke 2:7

It is astounding that the King of kings and Lord of lords was born in a barn because no one would give His parents a room in the inn. If we were God, we would have saved Herod the trouble of killing all the newborn baby boys in Bethlehem by retaliating and doing it ourselves. Jesus was the Creator, and His creation had no room for Him. That could really bother a selfish, self-centered God!

I believe the Father delighted in the setting in which Jesus was born. After all, a room in the greatest palace on earth would still have been a shambles compared to the splendors of heaven Jesus had left. Nothing could compare, so why try? Besides, love and humility motivated this awesome act of God becoming man. (Phil. 2:8.) Jesus said Himself that He was meek and lowly of heart. (Matt. 11:29.) We serve a humble God.

The Lord could have come in some spectacular way. He could have been born in the greatest palace. He could have mesmerized everyone into believing on Him, manifesting such awesome things that it took no faith to believe He was the Messiah, but that is not His way. He loves to see faith in people, just simple faith. That is why it is impossible to please Him without faith. (Heb. 11:6.)

Are you missing God's subtle miracles all around you just because you are looking for something spectacular? If you had found Jesus lying in a manger of a barn, would you have had the faith to believe? The Lord delights in revealing Himself in subtle ways. Don't miss Him today.

The War Is Over
Luke 2:8-20

Glory to God in the highest, and on earth peace, good will toward men.
Luke 2:14

A couple of Japanese soldiers were found on one of the South Pacific islands years after the end of WWII. Due to temporary deafness from bomb explosions, they had missed the announcement via airplane and were unaware of the war's end. Many years later, they were still hiding in the jungle fighting the war. How sad. However, many Christians still think that the war is on between God and man. That's even sadder!

These angels weren't proclaiming that there would be peace among people. That certainly hasn't happened since Jesus came, and it's not what we see happening now. Jesus even declared that He didn't come to bring peace between people. (Matt. 10:34-36.) These angels were praising God that the war between God and people was over.

Prior to Christ coming to the earth, God dealt with mankind through the Law. The Law was a system of rules and regulations with appropriate punishments for disobedience. The only thing wrong with that system was that we all broke the Law. Therefore, we all came under the curse instead of the blessing. There was no peace because of our sins.

Jesus ushered in a new way for God to deal with us. We can now be totally free of all sin, not because of our performance, but because of our faith in Jesus Christ. The war between God and us is over. The peace treaty has been signed in the blood of the Lamb. Are you enjoying that peace, or are you still suffering the hardships of war because you missed the announcement? There is peace and goodwill toward you from your loving, heavenly Father today.

In Him
Luke 2:8-20

For unto you is born this day in the city of David a Saviour, which is Christ the Lord.
Luke 2:11

Jesus did not grow into being Lord and Savior. He was born the Lord of Glory. Jesus was God manifest in the flesh. (1 Tim. 3:16.) What a great mystery! How could Almighty God limit Himself to the form of a man? Even if He did, how could he possibly start as a baby?

These questions defy our ability to fully understand. At the dedication of the first temple, Solomon said, "But will God in very deed dwell with men on the earth? Behold, heaven and the heaven of heavens cannot contain thee; how much less this house which I have built" (2 Chron. 6:18). How much less the body of a little child!

Part of the answer is that God is a spirit (John 4:24), and spirits are not limited by time and space. In Jesus' spirit, He was the eternal God who created the universe. The physical body of Jesus was just His earth suit that He used to walk among us. All of Jesus' deity could not fit inside His physical body; it could reside in His spirit.

Even though this is still hard to grasp, it helps us understand how Christ can live in us as believers. (Col. 1:27.) If all the glory of God could fit inside the spirit of Jesus, then all the fullness of God can dwell in our born-again spirits too. (John 1:16.)

The revelation of who you are in Christ and who He is in you will change your whole perspective on your life as a Christian. Today, meditate on the truth that He really lives in you and you really live in Him.

Daniel's Influence
Matthew 2:1-11

Now when Jesus was born in Bethlehem of Judaea in the days of Herod
the king, behold, there came wise men from the east to Jerusalem. Saying,
Where is he that is born King of the Jews? for we have seen his
star in the east, and are come to worship him.
Matthew 2:1-2

It is remarkable that these men from the East would interpret the appearance of any star, regardless of how unusual it might be, as a sign of the birth of the Jewish Messiah. What did they know about Jewish prophecy?

Matthew 2:1 calls these men "wise men." The actual word used in the Greek text was *magos*, which was of foreign origin, denoting a Magian (hence Magi) or an Oriental scientist or magician. It is commonly believed they came from Persia. This is significant because Babylon was where Daniel was taken as a captive and elevated to the head of all the magicians. He came through the lions' den victoriously and had gained the reputation as the greatest wise man of all. (Dan. 6.) Eventually he was promoted to be the head of all the wise men. (Dan. 2:48.)

Daniel was the prophet to whom God gave the interpretation of Jeremiah's seventy-weeks prophecy, which pinpointed the coming of the Messiah. (Dan. 9:2,24-27; Jer. 25:11.) As head of the magicians (or scientists) in Persia, Daniel made this knowledge known to his colleagues. No doubt, through the centuries their successors continued to study his prophecy and anticipated the event. It is very understandable that the appearance of a new star moving in a different fashion would be taken as a special sign of the Jewish Messiah's birth.

The religious Jewish scholars were taken by surprise, but the Persian magicians were not. They had been studying God's Word through Daniel. The Word makes us wise unto salvation. (2 Tim. 3:15.)

Let the Word instruct you today, and you will be wise to make good decisions and to know the season you are in.

Revelation Knowledge
Luke 2:25-35

And it was revealed unto him by the Holy Ghost, that he should not see death,
before he had seen the Lord's Christ.
Luke 2:26

A pastor friend of mine told me that before he received the baptism of the Holy Spirit, the thing that upset him the most about Charismatics was what we called "revelation knowledge." He had two doctorate degrees and had been through seminary, yet he would hear ministers like me on the radio (whom he could tell had no formal training) expound the Scriptures in ways he had never heard before. He said he had studied those same Scriptures hundreds of times and had missed the simple, obvious truths that we brought out. It upset him and, at the same time, made him desire what we had.

This was how Simeon operated. "It was revealed unto him by the Holy Ghost." This wasn't something he was taught by man. It was revelation knowledge: knowledge that didn't come from observation or instruction but was intuitive. This revelation knowledge is available to all born-again believers who will receive this ministry of the Holy Spirit.

Simeon had no natural way of knowing which of the thousands of babies he saw would be the Christ. He simply kept his heart in tune with the Holy Spirit, and that knowledge was supernaturally imparted to him at the right time. This shouldn't be hard to believe. In nature we see birds, fish, and animals migrate to the exact spots their parents came from without ever being there before. They didn't learn that in school.

If God can speak to His animal creation, doesn't it make sense that He can also speak to you? Listen for the voice of God on the inside of you today, and ask Him to give you revelation knowledge of Him and His will for your life.

God's Chosen
Luke 2:36-40

And she was a widow of about fourscore and four years, which departed not from the temple, but served God with fastings and prayers night and day.
Luke 2:37

L et's suppose Anna was fourteen years old when she married. That would have made her ninety-eight years old at the writing of this passage. Yet she was still fasting and praying night and day. This was an amazing woman for any time.

Satan tries to convince us that God won't use us. He may cite things like age, lack of ability, or failures in our past; but just like Anna, there are many scriptural examples of God using those who would be considered unusable by worldly standards.

Moses was eighty before he began to fulfill God's plan for his life, and he worked until he was one hundred twenty years old. Abraham was in his nineties before he had the son God had promised him. Obviously, age is not a factor when God chooses to use someone.

Gideon was another person who looked unusable. He was hiding from the Midianites when the angel of the Lord appeared and told him he was a mighty man of valor. (Judg. 6:11,12.) He couldn't believe it at first and had to have the Lord confirm it three times! Gideon is one of many examples that, truly, "God hath chosen the foolish things of the world to confound the wise; and God hath chosen the weak things of the world to confound the things which are mighty" (1 Cor. 1:27,28).

If you feel foolish or weak, then you qualify to be chosen by God for a great mission. Look into the Word of God and see yourself as He sees you. Let Him use you today.

To Resolve or Not to Resolve
Proverbs 4:20-27

Ponder the path of thy feet, and let all thy ways be established.
Proverbs 4:26

The end of the old year and the beginning of a new one is a great time to take inventory of what has happened in your life and plan for what's ahead. Some people don't think it's good to look back, and they certainly don't think it's good to make New Year's resolutions. But this passage of Scripture tells us to "ponder the path of thy feet."

Ponder means "to weigh mentally." You can't weigh something unless you have something to weigh it against. If you don't have any goals, there's no way to evaluate whether or not you're making progress. We all need something to shoot at. Otherwise, we'll shoot at nothing and hit it every time!

There are dangers associated with setting goals and making resolutions. If we stretch ourselves too far, we are destined to fail. This just adds to our sense of guilt and frustration. The Bible advocates vision and goal setting, but we need to exercise wisdom. We shouldn't set goals arbitrarily, independent of God. Establishing goals contrary to His will just absorbs all our time and keeps us from Him.

It's beneficial to look back and remember the good and learn from the bad. In order to plow a straight row, we must fix our eyes on a point far out in front of us. Use this time to see if your life is going in the direction the Lord wants it to. If it's not, then there needs to be some changes. It's foolish to keep doing the same things expecting different results. Ponder the path of your feet today, and take the appropriate steps.

List of References

Definitions of English words are from *The American Heritage ® Dictionary of the English Language* (Boston, MA: Houghton Mifflin, 2000).

Definitions of Greek and Hebrew words are from *James Strong, Exhaustive Concordance of the Bible*, "Greek Dictionary of the New Testament" and "Hebrew and Chaldee Dictionary" (Nashville, TN: Thomas Nelson Publishers, 1984).

Fritz Rienecker, *A Linguistic Key to the Greek New Testament* (Grand Rapids, MI: Zondervan Publishing House, 1980).

Receive Jesus as Your Savior

Choosing to receive Jesus Christ as your Lord and Savior is the most important decision you'll ever make!

God's Word promises, "That if thou shalt confess with thy mouth the Lord Jesus, and shalt believe in thine heart that God hath raised him from the dead, thou shalt be saved. For with the heart man believeth unto righteousness; and with the mouth confession is made unto salvation" (Romans 10:9,10). "For whosoever shall call upon the name of the Lord shall be saved" (Romans 10:13).

By His grace, God has already done everything to provide salvation. Your part is simply to believe and receive.

Pray out loud: Jesus, I confess that You are my Lord and Savior. I believe in my heart that God raised You from the dead. By faith in Your Word, I receive salvation now. Thank You for saving me.

The very moment you commit your life to Jesus Christ, the truth of His Word instantly comes to pass in your spirit. Now that you're born again, there's a brand-new you.

Receive the Holy Spirit

As His child, your loving heavenly Father wants to give you the supernatural power you need to live this new life.

For every one that asketh receiveth; and he that seeketh findeth; and to him that knocketh it shall be opened...how much more shall your heavenly Father give the Holy Spirit to them that ask him?

Luke 11:10-13

All you have to do is ask, believe, and receive!

Pray: Father, I recognize my need for Your power to live this new life. Please fill me with Your Holy Spirit. By faith, I receive it right now. Thank You for baptizing me. Holy Spirit, You are welcome in my life.

Congratulations—now you're filled with God's supernatural power.

Some syllables from a language you don't recognize will rise up from your heart to your mouth. (1 Cor. 14:14.) As you speak them out loud by faith, you're releasing God's power from within and building yourself up in the spirit. (1 Cor. 14:4.) You can do this whenever and wherever you like.

It doesn't really matter whether you felt anything or not when you prayed to receive the Lord and His Spirit. If you believed in your heart that you received, then God's Word promises you did. "Therefore I say unto you, What things soever ye desire, when ye pray, believe that ye receive them, and ye shall have them" (Mark 11:24). God always honors His Word—believe it!

Please contact me and let me know that you've prayed to receive Jesus as your Savior or be filled with the Holy Spirit. I would like to rejoice with you and help you understand more fully what has taken place in your life. I'll send you a free gift that will help you understand and grow in your new relationship with the Lord. "Welcome to your new life!"

About the Author

For over four decades, Andrew Wommack has traveled America and the world teaching the truth of the Gospel. His profound revelation of the Word of God is taught with clarity and simplicity, emphasizing God's unconditional love and the balance between grace and faith. He reaches millions of people through the daily Gospel Truth radio and television programs, broadcast both domestically and internationally. He founded Charis Bible College in 1994 and has since established CBC extension schools in other major cities of America and around the world. Andrew has produced a library of teaching materials, available in print, audio, and visual formats. And, as it has been from the beginning, his ministry continues to distribute free audio materials to those who cannot afford them.

To contact Andrew Wommack please write, e-mail, or call:

Andrew Wommack Ministries, Inc.
P.O. Box 3333
Colorado Springs, CO 80934-3333
E-mail: awommack@aol.com
Helpline Phone (orders and prayer): 719-635-1111
Hours: 4:00 AM to 9:30 PM MST

Andrew Wommack Ministries of Europe
P.O. Box 4392
WS1 9AR Walsall
England
E-mail: enquiries@awme.net
U.K. Helpline Phone (orders and prayer): 011-44-192-247-3300
Hours: 5:30 AM to 4:00 PM GMT

Or visit him on the Web at: www.awmi.net

Living in the Balance of Grace and Faith

Taking on one of the biggest controversies of the church, the freedom of God's grace verses the faith of the believer, Wommack reveals that God's Power is not released from only grace or only faith. God's blessings come through a balance of both grace and faith.

Addressing many of the misconceptions believers are taught in the church today, this book opens up the Scriptures revealing the vital connection between grace and faith. Many believers think they walk in both grace and faith when actually they are misusing one or both of these principles. Andrew addresses:

• Some believers willingly sin believing God's grace will cover them, while the blessing of grace is not to sin, but to release guilt and condemnation when they make a mistake.

• Other believers think they must "work" their faith by ritualistic prayer, confession, or Bible study. Although all these things are good, Jesus Christ set believers free from works of the law. God wants a relationship where He can communicate directly to each believer.

• Grace and faith work together. When believers receive the unmerited favor or grace of God, they can release their faith without doubt or reservation and receive God's blessings.

Wommack, in his logical, practical style, brings believers back on track in their Christian walk through living in the balance of grace and faith.

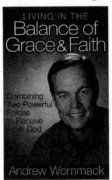

ISBN: 978-1-57794-918-3 Paperback
Available at bookstores everywhere
or visit www.harrisonhouse.com

The Believer's Authority

The controversial subject of the authority of the believer in Christ is widely discussed in the church today. Andrew Wommack brings a fresh perspective to this important spiritual truth that may challenge everything you've been taught including:

• If believers have been given authority, then when, how, and toward what should it be exercised? Don't assume the answer; discover the true battleground, and learn how to recognize the real enemy.

• Most people believe God created our enemy, Satan, but did He? Understanding the answer will set you free to exercise your authority as a believer.

• Is spiritual warfare, as taught in many churches today, valid? Can believers use their authority to fight the devil and his demons in the air, or is the real battle in the mind? The answer is an important prerequisite to winning spiritual battles.

Digging into the Scriptures, Andrew reveals the spiritual significance of your choices, words, and actions; and how they affect your ability to stand against the attacks of Satan and to receive God's best. Discover the powerful truths behind true spiritual authority and begin seeing real results.

Item Code: 1045-C, 6-CD album

Item Code: 1045-D, 5-DVD album (as recorded from television)

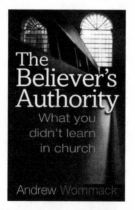

ISBN: 978-1-57794-936-7 Paperback
Available at bookstores everywhere
or visit www.harrisonhouse.com

Other Teachings by Andrew Wommack

Spirit, Soul & Body

Understanding the relationship of your spirit, soul, and body is foundational to your Christian life. You will never truly know how much God loves you or believe what His Word says about you until you do. In this series, learn how they're related and how that knowledge will release the life of your spirit into your body and soul. It may even explain why many things are not working the way you had hoped.

Item Code: 318   Paperback
Item Code: 1027-C   4-CD album

The True Nature of God

Are you confused about the nature of God? Is He the God of judgment found in the Old Testament or the God of mercy and grace found in the New Testament? Andrew's revelation on this subject will set you free and give you a confidence in your relationship with God like never before. This is truly nearly-too-good-to-be-true news.

Item Code: 308   Paperback
Item Code: 1002-C   5-CD album

The Effects of Praise

Every Christian wants a stronger walk with the Lord. But how do you get there? Many don't know the true power of praise. It's essential. Listen as Andrew teaches biblical truths that will spark not only understanding but will help promote spiritual growth so you will experience victory.

Item Code: 309   Paperback
Item Code: 1004-C   3-CD album

God Wants You Well

Health is something everyone wants. Billions of dollars are spent each year trying to retain or restore health. So why does religion tell us that God uses sickness to teach us something? It even tries to make us believe that sickness is a blessing. That's just not true. God wants you well!

Item Code: 1036-C   4-CD album

CHARIS BIBLE COLLEGE

COLORADO SPRINGS CAMPUS

Equipping the saints for the work of the ministry

Combining the rich teaching of God's Word with a practical hands-on ministry experience in a Two Year Program.

Night Classes and Distance Learning/Correspondence courses also available

For more information, call

Charis Bible College
at
719-635-6029,
or visit our website at
www.charisbiblecollege.org

Ask about Extension School locations

Fast. Easy.
Convenient.

For the latest Harrison House product information and author news, look no further than your computer. All the details on our powerful, life-changing products are just a click away. New releases, e-mail subscriptions, testimonies, monthly specials—find it all in one place. Visit harrisonhouse.com today!

harrisonhouse